Guide to Brazil

Other Bradt guides to Central and South America

Guide to
Brazil

Amazon • Pantanal • Coastal Regions

Alex Bradbury

with Ric Goodman and Geoffrey Roy

Bradt Publications, UK
The Globe Pequot Press Inc, USA

First published as *Backcountry Brazil* in 1990 by Bradt Publications.
This edition published in 1997 by Bradt Publications,
41 Nortoft Road, Chalfont St Peter, Bucks SL9 0LA, England.
Published in the USA by The Globe Pequot Press Inc, 6 Business Park Road,
PO Box 833, Old Saybrook, Connecticut 06475-0833.

British Library Cataloguing in Publication Data
A catalogue record for this book is available from the British Library
ISBN 1 898323 59 3

Library of Congress Cataloging-in-Publication Data
Bradbury, Alex
  Guide to Brazil : Amazon, Pantanal, Coastal Regions/Alex
  Bradbury with Ric Goodman and Geoffrey Roy. — 2nd ed.
    p. cm.
  Rev. enl. ed. of: Backcountry Brazil, 1990.
  Includes index.
  ISBN 1-898323-59-3
    1. Brazil–Guidebooks. 2. Natural history—Brazil—Guidebooks.
  3. Pantanal (Brazil)—Guidebooks. 4. Amazon River Region—
    Guidebooks. 5. Beaches—Guidebooks, Northeast—Guidebooks.
  I. Goodman, Ric. II. Roy, Geoffrey. III. Bradbury, Alex.
  Backcountry Brazil. IV. Title.
  F2509.5.B68   1997
  918.104'64—dc21   97-13873
                                                   CIP

Cover photographs
Front: Hilary Bradt
*Back: Blue and yellow macaw (*Ara ararauna*)* Geoffrey Roy
Colour Photographs Jayne Bradbury (JB) Ric Goodman (RG), Geoffrey Roy (GR),
Journey Latin America (JLA)
Illustrations: Alex Bradbury
Maps *Inside covers*: Steve Munns   *Others*: Alex Bradbury

Typeset from the author's disc by Patti Taylor, London NW10 1JR
Printed and bound in Great Britain by The Guernsey Press Co Ltd

CONTENTS

ACKNOWLEDGEMENTS

Alex Bradbury owes special thanks to two long-time Brazilian friends: Wellington Franklin, who over the years has accompanied us on numerous trips throughout the Northeast; and Ricardo Silva Pereira, who shared his insights into Brazilian life and showed us how to play *samba* on tiny wooden matchboxes. Ziza Franklin and Amanda Pereira were gracious hosts and travel companions. Veleda Furtado continues to school us in Portuguese prior to every trip. Katy Ranzoni joined us in updating the Pantanal and Northeast chapters, and kept us company on the long road trips. My mother, Ann Bradbury, never flags in her support of my writing career and always gives the cat a home during our frequent travels. Many thanks to my editors, Hans van Well and Tricia Hayne, for their attention to detail and good taste. Finally, this book would never have happened without the encouragement of publisher Hilary Bradt.

Ric Goodman would like to thank the família Almeida Tavares, Jaci, Roberto, Fábio, and Eliete for unsurpassed hospitality during his stay in Brazil. He also expresses his deep thanks to his wife Nádia for endless patience and love.

Geoffrey Roy gives huge thanks to David Gilmour who was inspirational in getting him to South America in the first place. He also thanks Debra Fleming, his home back-up and go-between. He has no doubt that she's a star! In Brazil, Geoffrey would like to thank three people: Dr Ning Labbish Chao of Projeto Piaba, for his hospitality and staff; Greg Prang, for his great company and for introductions to anyone who is anyone in Manaus; and, most importantly, Lucy 'The Stingray Girl', who was his eyes, ears and translator, and who put up with his demands and got nothing in return. He wishes her the very best of luck with her research into Amazonian stingrays. Lastly, he thanks his parents "who for years have put up with a wayward son, provided financial backing and often bailed me out of trouble".

Introduction

In the last few days of 1983, my wife and I quit our comfortable jobs, collected the damage deposit on our rented home, and boarded a jet for Belém do Pará, Brazil's sprawling port at the mouth of the Amazon River. Arriving after dark in a city named after Bethlehem, I remember drawing all sorts of pretentious mystical connections. But our year-long pilgrimage – the first of many to Brazil's wild places – was merely starting in Belém, not ending there. And if we were guided by a star, it shone not on Brazil's cities, but rather on its jungles, fishing villages, mountain ranges and quiet backwaters.

This book was written for fellow pilgrims in search of those wild places. Brazil boasts more undisturbed backcountry than any other country on the continent, most of it accessible to travellers of modest means and limited wilderness experience. I've concentrated here on the four regions which, to my mind, offer the best and most uniquely Brazilian experience for the backcountry traveller: Amazônia for the jungle buff; the Pantanal for wildlife lovers; the northeast coast for aficionados of deserted beaches and rustic fishing villages; and the rugged Serra do Mar for hikers and spelunkers.

Like most travellers, I'm not immune to Brazil's urban charms, but there are two good reasons for the backcountry focus of this guide. Firstly, the bookshelves are already crammed with advice on navigating Copacabana and Carnaval; tips on finding alligators in the Pantanal and fishing for piranhas in the Amazon are much harder to come by. Secondly, Brazil's wild places, like those elsewhere, are disappearing at an alarming rate. Twenty years from now, Carnaval, Copacabana and the urban guidebooks will probably look terribly familiar, whereas your chances of spotting a herd of capybaras or a flock of roseate spoonbills will be vastly diminished.

But this see-it-while-you-can cynicism can be overdone. There is much that has changed for the better in Brazil, and I've tried to capture as many of those changes as possible in this new update. For example, since the first edition, low-impact camping trips have made the Pantanal's spectacular wildlife more accessible to amateur naturalists, while at the same time focusing national attention on the benefits of preserving the region. Travellers to Amazônia can now sign on as volunteers in sustainable-use projects involving tropical aquarium fish. In the northeast, a resurgence of pride in the region's Afro-Brazilian culture is making it easier to see traditional *capoeira* dances and *candomblé* ceremonies. In fact, so many

changes have occurred in Brazil's backcountry that they would have swamped a single writer. Nature photographer and journalist Geoffrey Roy has completely updated the Amazon section, while I returned to research the Pantanal and the northeast coast. Ric Goodman has contributed a brand new section on the mountainous parks of the Serra do Mar, a region of virgin forests and limestone caves that is scarcely mentioned in most guides. Jungle lodge listings have been expanded, maps revised, and transportation tips updated. Once again, our goal has been to offer a limited menu of travel 'recipes' within each region as a starting point for experimentation.

Much of the information is arranged around the concept of 'gateway cities' – those you'll most likely use as base camps for your forays into the backcountry. Some of these cities are interesting in their own right, so we've expanded the sections on what to see, lodging, and transport. But we've deferred detailed urban sightseeing and hotel/restaurant listings to other guidebooks and concentrated instead on getting you to a Brazil that even many Brazilians never see – the untamed soul of this vast country.

We've been drawn back to those wild places, extending a pilgrimage that began over fourteen years ago. There are always the disappointments: places eroded by time, progress, an overabundance of pilgrims like ourselves. At some point in your trip, however, we hope you'll share the enthusiasm of a Brazilian friend from the northeast coast. Standing in the back of a pickup truck, surveying a fishing village surrounded by miles of windswept sand dunes, he told us: *'Isto é o Brasil. Isto eu gosto'* – *'This is Brazil. This I love.'*

Vitória Régia waterlilies outside Porto Jofre, Pantanal

BRAZIL

States and Major Cities

Chapter One

General Information

GEOGRAPHY

Geographically speaking, Brazil is not a land of many contrasts. Crystalline shield rocks underlie most of the country and make for a landscape of flat horizons, hilly uplands, plateaux and low-lying mountains. Even before the scientific community accepted the theory of plate tectonics, geologists noted the similarity between landforms in Brazil and some of those in southern Africa; we now know that the two continents separated some 200 million years ago.

At the expense of some geological detail, the whole country can be pictured as two vast areas of shield rocks – the Guyana Highlands and the Brazilian Highlands – neatly divided by the Amazon River basin. The Guyana Highlands extend from Venezuela and the Guianas into the northern Brazilian states of Amapá, Pará, Roraima and Amazonas. The Brazilian Highlands run northward from Argentina to the Amazon River Basin. The two highlands almost touch at Óbidos, where the Amazon Basin narrows to less than 2km in width.

These highlands represent some of the oldest geological formations on earth, ancient crystalline rocks such as granite, gneiss and schist. Such shield rocks are easily eroded, and the low rolling topography of both highlands testifies to the work of countless years of tropical rain. The average elevation of the Guyana and Brazilian Highlands is 900–1,200m, but newer mountains have pushed up in places; the Serra do Espinhaço range in east-central Brazil, for example, boasts the second highest peak in the country (Bandeira, at 2,890m). Pico da Neblina, the tallest mountain at 3,014m, rises out of the Guyana Highlands near the Venezuelan border. More than mere geological curiosities, the highlands have played a major role in Brazil's boom-and-bust history, for the shield rocks are veined in spots with gold, diamonds, and other semi-precious stones.

From Salvador all the way south to Florianópolis, the Brazilian Highlands plunge to the Atlantic in a series of steep folds. Known as the Great Escarpment, this mountainous dropoff has historically hampered travel and communication between the coast and the interior.

A vast sedimentary basin surrounding the Amazon River separates the two highlands from west to east. The Amazonian floodplain lies perfectly flat for thousands of miles, and geologists estimate that the sediment beneath it may run to as much as 4km deep. The basin is widest at the western edge of Brazil, and slims to a narrow, 2km-wide ribbon just east of Manaus before expanding again.

There are no volcanic areas in Brazil and, because of the predominance of ancient weathered rocks, no dramatic mountain scenery of the sort seen in the Andean countries.

CLIMATE

Brazil boasts a climate which, like its geography, is remarkably uniform. Draw a line from Recife, near Brazil's eastern bulge, southwesterly to Paraguay, and you'll have described an area with mean temperatures that vary no more than four degrees Celsius all year long. Only in the extreme south do winter temperatures – and keep in mind that July is the chilly heart of winter down here – plummet to 12°. Frosts occur in parts of São Paulo, Rio Grande do Sul and Paraná – you can buy postcards in Curitiba of their famous 'snowfall' in 1977 – but the areas described in this book rarely get cooler than 22° or warmer than 27° at any time. In terms of temperature, then, the terms 'summer' and 'winter' become pretty meaningless. Daily temperature fluctuations are usually greater than seasonal changes; anyone who has spent an evening aboard a cargo boat in Amazônia can appreciate the old saying, 'Night is the winter of the tropics'.

Rainfall is the chief climatic variable in Brazil. Since everything from mosquito hatches to road conditions to river heights depends on the rain level, much of your itinerary will have to do likewise. The statistics can be deceptive. Judging by annual rainfall alone, Brazil seems neither drenched nor parched. Most of the country receives less than 1,000mm, and mean annual rainfall exceeds 2,000mm in only a few areas: a thin coastal strip running north from São Luis to French Guiana, portions of eastern Amazonas, and Roraima. Even the notorious 'drought polygon' of northeastern Brazil receives, for the most part, between 600 and 1,000mm of rain annually. Yet rainy seasons – some more distinct than others, depending on the area – end up dumping much of the year's allotment in a few short months. Precipitation can be surprisingly concentrated even within the space of a single day. Bars and restaurants in Belém do a land-office business during the half-hour of intense rain that drenches the city most afternoons during the wet season. Unfortunately, Brazil's rainfall isn't always so predictable. We've taken boats in the Pantanal because the roads had washed out during the 'dry' season'; we've tramped down those same roads, dusty and lined with parched, tinder-dry vegetation, in the 'wet' season. The drought season which normally lasts six months in the northeast had already stretched to four years by 1984. Rainy and dry seasons in Amazônia, the Pantanal, and the northeast coast are discussed in more detail in their respective chapters. Always be prepared for a surprise, however.

HISTORY

Portuguese navigator Pedro Alvares Cabral assumed his ship had been blown off course when he bumped into northeastern Brazil in April 1500. Cabral was headed for India as part of the lucrative spice trade there which kept Portugal largely occupied for the next half century. Meanwhile, colonists began exporting *pau do brasil*, a jungle wood which produced both a red dye and a new name for the fledgling colony. By mid-century, wealthy Portuguese colonists in the northeast established sugarcane as a cash crop and imported African slaves to work it. To the south, near present-day São Paulo, Jesuit missionaries and poor Portuguese adventurers began pushing west into the vast interior of Brazil, toward Spanish territory.

Spain and Portugal had already demarcated their claims in South America; the Treaty of Tordesillas ceded most of the continent east of longitude 45°W to the Portuguese crown. The throne was inherited in 1580 by the Spanish, who controlled Brazil for over fifty years. During this period, the Dutch captured a number of important cities on the northeast coast. Portugal regained control of the country, but continued to neglect it for another century and a half.

The feudal principalities established by the crown in northeast Brazil became the most important world source of sugar. But the lower-class colonists near São Paulo had neither the capital nor the desire to establish farms. Instead, they pushed west, searching for gold and Indian slaves. Called *bandeirantes*, these soldiers of fortune clashed violently with Jesuit missionaries protecting the native Indians.

Just as the 17th century dawned, vast quantities of gold and diamonds were discovered in Minas Gerais. More gold turned up in Mato Grosso and Goiás, and Brazil's first 'boom' began. Gold soon replaced sugar as the colony's economic mainstay, especially as competition from the cane-growing Caribbean isles had gradually eroded Brazil's sugar markets. The Portuguese crown took a renewed interest in its colony, extracting heavy taxes on the gold. One particular gold-shipping port assumed pre-eminence and became Brazil's new capital – Rio de Janeiro.

The Jesuits' success in protecting Amerindians from the slave-trading *bandeirantes* eventually angered the crown. In 1759, all Jesuits were ousted from Brazil. The *bandeirantes* pushed the remaining Indians into the interior; farmers usurped their land, as did gold prospectors, and later, industrialists. São Paulo thus gradually became the wealthiest state in the viceroyalty.

In 1789, Brazilian nationalists under Tiradentes rebelled for the first time. They failed and Tiradentes was summarily executed, but the stage had been set for independence. When France invaded Portugal in 1808, King João VI sailed to Brazil and from there ruled the Portuguese empire. He returned to the mother country in 1821, leaving his son Pedro in charge of Brazil. A year later, Pedro I refused an order to return, and declared Brazil independent. Colonists crowned him constitutional emperor late that year. Brazil is thus the only country in the western hemisphere that chose a monarchal system over a republican one following independence.

Pedro I eventually fell into disfavour with the colonists, and they crowned his 15-year-old son. Pedro II turned out to be a charismatic and popular ruler, introducing liberal policies, promoting education and pulling Brazil into a cohesive nation over the next half century. But Pedro's liberalism proved his downfall; his outspoken stance against slavery (which was abolished in 1888) alienated the plantation owners who deposed him and proclaimed the Republic. A series of military and civilian leaders ruled the country for the next forty years, under a 'democratic' constitution which was actually more restrictive than the monarchal one. As for Pedro II, Brazil's most popular ruler died penniless in a French flophouse.

When gold production slowed to a trickle, coffee became the next 'boom crop'. Italian and Japanese immigrants came in their thousands to work the plantations near São Paulo. Amazônia provided the next boom – rubber – and Manaus became the Paris of the Western Hemisphere for a brief time. The end came in 1910, when Asian rubber plantations swiftly out-distanced Brazil's wild harvest.

The military gained control of Brazil during the world depression in the 1930s. Getúlio Vargas ruled for the next 15 years, a popular but iron-fisted dictator who succeeded in setting the country's finances right. He finally permitted elections in 1945, and was re-elected himself in 1950. Corruption marked his second term, however, and Vargas committed suicide four years later. His elected successor, Juscelino Kubitschek, built the new capital of Brasília and pushed the country near bankruptcy. By 1960, Brazil had become rife with corruption and was essentially leaderless, with the military pressing for renewed powers.

The generals made their move in 1964, installing a military dictatorship that would rule for the next 21 years. In 1968, the 'elected' president Marshal Costa e Silva dissolved Congress, exiled the opposition, and censored the press. The succession of military dictators borrowed millions from the International Monetary Fund (IMF), creating an illusion of prosperity and growth. While the world marvelled at the 'Brazilian miracle,' repression and torture came to a peak in the late sixties.

Finally, in 1979, military leaders announced a gradual return to democracy and Brazil re-opened politically. 1985 saw indirect elections; Tancredo Neves, an elderly and extremely popular statesman, won the presidency over the military's hand-picked candidate. But as Brazilians prepared for a political celebration of Carnaval-like proportions, Neves became ill. He died suddenly on the day before inauguration.

Neves' vice-president José Sarney – a colourless former backer of the military – succeeded him, or tried to. Brazil at that moment was reeling under a series of labour strikes, record unemployment and runaway inflation that topped 40,000% annually. After an initial period of timid rule, Sarney announced a sweeping economic programme (the Cruzado Plan) similar to Argentina's. He froze prices, abolished the old currency, raised wages and taxes, began implementing land reform and suspended payment of the huge national debt to the IMF indefinitely. The plan was as flawed as it was bold; black markets sprung up, undermining the plan from the start, strikes accelerated, and Sarney ended up backpedalling on most of the programme.

Brazil's first direct presidential election in 29 years took place in December 1989. Fernando Collor de Mello, a wealthy conservative, narrowly defeated charismatic labour leader Luiz Inácio da Silva. A former car factory lathe operator known popularly as 'Lula', da Silva had vowed to suspend debt payments indefinitely.

Collor campaigned as a reformist, and tried to maintain that image even as he was implicated by his own brother in stealing from the national till. Meanwhile, the economy continued to nosedive. Collor's entire cabinet resigned in spring 1992, his approval ratings having sunk to 16%, and his wife was indicted on charges of embezzling funds from a national charity. Calls for impeachment came from every sector of the country, and rumours even circulated of another military takeover if Collor wasn't quickly removed from office. The day before formal impeachment hearings, Collor resigned the presidency in disgrace. His vice president and successor, Itamar Franco, began the country's economic stabilisation with the Plano Cruzeiro Real.

This was mere preparation for the next economic plan, the Plano Real, ushered in by government minister Fernando Henrique Cardoso in 1994. Later that year, Fernando Henrique won the presidential elections handily, and Brazilians remain generally pleased with the economic stability that had so long eluded their nation. Annual inflation in 1996 was less than 10% and the economy continues to grow slowly but steadily. The next presidential elections are scheduled for 1998, and Fernando Henrique's re-election hopes will hinge on a constitutional amendment permitting a second term.

Brazilians have always been cynical regarding politics, but Collor's peaceful removal from office – and the economic stability which followed – has given them reason for cautious optimism. Still, Collor and his cronies remain newsworthy. In summer 1996, a business associate about to testify on his dealings with the ex-president was found shot to death in bed along with his young girlfriend. Collor himself lives in comfortable self-exile in Miami.

PEOPLE

Brazil's population has increased tenfold in the last century, so that it nearly exceeds that of the rest of the continent combined. 1994 estimates put the population at 160 million, most of whom are concentrated along the narrow coastal strip.

São Paulo, with over 11 million inhabitants, is now the world's third largest city and typifies the disturbing pattern of growth in modern Brazil: rural Brazilians have flocked to the large cities in such numbers that housing, employment and health needs will never be met. Every urban centre has its *favelas* – pathetic shantytowns, largely populated by refugees from the impoverished and drought-plagued northeast portion of the country. At the same time, the vast interior states of Pará, Amazonas, Goiás and Mato Grosso contain less than one person per square kilometre. The country's leaders have been trying to lure colonists into the interior for at least three decades now, with schemes ranging from the symbolic founding of Brasília near the country's geographical centre to recent land giveaways in Rondônia. They have met with little success.

Brazil is a nation of young people; over half the population is under 20 years of age. Recent surveys indicate that literacy is 80% and that the average life expectancy is 65 years, although both figures seem far too high once you've visited poor rural areas. And Brazil remains a nation of poor people: 1% of the population controls 45% of all the agricultural land; and 10% of all Brazilians spend 51% of the national income.

Brazil's cultural mosaic, originally shaped from Portuguese, African, and Amerindian elements, remains unique. Europeans and Amerindians interbred throughout South America, but nowhere else on the continent (with the exception of the Guianas) will you find such a pronounced and widespread African influence. This should come as little surprise: Brazil imported fully 31% of all the slaves sold in the New World while the Spanish-speaking countries together bought a mere 9%. By the beginning of the 19th century, blacks were the dominant element in the country's population. Whites gradually became more numerous with racial mixing and increased European immigration in the 19th and 20th centuries. During this period, thousands of Italians, Germans, Poles and Swiss settled in Brazil, mostly from São Paulo southward. Mosques in cities like Curitiba attest to the country's Lebanese and Syrian immigrants, while the Japanese population of São Paulo is equalled nowhere else outside Japan.

Despite this varied racial mix and the sheer size of the country, Brazil has managed to achieve an amazing cultural unity. *Brasileiros* of all skin colours, from Amazonian jungle town to the boutiques of São Paulo, retain a strong and deep-rooted sense of themselves as a distinct people. Along with this goes the national pride in Brazil as the world's greatest 'racial democracy.' Sociologists have been debunking that claim for years, and no objective observer can deny that discrimination and prejudice do exist in

Brazil. We've heard some shocking racial slurs levied against '*os pretos*', often from Brazilians who, in the United States, would themselves be considered coloured!

Still, 'racial democracy' is not entirely a myth. Most Brazilians give at least lip service to the country's strong African heritage. Brazil's most popular author, Jorge Amado, has promoted Afro-Brazilian culture in at least a half-dozen best-selling novels. The words *nego* and *nega* have long been terms of affection, applied to even the blondest of Brazilians. The noticeable lack of racial tension makes far more sense when you realize that Brazilians recognise at least a dozen colour distinctions; a 'black' American, for instance, might be described by Brazilians as either a *morena*, *morena clara*, *sarará* or any of ten other names depending on skin colour, hair texture, and facial features. With so many teams playing, it's not easy to choose sides for a racial tug-of-war. And, as a result, there are no Brazilian social classes based on skin colour alone.

The forgotten element is the Amerindian. Like all American Indians, Brazil's first immigrants came from Asia some 30,000 years ago via the Bering Strait. The Tupi bands, however, never formed cohesive political units – indeed, many had no concept whatsoever of a leader – and never became 'civilised' in the sense of the Mayas, Aztecs or Incas. Their agriculture, tools, and housing remained primitive; they never developed a written means of communication. Yet it was these Indians who taught the European settlers how to survive in the New World: how to cultivate new crops, how to hunt and fish, how to navigate the rivers and penetrate the jungle. There are now fewer than 150,000 Amerindians living in Brazil, roughly one-sixth of the estimated population when the Portuguese landed. The now-defunct Indian Protection Service itself was responsible for aerial bombing raids on native villages and other campaigns designed to dispossess Amerindians of their land. The National Indian Foundation (FUNAI), inaugurated in the aftermath of scandals involving the Indian Protective Service, is still largely ineffectual in its attempts to protect native land from gold-seekers, farmers, and ranchers. The tribes themselves have won some recent land battles through demonstrations, road seizures, and the work of charismatic chiefs such as Raoni.

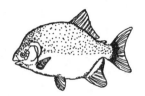

Chapter Two

Preparations

RED TAPE
Entry requirements
Everyone travelling to Brazil needs a valid passport. You may also need a visa, depending on your nationality. Brazil's reciprocal visa requirement means that citizens of countries requiring Brazilians to carry visas (currently including the United States, France, Canada and Australia) will need a visa *prior* to arriving in Brazil. British, West German, Dutch, Swiss and Italian citizens do not need a visa, but must show an onward ticket upon entering Brazil (or proof that they can pay for a return ticket, see below). These regulations could change, so check with the local Brazilian consulate before your trip.

Citizens of countries requiring Brazilian visas must get them by one of two methods: personally applying at a Brazilian consulate; or applying by mail to a private agency contracting with the Brazilian government to issue visas. You can no longer receive visas via mail from Brazilian consulates. Visas are good for 90 days from the date of issue, and you must arrive in Brazil within 90 days of issuance. Visas allow multiple entries and can be renewed for another 90 days. Travel agencies will furnish you with the addresses of agencies which issue visas for the Brazilian government. You'll need to telephone or write to the agency well in advance of your trip. To issue the visa, they'll require the following:

- the completed application form, a passport valid for at least six months from your intended date of arrival
- proof of a bank account (usually a letter from your bank will suffice, or a recent monthly bank statement)
- proof from your employer that you have a job
- a photocopy of your plane ticket out of Brazil, or other proof that you'll be able to leave
- two standard passport photos
- fee (currently about US$35, but this may depend on how many applications are requested)

The 90-day visa may be renewed within Brazil for longer stays (but see *Visa Renewals* in *Chapter Four* for restrictions).

Other documents

Brazil does not require any proof of immunisation when adults enter the country from North America, Europe, or Australia (children between the ages of three months and six must have proof of polio vaccination). Nevertheless, if you plan to visit either the Amazon or the Pantanal (or if you plan to re-enter Brazil from any country near the Amazon), you should get at the very least a yellow fever immunisation and carry the International Vaccination Certificate as proof (see *Immunisations* in *Chapter Three*).

If there's even the remotest chance that you'll rent a car in Brazil, bring an International Driver's Permit, your driver's licence, and a credit card. We've rented before without a credit card, but it required that we furnish the agency with our return airline tickets, a tactic that might not always work (see *Chapter Four*). If you plan to do any scuba diving, don't forget your C-card and perhaps a few recent logbook entries.

NOTE: Make a photocopy of your passport, including the visa page, to smooth the way if it's lost or stolen. Also make copies of your return airline tickets; on extended trips, these will suffice in renewing your visa, allowing you to leave the originals with friends or in a hotel safe. Make sure you've written down your credit card number and the telephone number to call if the card is stolen.

Brazilian consulates/diplomatic offices

US
Brazilian Consulate General, 630 Fifth Ave, New York, NY10111 (tel: 212 757 3080). Consulates also in San Francisco (tel: 415 981 8170), Los Angeles (tel: 213 651 2664), Washington, DC (tel: 202 745 2700), Boston (tel: 617 542 4000), Chicago (tel: 312 464 0244), Miami (tel: 305 285 6200).

Canada
Brazilian Embassy, 255 Albert St, Suite 900, Ottawa, Ont K1P-6A9 (tel: 613 237 1090).

England
Brazilian Consulate, 32 Green Street, London W1Y 4AT (tel: 0171 499 0877).

Germany
Kurfurstendamm 11, 1 Stock, 1 Berlin, 15 (tel: 30 883 1208).

France
34 Cours Albert, 1er, 75008 Paris (tel: 1 259 9250).

Australia
19 Forster Crescent, Yarralumla, Canberra, ACT 2600 (tel: 062 732 372).

MONEY: HOW MUCH TO BUDGET

Brazil is currently one of South America's most expensive countries, outranked only by Chile, Argentina, and French Guiana.

Obviously, how much you'll spend depends on your style of travel. As a couple, Jayne and I spent around US$2,300 for a recent month-long trip, or US$38 per day per person; this includes some time spent in both the backcountry and in cities and towns, some camping as well as some paid lodging in houses or budget hotels, guide fees, all food and drink, and transportation by bus, boat and rental car. The most frugal travellers we met in Brazil during this same period spent about US$750 pp per month. Your biggest expenses will be lodging, transportation, and guide fees; one can still eat very cheaply in Brazil. If you're planning to travel through Brazil by bus, budget around US$0.04 per kilometre of highway.

In towns and cities, a couple can travel almost as cheaply as a single person, since most rooms have double beds and you're charged accordingly. Meals are huge, and as a couple you can often split one, further reducing costs.

Figure on your daily living expenses being about the same for days spent in the backcountry and days spent in towns and cities. This may seem illogical at first – after all, lodging costs little or nothing at all in the backcountry – but you'll soon find that everything else is pricey as you leave the metropolitan centres. For example, the cost of living in Mato Grosso is double that of São Paulo, due mainly to high food prices. Transportation also gets expensive when you run out of road and have to hire boatmen or four-wheel drive vehicles. Gasoline is costly in Brazil (they have to import it), and costlier still when it has to be trucked or shipped into the wilder regions of the country. Finally, your average price per day will escalate sharply if you plan to rent a car or travel by air.

Average costs of such things as bus travel per hour and per kilometre, hotels, car rental, and meals can be found in *Chapter Four*. You'll find further price information by area in *Chapters Five, Six* and *Seven*.

The US dollar is the only reliable medium of exchange in Brazil, whether using cash or cheques. You can now get cash advances on VISA credit cards at many Brazilian banks, so if you've got one, bring it. Bring the bulk of your money (about 75%) in the form of travellers cheques and the remainder in cash dollars. Banks and black marketeers accepting travellers cheques have never once turned down our American Express cheques, and we have exchanged them in virtually every state in Brazil; according to reports, Thomas Cook and Barclays are also accepted, though not quite as widely as American Express. The handiest denominations for exchange are US$100 and US$50 notes and cheques. See *Chapter Four* for a detailed discussion of currency exchange and cash advances in Brazil.

WHAT TO BRING

Whether you're visiting the Amazon, the northeast coast, or the Pantanal, remember that you'll often be hauling your luggage around on foot, cramming it into tiny luggage racks in buses, manoeuvring it through mobs of people, suspending it from trees, and stowing it in small boats. We get by with a nylon duffle bag and a small daypack apiece. Any of the non-rigid nylon 'suitcases' will work, but make sure they've got a comfortable shoulder strap. Internal-frame backpacks are another excellent choice; local prejudice against *muchileiros* (backpackers) seems to be waning in Brazil. Avoid standard (rigid) suitcases; and remember that you can always buy cheap nylon bags in Brazil if you need more space. Our luggage doesn't allow for buying much along the way, so we try to plan our trip with a shopping spree at the very end, purchasing extra bags for the trip home.

Clothes

Most people take far more clothing than they need. Again, remember that you can easily buy extra clothing if you need it in Brazil (shoes larger than size 39 are the exception). Choose clothing that you can easily wash by hand and which dries quickly; if you spend several months in the backcountry, this routine will quickly wear out your clothes, so don't bring anything you can't part with. We generally throw away or give away half the clothing we take to Brazil by the end of a trip.

Take one pair of loose-fitting athletic trousers made of synthetic fabric. These are cool, they pack well and dry quickly. Bring also a pair of hiking shorts with pockets, and a pair of nylon jogger's shorts. Avoid jeans – they're hot, bulky, they soak up water like a blotter, and you'll turn homicidal trying to wash and dry them.

My favourite shirt for all purposes is a loose-fitting cotton/synthetic blend workshirt with long sleeves and snaps rather than buttons. You'll need long sleeves against the sun and insects, and the snaps never catch and pull off in the rainforest. Take also a couple of T-shirts for beach use and as layering against the cold at night.

Swim suits are a must along the northeast coast – you'll spend virtually all day in them – and they'll see some use in the Amazon if you're bathing in crowded areas. To avoid offending the locals, women should bring a fairly modest swim suit for use in the backcountry.

Rubber sandals (thongs) are invaluable, especially along the northeast coast where they're all the footwear anyone owns. Except in insect-plagued areas, they're also great for jungle camp use in the Amazon, boat travel, and for much of the Pantanal. Unlike shoes, extra pairs can be purchased in Brazil up to size 44.

Take along a pair of tennis or running shoes; they're practical for everything from muddy jungle trails to sandstone cliffs. Some rainforest buffs, including a number of guides and camp workers, swear by army surplus jungle boots, which feature canvas uppers and thicker soles than running shoes. Leave your standard leather hiking boots at home. As noted earlier, if you wear a size larger than size 39 and plan to spend more than a couple of months in the hinterlands, bring extra footwear from home.

It doesn't often get cold in the areas described in this book, so you needn't pack bulky items like sweaters. But the person who tries to convince you that it's *always* warm in Brazil has probably never done much camping there. I'm a seasoned high-mountain camper and skier, yet one of the most miserably cold nights I've ever spent was huddling in a tent in the Brazilian Pantanal. The Pantanal can experience bitter cold fronts in June and July, while the Amazon jungle and river boats get unbelievably chilly at night. Practice layering with T-shirts, a sweatshirt, or even lightweight polypropylene long underwear in the Pantanal. In Amazônia, bundle up for the night with extra T-shirts and a woollen blanket (see below). A woollen knitted cap is a good idea, since it is easy to pack and prevents heat loss from that most important part of your body, the head.

You probably won't spend your entire trip in the backcountry, so bring one set of nice clothes which need no ironing: a short-sleeved dress shirt and a pair of slacks. Dress shoes take up far too much room when toting a single bag, so I get by with a single pair of black leather tennis shoes for both backcountry and city use. As soon as I hit the city I wash off the jungle mud, let them air-dry, and pay a shoe-shine boy to apply some black polish.

You'll want a cap or visor to shade you from the sun, at least in the Pantanal and the northeast coast.

Toiletries

You can buy most toiletries in Brazil, with the following four exceptions: sun screen lotions, especially with protection factors greater than 8; tampons, which are extremely difficult to find, especially in rural towns; contact lens solutions; and moisturizing creams for use on sunburned skin.

Camping, fishing, and wildlife-viewing equipment

If you can get hold of a hammock from Mexico's Yucatán peninsula, do so; they compress to less than half the size of any other hammock I've ever seen, they dry quickly, and they're lightweight. Otherwise, wait until you're in Brazil to buy a hammock and mosquito net. Those who aren't comfortable in hammocks may want to bring along an internal-frame mosquito net for use with a sleeping bag. They can also be placed on a bed in mosquito-ridden hotel rooms, and barely weigh more than 1kg; Long Road Travel Supply, PO Box 638, Alameda, California, 94501 USA, markets several models. Bring along a bedsheet to cover yourself in the hammock. In Amazônia, you'll need a woollen blanket to keep warm at night, both in the jungle and aboard cargo boats. We prefer, however, to buy these in Brazil just prior to entering the backcountry; then we give them away rather than have them take up valuable space in our luggage.

You'll want to bring along a flashlight (lantern) and extra batteries. Anyone visiting the Amazon rainforest who wants to see animals should also carry a headlamp for night walks (see *Chapter Six*). Recreational Equipment, Inc. in the US markets a lithium-powered model with two lamps that operates for up to eight hours on the highest amperage lamp (17 hours on the lower). It uses two six-volt lithium batteries, and retails with batteries at about US$60. Ray-O-Vac makes a much cheaper model which utilizes a heavy duty six-volt lantern battery suspended from your belt.

Binoculars are absolutely vital for wildlife-viewing in the Pantanal, and helpful at times in the Amazon. I'm still amazed at the number of travellers who visit wildlife areas without binoculars and then have to borrow them. They make a huge difference, allowing you to get eyeball-to-eyeball with an alligator or a nesting stork. We carry a lightweight (20 ounce) 7x35 model, although serious birdwatchers may want an 8-or even 10-power model.

A camping stove is by far the most practical way to cook in the backcountry. During our first trip to Brazil we packed a butane stove, but found few places selling Camping Gaz cartridges. For short trips you may be able to bring an adequate supply from home, but remember that it is technically illegal to take such cartridges aboard aircraft. Unfortunately, many of the camping stoves available in the United States and Europe rely on white gas (paraffin), which is virtually unheard of in Brazil. You can manage by burning unleaded gasoline in these stoves, but it will produce a dirty yellow flame of lower heat and will constantly plug up the works. Much more practical are multiple-fuel stoves such as the MXR X-GK, or kerosene-burning stoves such as the Optimus 00. Kerosene (*querosene*) is available throughout Brazil and is dirt cheap. At a pinch, unleaded gasoline can be burned in kerosene stoves.

Some sort of water purification system is essential if you'll be camping, be it chemical treatment with iodine or one of the filter kits. See *Chapter Three* for a list of options.

A small cooking set of nesting aluminium pots, along with cutlery and plastic cups completes your camp kitchen. Don't forget a small plastic bottle of dishwashing detergent and a dish scrubber or scouring pad.

Bring plenty of strong nylon cord for tying and hanging things in camp, as well as for suspending your hammock. Polyethylene sheeting works well as a dry groundcover and as a roof over your hammocks in the rainforest. Get the kind with metal grommets along the edges, allowing it to be stretched tightly with cord. This stuff is quite bulky, so don't unpack it from its original bag until you're ready to use it.

Buy several plastic bottles of insect repellent. The best stuff contains 95% DEET (diethyl-meta-toluamide). DEET-based repellents are now available in Brazil, but they aren't any cheaper than buying them beforehand.

A compass is essential for walking in the rainforest or trackless Pantanal grasslands. Practise using it before you leave home. Another aid in finding your way back is plastic flagging tape in bright orange or red; you can buy rolls of it wherever surveying equipment is sold.

Serious anglers will want to bring fishing gear from home. See page 93 in *Chapter Five* for recommended tackle; what works in the Pantanal also works in the Amazon. If you're just out for piranhas, you can easily buy hooks and line in Brazil.

Bring at least one plastic water bottle – they're far sturdier than the litre plastic bottles sold in Brazil, which can puncture or crack in your pack. On an average day-hike in the hot Brazilian sun, you'll probably need several water bottles.

Miscellaneous

Don't forget your malaria pills and other medicinal items (see *Chapter Three*).

Clear plastic Ziplock sandwich bags are a traveller's godsend. We pack everything from matches to pills to dishwashing equipment in Ziplock bags, and they invariably take up less space than the original container. Bring along plenty of extras.

You'll use a pocket knife hundreds of times in a trip; try to get one with scissors. Bring slow-burning candles to cope with the frequent power cuts in the backcountry towns. Film is difficult to find and very expensive, so bring far more than you think you'll need, along with all other photographic equipment, including extra photocell batteries and a tripod (see *Chapter Four* for more information).

Buy a fabric money pouch for concealing your valuables under your clothing. These are available in many travel accessory stores and are far superior to leather money belts worn outside the clothing. The pouch should be large enough to hold your passport, with a thin elastic strap securing it around your waist.

Additional items you may want to bring along include: spare glasses or contact lenses and your glasses prescription; sunglasses; Portuguese-English dictionary and phrasebook; photos of your home, family, and friends; postcards from home (your new-found Brazilian friends will want to see these); a sewing kit; pens and notebooks; a hand-held calculator (for figuring currency exchange); a battery-operated travel alarm clock (much wildlife-watching requires that you get up before dawn); toilet paper; and earplugs for noisy hotels or night buses.

LEARNING THE LANGUAGE

With the obvious exceptions of money and passport, the most valuable thing you can possibly take with you on the plane to Brazil is a rudimentary knowledge of Portuguese. Nothing else is spoken outside the large cities. I once listened in on an American bragging to his breakfast companions that he could communicate virtually anything with body language, gestures, and facial expressions. 'The eyes speak,' he said. As soon as the waiter appeared, however, Mr Body Language relied on his bilingual Brazilian friend to order breakfast. I'd been anxious to see how he was going to order scrambled eggs, toast, and black coffee with those eloquent eyes of his.

This doesn't mean that you have to be fluent before catching the plane. For that matter, we have known gringos who managed to stumble into some fairly remote backwaters with nothing more than hand signals and sheer bravado. Headed out of Santarém on the way to the jungle gold fields of Serra Pelada, we met a German who had somehow found his way there – apparently by bus – without knowing the word for bus station. Then there was the Israeli who'd spent three months in Brazil and couldn't count to ten in Portuguese. When he needed to bargain, he would get out his pen and scribble numbers. When he needed to use the toilet, he merely pointed to his crotch.

While it's possible to travel this way – like a pinball careening blindly from post to post – it can't be much fun. From a purely practical standpoint, the inability to communicate costs both time and money. There can even be an element of danger involved; the linguistically deficient river traveller may not discover the meaning of the words *cascata perigosa* until his canoe is pitching headfirst down a frothy chute.

Travellers who can speak some Portuguese, on the other hand, will find themselves invited into homes, given lifts, fed meals and, far more importantly, offered friendship. Brazilians are a gregarious people, even more so than most other South Americans; if you can do more than ask directions in Portuguese, you'll be included in all sorts of cultural activities, the kind of things that transform a mere tourist into a traveller. We've ended up guests at rural weddings and pig barbecues, birthday parties and basketball games, gone catfish fishing and wild-fruit browsing.

Leave your Spanish at the border. Brazilians are fond of saying that 'Spanish is but Portuguese badly spoken,' which fairly sums up their pride in the national tongue. Speaking *castelhano,* as Brazilians refer to Spanish, will neither earn you friends nor get you very far. Many Brazilians can understand rudimentary Spanish, but sadly, it doesn't work the other way around. Even native Spanish speakers throw their hands up in exasperation when forced to decipher spoken Portuguese for the first time. A Mexican friend of ours who boarded a Rio-bound Varig jet confident in his ability to understand this sister tongue found himself, within five minutes, begging the flight attendant to speak English. The similarities between the two languages become far more obvious in print; Spanish speakers will have little trouble reading signs, newspapers, and documents in Portuguese.

For a select list of Portuguese grammar books, see the *Further Reading* appendix. I've recommended some tapes and records as well, since they're an excellent way to learn pronunciation. Still, nothing beats a tutor. For US$10 an hour, Jayne and I hired a Brazilian woman to converse with us one hour a week for several months before our first trip. It turned out to be the best travel investment we've ever made.

Not surprisingly, Brazil boasts a number of distinctive regional accents (*sotaques*), but don't let that discourage your language studies. Our first day in the arid badlands of northeast Brazil came as a linguistic shock; sharing the back of a flatbed truck with thirty leathery *sertanejos*, we had to wonder if this was the same language taught by our city-bred tutor from the south of Brazil. It didn't help that the average passenger owned fewer teeth than a professional hockey player. Nevertheless, they understood *us* perfectly, and before the day was out we had begun to adjust ourselves to their sing-song, hillbilly version of Portuguese.

See also *Appendix One*.

GETTING THERE

Airline tickets to Brazil vary greatly in price, and you can save enormous amounts by planning your trip well in advance. For example, we were just about ready to dish out US$1,400 per round-trip ticket to Rio from our home in the northwest United States when we found a fare on another airline which cut that cost to US$900. Unfortunately, prices and airline routes change all the time, so the information below is necessarily vague.

Work through a travel agent; many specialise in South America and are able to discount tickets bought in bulk. But do your own fare and route research – before signing the cheque – to make sure you're getting the best deal. Constantly check ads in the travel section of your newspaper; your travel agent may not deal with a particular airline offering budget fares, and you can either bring such fares to his/her attention or else deal with the agent advertising them. Many agents will assume you want to fly directly to your destination – New York to Rio, for example – even when a two-hour layover in Paraguay or Peru might save you hundreds of dollars. Ask to see your agent's IATA airlines' schedule book and learn how to use it. Even good agents don't have the time to research creative and unusual routes, and we've discovered some on our own with the IATA 'Bible.' Remember, however, that some budget airlines are non-IATA. In many cases, the cheapest fare will end up being a circuitous route with several airlines rather than a direct one (Miami-Guadeloupe-Cayenne-Belém, for example). Airline fares obey no human laws of logic or reason; never assume that the lengthiest route is the most expensive.

Besides the travel agents and flight information sources listed below, *South American Explorer*, the quarterly magazine of the South American Explorers Club, is an excellent source of up-to-date information and advertisements on bargain fares to Brazil. See *Information,* below, for information on the Club.

Direct flights from Europe

From London, both Varig and British Airways fly to Rio and São Paulo, the latter twice weekly. Air France flies to both Rio and Recife from Paris. Lufthansa provides service from Germany to Rio and São Paulo. TAP runs flights from Lisbon to Rio and Recife. Varig flies to Brazil from Rome and Milan. Transbrasil has flights from Vienna and Amsterdam to Brazil. Iberia, SAS and Swissair also serve Rio from Europe. Cheap charter flights are reportedly available, especially from Lisbon and Madrid. Journey Latin America, 14-16 Devonshire Road, Chiswick, London W4 2HD (tel: 0181 747 3108) is an excellent source of bargain flights and combined Central and South America airpasses, and publishes a magazine, *Papagaio,* listing bargain fares. Also try Trailfinders, 42-50 Earls Court Road, London W8 6FT (tel: 0171 938 3366), STA Travel (tel: 0171 937 1221 in London), and South American Experience, 47 Causton Street, Pimlico, London SW1P 4AT (tel: 0171 976 5511). Last Frontiers, Long Crendon, Buckinghamshire (tel: 01844 208405) offer tailor-made tours as well as flights.

Direct flights from the US and Canada

From the US, the primary carriers are United, American, Varig, Transbrasil, Vasp, JAL, and Aerolíneas Argentinas. From Los Angeles, both Varig and JAL fly twice a week to Rio (with a stop in Lima) and then on to São Paulo. Flying time averages about 13 hours from Los Angeles. Currently, the cheapest round-trip airfares from Los Angeles-Rio cost around US$600. Varig, and Aerolíneas Argentinas both fly to Rio from Miami, though not all directly. Flight time from Miami is about seven hours, and the cheapest current Miami-Rio round-trip airfares cost around US$580. You can also reach Manaus twice weekly from Miami on Varig. Vasp (until recently a strictly internal carrier) is now running flights from Miami and Los Angeles to Rio and São Paulo. Varig offers flights once a week from Miami to Belém, then on to Recife and Salvador. Varig flies to Rio from New York (flight time around nine hours), while Canadian Pacific provides service from Toronto to Rio. The current cheapest New York-Rio round-trip airfares cost around US$650. Flights from Miami are generally the cheapest, even if you live much closer to Los Angeles, as we do. One of the very cheapest fares to Brazil used to be the Lineas Aereas Paraguayas (LAP) Miami-Asunción-Rio flight, but at this writing, LAP has gone out of business and has been replaced by LAPSA, which is not flying from the US. Manaus may well be the cheapest airfare destination in Brazil from the US, so even if you're headed to Belém, the Pantanal, or the northeast coast, you should investigate the cost of a flight to Manaus followed by a domestic flight rather than flying to Rio.

Cheap fares are available from travel agents including Brazil Tours, 8416 Lankershim Bd, Suite 204, Sun Valley CA 91352 (tel: 1 800 927 8352), Around the World Travel (tel: 1 800 471 6333), and Brazil Air Travel and Tours, 10700 Santa Monica Bd, Suite 15, Los Angeles CA 90025 (tel:

1 800 441 8515). One of the best sources of current information on bargain flights from the US to Brazil, as well as travel agents specialising in such flights, is the monthly magazine *Brazzil*, subscriptions available from PO Box 42536, Los Angeles CA 9005-0536.

Flights from Australia

The most direct flight is with Aerolíneas Argentinas, which flies once or twice a week from Sydney to Rio, via Buenos Aires. Qantas/Varig flies to Rio via Los Angeles. Alternately, fly Lan Chile from Tahiti to Santiago and change there. I'm told that many Australians combine trips to South America and Europe, since it's scarcely more expensive to visit Europe than Brazil.

Brazil Airpass

Three Brazilian airlines – Vasp, Varig, and Transbrasil – are currently offering airpasses which allow almost unlimited flights within Brazil during any two to three week period for a fixed price of around US$330-450. Depending on your itinerary, it can be either a great deal or a waste of money. Although the Brazil Airpass deal is good only for flights within Brazil, it deserves mention here because you can only purchase it from a travel agent *outside* the country. There are numerous limitations and variations on airpasses, and travellers will want to carefully consider their itinerary before purchasing one; see *Chapter Four* for details.

Extended trips

Most economy airline tickets stipulate a stay of less than 90 days. Some bargain fares are restricted to 30 days, and charter flights often restrict you to three weeks or less. So if you plan to spend more time in Brazil, you'll be restricted to standard fares which often cost considerably more.

You can always buy a one-way fare, although these are almost always far more than half a bargain round-trip fare. For those of us requiring a visa, there's also the problem of the onward-ticket stipulation of the Brazilian government: no return ticket, no visa. This problem, however, can almost always be circumvented by providing, along with your application for a visa, a letter from your travel agent stating that you have a round-trip ticket. If you can't convince your agent to provide such a mendacious letter, a bank statement showing that you have sufficient funds to purchase a return ticket will also work.

A second option is a round-trip ticket with no set return date. Such open airline tickets are available for stays of up to a year, but with few exceptions these aren't nearly as cheap as the limited-time fares, and you may have to pay any return-trip fare increases that occur during that time. Do check around, however, because you can occasionally find a good open fare. For instance, at this writing there is a fare good for a year from Los Angeles to São Paulo for the same price as a bargain Los Angeles-Rio fare. There are other problems with such tickets, however. Carrying a return ticket around for months on end gets to be a security worry; leaving it in a Brazilian safety deposit box, a trusted hotel or with a Brazilian friend is a good idea, but problems arise if you have to leave Brazil in order to get a visa renewal. One solution already mentioned is a letter to the Brazilian consulate from your bank assuring them that you have sufficient funds to get home. Some travellers told us they sold back their return ticket but kept the travel agent's receipt to show the authorities; this ruse may work for the initial 90-day visa, but I can't imagine it would work for a visa renewal within Brazil.

Long-term visitors not requiring a visa were once better off buying a one-way ticket to Brazil and worrying about the return ticket later. Flights purchased within Brazil aren't cheap however, and the government is charging a whopping 25% tax on international airlines tickets. So you're best off either buying an open-jawed two-way ticket at home or else leaving Brazil by overland routes and flying home via another South American country. Once again, check with a travel agent at home experienced in such matters before deciding.

Anyone planning a trip over 90 days should refer to *Chapter Four* before fixing an itinerary.

Overland routes

From **Venezuela**, the only point of entry is the border 16km from Santa Elena de Uairén. Overland travellers may take the daily buses from either Carácas, Ciudad Guayana, or Ciudad Bolívar to El Dorado and onward over the newly-paved road to Santa Elena. Alternatively, Orinoco operates a direct daily bus from Ciudad Bolívar all the way to Santa Elena (14 hours, US$20). The easiest way to reach Brazil, however, is to catch the direct bus from Ciudad Bolívar to Boa Vista, Brazil (18 hours, US$36). Buses also leave for Santa Elena from Tumeremo, a town north of El Dorado; travellers report that it may be easier to catch a bus here than further down the line at El Dorado, by which time it may be full. The trip is scenic but rough, and all vehicles get stopped frequently by Venezuelan border police. União Cascavel buses leave Santa Elena daily at 08.30 and 15.00 for Boa Vista, Brazil (four hours, US$16), a trip that used to take nine hours until the road was paved. Get exit stamps at the immigration police station next to the bus terminal in Santa Elena, and get rid of your Venezuelan currency before heading to Boa Vista, where it cannot be exchanged. Despite the newly-paved road, this route remains one of the worst overland routes into Brazil, due to frequent, lengthy, and rude inspections by police.

From **Bolivia**, travellers may enter Brazil nearest the Pantanal by catching either the *ferrobus* or the regular train from Santa Cruz de la Sierra to Quijarro, which is the Bolivian border town close to Corumbá, Brazil. The *ferrobus* runs from Santa Cruz to Quijarro on Tuesday, Thursday and Saturday (12 hours, US$25, frequently sold out a week in advance), and the regular train – the famous 'Trem da Morte' (Death Train) makes the trip on Mondays and Fridays (roughly 20 hours, but often taking several days in wet weather, US$15-30, depending on class). You can get a visa for Brazil at the Brazilian consulate in Santa Cruz, Av Busch 330, but it could take up to a day to process. Without a visa, however, you'll be turned back at the border. If you know you're coming this way, get your Brazilian visa at home. Taxis, collectives, and buses meet the *ferrobus* and trains in Quijarro and take travellers over the Paraguai River to Corumbá, Brazil. This area is rife with cocaine and alligator-hide smugglers, and plainclothes police on both sides of the border make frequent and often unpleasant searches of baggage and clothing. You may need to show proof of yellow fever vaccination to enter Brazil. Further details on the Quijarro-Corumbá crossing can be found in the section on Corumbá in *Chapter Five*. A second point of entry from Bolivia is at Guayaramerín on the banks of the Mamoré River. Get an exit stamp at the Bolivian immigration office on Av Costañera next to the docks, and take the ferry or hired boats across the river to Guajará-Mirim, Brazil. If you don't have a Brazilian visa, you can get one from the Brazilian consulate on Calle Beni near the town plaza (visas aren't necessary if you're merely visiting Guajará-Mirim, but are required for going any further into Brazil). The Brazilian federal police across the river will stamp your passport (sometimes requesting to see proof of yellow fever vaccination), and from there, daily bus and riverboats travel to the Amazonian metropolises of Porto Velho and Manaus. A third entry point from Bolivia, also near the Pantanal, is at the Bolivian town of San Matías, accessed via bus from San Ignacio. From San Matías, there's a single daily bus to Cáceres, Brazil.

The only route from either **Peru** or **Colombia** involves a border crossing along the Amazon River (this portion above the confluence with the Rio Negro is known in Brazil as the Solimões). From Peru, riverboats leaving Iquitos are virtually the only option; some cargo boats go all the way downriver to Manaus, but most go only as far as Ramón Castilla, near the border towns of Tabatinga, Leticia, and Benjamin Constant. Travellers requiring a visa to enter Brazil should get it in Iquitos; all boats stop for Peruvian exit stamps at a river post called Puerto Alegría, two hours upstream from Benjamin Constant. Canoes run from Ramón Castilla across the river to Benjamin Constant, Brazil. Virtually all boats headed downriver to Manaus leave from Benjamin Constant. Canoes also go from Ramón Castilla to Tabatinga, Brazil, on the opposite bank from Benjamin Constant. Entry to Brazil from Colombia is via Leticia; motorized canoes will take you from here to Benjamin Constant.

From **Paraguay**, travellers headed for the Pantanal may cross the border at Pedro Juan Caballero. The 'border' here is nothing more than a wide, dusty boulevard, and travel to Ponta Porã, Brazil, on the other side is totally unrestricted. You must have an exit stamp from Paraguay, however, before going any further into Brazil. Buses leave Ponta Porã daily for Campo

Grande, Brazil. A second point of entry is at Ciudad del Este (formerly
Puerto Stroessner), a Paraguayan casino town near the Iguaçu Falls and the
huge Itaipu dam. Simply take a bus across the Friendship Bridge to Foz do
Iguaçu, Brazil.

There are no roads connecting Brazil and **Suriname**, and those wishing
to go overland to or from Suriname must do so via French Guiana. However,
only French and Brazilian citizens can enter Brazil from **French Guiana**
at Saint-Georges (this according to our friend Robert, an immigration
policeman in French Guiana; check in Cayenne to see if things have
changed). From **Guyana**, you must fly first from Georgetown to Lethem
(a road is being built but is presently virtually impassable), then cross the
Takutu river by boat, and finally walk or hitch three kilometres to Bom
Fim. A bus departs Bom Fim at 08.00 on Tues, Thur, and Sat for Boa
Vista, from where there is daily bus transport to Manaus.

WHEN TO GO AND HOW LONG TO STAY

The Pantanal, the Amazon, and the northeast coast to a lesser extent, all
have periods of the year when travel is best, mostly weather-dependent.
But those periods vary somewhat depending on what you plan to do and
see. Read the sections on *When to Go* in *Chapters Five* to *Eight* for details
by area. In general, the best time to see the regions described in this book
would be between late June and early October, avoiding the rainy seasons
as well as the hordes of Brazilians on vacation.

Backcountry travel requires more time than, say, a whirlwind tour of
major Brazilian cities. For this reason you probably shouldn't attempt a
visit of less than two weeks. Even so, you won't have time to sample more
than two of the regions described in this book on a 14-day jaunt. We have
never felt it worth our airfare to spend less than a month in Brazil. If you
do plan a trip lasting less than a month, you should definitely fly between
gateway cities rather than taking the bus.

INFORMATION

Brazil's national tourism authority Embratur has its headquarters at Setor
Comercial Norte, Quadra 2, Bloco G, Brasília, DF 70710, Brazil, and mails
general information and brochures on request.

A great source of information is the venerable South American Explorers
Club, which publishes a quarterly magazine, sells books, and operates
clubhouses in Lima, Peru and Quito, Ecuador. The club's magazine, *South
American Explorer*, is full of current information and ads for guide services,
lodging, research opportunities, airfares, arts and crafts, and books on Brazil
and the rest of the continent. The classifieds are full of travellers looking
for companions on the road, the feature articles in any given issue cover
subjects ranging from leech collecting in Suriname to socio-political

analyses of Nicaragua, and the whole thing is put together by a witty gang of folks who happen to love South America. From a practical standpoint, perhaps the most useful thing the club offers is a series of unsolicited trip reports from members, describing the best and worst of their travels, including tips on guides, hotels, exchange rates, transportation, etc. You can, for instance, have the club send you all the most recent trip reports from the Pantanal, or Brazilian Amazônia prior to your trip. Yearly memberships, including a subscription to the magazine, cost US$40 for an individual, US$60 for a couple. The club's headquarters in the US are at 126 Indian Creek Road, Ithaca, NY 14850 (tel: 607 277 0488, email: explorer@samexplo.org).

Another good source of information is a lively magazine produced by Brazilian expats in the Los Angeles area, *Brazzil*. This monthly magazine features an eclectic blend of articles ranging from the scholarly to the trashy, with the emphasis on Brazilian culture, music, and politics. There are also lots of ads for cheap airfares to Brazil from the US. For subscriptions, write to PO Box 42536, Los Angeles, CA 90050-0536, fax: 213 257 3487, email: brazzil@brazzil.com.

Collared peccary

Chapter Three

Health and Safety

HEALTH

This section describes only those problems particular to travel in tropical Brazil. All travellers, and especially those spending long periods of time in the backcountry, should also be prepared to deal with the whole spectrum of common ailments and first aid crises. The appendix on *Further Reading* lists several good reference books on staying healthy while travelling.

Before you go

Disease patterns and health regulations constantly change, so get the latest information just before you travel. Americans should write to the US Government Printing Office, Washington, DC, USA 20402, and request a copy of the most recent *Health Information for International Travel* bulletin published by the US Center for Disease Control. British readers should contact MASTA (Medical Advisory Service for Travellers Abroad) or a BA Travel Clinic or similar. Among their many services is a Concise Health Brief giving up-to-date advice on health hazards in specific regions. They also operate vaccination centres and sell tropical supplies. Telephone the Traveller's Health Line on 0891 224100.

Malaria

Malaria is far and away the most serious threat to the backcountry traveller's health. Brazil was thought to have nearly eradicated malaria by1960, but in 1983 nearly 300,000 cases appeared in hospitals alone. Less than five years later, that figure had doubled, and by 1989, Brazil was accounting for 11% of the world's malaria cases outside Africa.

No drug can prevent infection itself, but there are several that stave off clinical attacks of the disease and may rid the parasites from your system should you become infected. Check with a doctor specialising in travel health or tropical diseases or follow travel clinic advice before deciding on anti-malaria prophylaxis for your trip. Both malaria and certain anti-malarial drugs are especially dangerous during pregnancy, so pregnant women and nursing mothers should get special advice. An overdose of anti-malarial drugs can be fatal, so keep them out of reach of children.

Four species of tiny, one-celled protozoan parasites cause malaria, but only two are widespread in Brazil: *Plasmodium vivax* and *Plasmodium falciparum*. Both are transmitted to humans via the bite of infected female *Anopheles* mosquitoes. At least five species of *Anopheles* – some of which invade houses and prefer human blood – are known to carry malaria in Brazil. Once in the bloodstream, the parasite invades and destroys red blood cells; doctors call this the primary attack, usually marked by chills, high fever, and finally, as the attack subsides, by a period of extreme weakness and fatigue. Untreated primary attacks of *vivax* or *falciparum* malaria generally last from two to four weeks, continuing this pattern of alternating chills and fever bouts. It is possible to be infected with both *vivax* and *falciparum* parasites at the same time.

Vivax parasites often disappear from the bloodstream for several weeks, either naturally or following drug treatment. Parasites that persist in the liver, however, can cause malarial relapses after this latent period. The natural duration of this cycle may last for 12 to 18 months, but sometimes as long as several years. *Falciparum* malaria, on the other hand, has no latent liver stage; when the parasites are gone from the bloodstream, they are gone for good – at least until the next bite from an infected mosquito. Untreated *falciparum* malaria lasts about 7-9 months, sometimes as long as a year and a half, and is frequently fatal.

Falciparum malaria is the most serious, partly because of the dangerous complications it can entail (blackwater fever, cerebral malaria) and also because this species has developed drug-resistant strains. A recent clinical test of Brazilian patients in Amazônia showed that nearly all were Fansidar-resistant, 84% of the cases were resistant to chloroquine, and 73% were resistant to amodiaquine. Currently, only one drug remains effective against malaria in Brazil: mefloquine (Lariam). Studies into side-effects suffered by Lariam users are still under review; it's worth seeking up-to-date expert advice.

Regardless of the drug(s) your doctor recommends, he or she will have you start them before your trip, generally one week before entering Brazil. This not only builds up a protective supply of the drug in your body, but allows you to get used to the stuff and to see how you react to it. In almost all cases, you're advised to avoid alcohol and to take the pills with meals or with milk so that you don't become nauseous. Get used to taking them on the same day each week, and don't miss a dose. You'll also be advised to continue taking pills for up to six weeks after you return home.

Always remember that no drug is 100% effective. If you develop any unexplained flu-like symptoms in Brazil or back at home, get to a doctor specialising in travel medicine. We have a friend whose *vivax* malaria appeared after she got home, but was discounted for a long time by doctors unfamiliar with tropical medicine.

For the latest malaria information, write to the Parasitic Diseases Division, Center for Infectious Diseases, Center for Disease Control, Atlanta, Georgia, USA 30333 (tel: 404 332 4559). Or, in Britain, call the Malaria Reference Laboratory on 0891 600 350.

Immunisations

As of this writing, Brazil does not require any vaccinations for travellers entering the country from North America, Europe, or Australia. You should definitely check with the Brazilian Embassy or Consulate (see *Chapter Two* for addresses) just before leaving on your trip, however. Regardless of government requirements, see a physician and consider getting the following vaccinations as insurance. Don't forget to carry your yellow International Vaccination Certificate as proof.

Yellow fever

Yellow fever, a mosquito-borne viral infection, is endemic in virtually all of Brazil except the coastal strip. Brazilian health authorities advise that the most infected areas are the states of Acre, Amazonas, Goiás, Maranhão, Mato Grosso, Mato Grosso do Sul, Pará, Rondônia, Amapá and Roraima. The disease is especially prevalent during the rainy season in forested, sparsely populated areas drained by tributaries of the Amazon. While yellow fever is serious – fatalities occur in up to 50% of the severe cases – a safe, effective, and long-lasting vaccine has existed for many years. These shots are good for ten years, and every traveller visiting Amazônia or the Pantanal should get one. Indeed, Brazilian authorities usually require proof of vaccination when travellers enter from Venezuela, Colombia, Ecuador, and Bolivia. Even within Brazil you may be required to show your immunisation card or else be re-vaccinated at certain checkpoints (Vilhena on the BR-364 highway between Porto Velho and Cuiabá is an example).

Hepatitis

Hepatitis is an infection of the liver caused by one of several viruses. Travellers in Brazil are mostly at risk from the form known as hepatitis A, which is spread via contaminated food or water. Symptoms may include high fever at the onset, jaundice, weakness, loss of appetite, nausea, and brown or tea-coloured urine. There is no specific medical treatment except bed rest. At best, hepatitis A disappears within 4-6 weeks, so it can easily finish your vacation; deaths are extremely rare. Safeguard yourself with an injection of either immune (gamma) globulin or the relatively new vaccine series before leaving home. If you travel a lot, it is probably wise to spend the extra money for the vaccine (Havrix), which is administered in two initial injections costing around US$100. It isn't cheap, but most public health officials are betting that it will provide somewhere between ten and twenty years of protection. Immune globulin, an antibody, is far cheaper, less effective and involves a single jab. Get it just before you leave, since it is only effective for about three months. If you're travelling longer than three months, you could consider repeat shots, since immune globulin is widely available from doctors and pharmacists in Brazil. But if you choose this route, make sure the immune globuline is manufactured in the US, since immune globulin produced elsewhere may not be adequately screened or processed against HIV contamination. Ask to see the bottle, and don't get the shot unless you can verify US manufacture. You're far better off with hepatitis A than with AIDS. For extended trips, you might consider getting a hepatitis A IgG test at home. A positive test result means that you're already immune, and no injection is needed.

Other forms of hepatitis (hepatitis B, C, and D) are spread via contact with infected blood or body fluids. Avoid unprotected sexual contact, blood transfusions, body piercings, and tattoos.

Speak to your doctor before leaving for advice on innoculations against tetanus, typhoid, diphtheria, polio, and hepatitis B. Most doctors and public health officials are now discouraging travellers from cholera vaccine, which is of little value against the disease.

Water sterilisation
Decide on a water sterilisation programme that best suits your trip and budget (see below), and buy the necessary equipment or chemicals before you leave.

Teeth
Have a dental check-up before you go. You can buy an excellent emergency dental kit in Britain which is every bit as useful as a first aid kit.

Insurance
Ask your travel agent about health insurance during your trip. Also write to IAMAT (International Association for Medical Assistance to Travellers), 417 Center St, Lewiston NY, USA 14092 (tel: 716 754 4883) for advice on this topic and a list of recommended English-speaking doctors in Brazil. Individual health insurance coverage can usually be had for about US$3 per day or less.

When you get there
Insects, parasites and other pleasantries
Teddy Roosevelt wrote: 'South America makes up for its lack ... of large man-eating carnivores by the extraordinary ferocity or bloodthirstiness of certain small creatures.' Unfortunately, the story doesn't end there. Not content merely to sting, bite, and otherwise puncture us, some of these insects leave us with even smaller, more insidious creatures swimming around in our systems.

Malaria, leishmaniasis, yellow fever, river blindness and Chagas' disease, among others, are all transmitted by insects. Avoiding contact with host insects is therefore the most obvious way to stay healthy. An ounce of prevention, after all, is worth a pound of cure – especially since some of these diseases are practically incurable. You'll never outfox the mosquitoes, *mutucas*, *piums* and sandflies 100% of the time; you're dealing with insects that often bite through clothing and invariably find their way inside your mosquito-netting. Nevertheless, not all mosquitoes carry malaria, and not all sandflies carry leishmaniasis; each bite you avoid therefore increases your chances of staying healthy.

Mosquito netting is a must. If you're not using a hammock, consider a lightweight internal-frame mosquito net, which works equally well with a sleeping bag or in bug-ridden rooms over a bed; Long Road Travel Supplies market several models (see the section on camping supplies in *Chapter Two*). Treating bednets with an insecticide such as Permethrin improves protection against anything which might bite you as you lean against the net and also repels sandflies which otherwise are small enough to get through the net. Bring repellent. You may have to apply this under your clothing as well as on exposed skin. Staying inside during the evening helps. In many jungle areas, this is a superfluous bit of advice; you'll be besieged by an almost opaque mass of mosquitoes as soon as the sun dips below the treeline. Planning your trip to avoid the rainy season can help reduce your insect worries. Finally, some disease-carrying insects such as the *barbeiro* require certain specific environments which you can steer clear of. See below.

Chagas' disease (Trypanosomiasis) is the work of yet another protozoan, *Trypanosoma cruzi*, transmitted by some six species of biting bugs in rural areas of Brazil. All six species are known collectively as *barbeiros*. One version has it that the striped bug resembles a barber's pole; others claim that the name derives from the bug's habit of biting mostly on the cheek. The *barbeiro* hides during the day, favouring thatched roofs and the deep cracks in mud walls. Naturally enough, Jayne and I first learned of the *barbeiro* only days before we visited a village composed entirely of mud-and-wattle huts with thatched roofs. Jayne finally approached one of the locals and asked the question point-blank: 'Tem barbeiro por aqui?' 'Tem,' nodded the old man, as the blood drained from Jayne's face. Then he added that the gentleman in question lived just up the path and would probably cut our hair for 200 cruzeiros a head.

The *barbeiro* – the six-legged one, that is – leaves its hiding place at night, feeding on humans as well as wild and domestic animals. Thousands of *barbeiros* can infest a single house, and bedrooms are normally prime habitat. The *barbeiro* defecates as it bites and parasites generally enter the bloodstream when the faeces are rubbed into the wound. The bite itself is often benign, and there may be no immediate symptoms in adults. Trypanosome parasites continue to multiply, however, invading the heart and other tissues. Heart damage and digestive problems may only surface ten to twenty years following infection, and sudden heart failure is not uncommon. Diagnosis is extremely difficult. Worse yet, the parasite has invaded many blood banks throughout South America within the last decade.

Since there is no drug both safe and effective against Chagas' disease, you'll have to protect yourself from *barbeiros*. If at all possible, avoid spending the night in mud-and-wattle houses; mud houses with smooth plastered walls and roofs of metal or tile are seldom colonized by the *barbeiro*. Hammocks and mosquito nets further decrease the risk, since adult *barbeiros* are poor fliers.

Leishmaniasis ('Leish') is the result of yet another insect-born protozoan, *Leishmania braziliensis*, and a particularly nasty one at that. Three forms of the disease exist, although all involve leprosy-like sores and lesions of the soft tissues, particularly the nose, mouth and lips. Fatal cases are rare, and it is a disease that, unlike malaria, is rarely contracted by travellers. Jayne and I stayed in a jungle camp in Amazônia which had reported 13 cases of the disease within a three-month period in 1987, but all were camp workers who had spent many months at the site. Still, leishmaniasis' hideous toll of disfigurement and its equally unsavoury cure – injections of poisonous sodium antimony gluconate – make it well worth avoiding. And within the last decade, leishmaniasis has expanded beyond the jungle, infecting domestic animals such as dogs and chickens in Brazilian cities. The parasite is carried via the bite of the small, creamy-white jungle sandfly *Phlebotomus*. Locals have told us that the bite is painless, and nothing may be apparent until the appearance of small sores on the skin. Once again, prevention is everything; the veteran camp workers in our leish-plagued area of Amazônia entered the jungle only with long-sleeved shirts buttoned at the collar and cuffs, and long trousers with socks rolled up over the legs. As a further safeguard, spread a film of good insect repellent on all exposed skin. Any unusual sores or lesions should be examined immmediately by a specialist in tropical parasitology. Sleep in an impregnated bednet.

Onchocerciasis (River Blindness) is caused by tiny nematode worms transmitted via the bite of either black flies or certain species of buffalo gnats. The disease owes its common name to the fact that immature black flies live attached to rocks in swift-flowing streams, and most infections occur within 10-20 kilometres of such fast water. Untreated, the microparasites often lodge in the cornea, causing blindness. Northern Amazonas state near the Venezuelan border and much of Roraima State are considered problem areas. (The Pantanal, since it is a land of mostly sluggish water, does not present much of a threat from river blindness). Adult black flies bite only outdoors and only during the daylight hours. Their bite is painless, however, and insect repellents are reported to be of little value. Thus, there is no way to be certain of avoiding the disease but, again, long trousers and long sleeves are a must. Fortunately, river blindness is very rarely contracted by travellers. If you begin to develop unusual skin rashes (particularly on the thighs, shoulders, arms, or head) after 12 to 20 months of being in an endemic area, consult a specialist immediately. Chemotherapy is the current cure.

Bicho de pé, jiggers, (known in Portuguese as *chigões*) are more of a nuisance than a threat. That's comforting news, because this tiny flea (*Tunga penetrans*) is quite common on the beaches of the northeast coast, particularly near fishing villages where pigs, chickens and dogs roam the shoreline. We've also got them while camping along muddy riverbanks in the Pantanal. In this kind of habitat, a fertilized female *Tunga* will hop about in search of a suitable host, penetrating any small crevice in the skin. She'll especially favour cracks between the toes, on the soles of the feet, and around the toe-nails, but any part of the body within hopping distance is fair game; more than one beach camper has found *bichos de pé* lodged in their buttocks, and I've discovered them underneath my fingernails. Once attached, the female *Tunga* burrows beneath the surface of the skin, swelling to the size of a small pea within 8-12 days and then laying her eggs. When the eggs hatch a new generation of *bichos de pé*, the mother flea dies and is expelled, leaving a small sore. I have a biologist friend who finds this so fascinating that he allows the whole process to go unhindered so that he can watch. To avoid turning your body into a parasitology experiment, check your feet and hands daily; look for tiny pepper-like dark spots. Enlarge the *bicho's* entrance hole with a sterilized needle and remove her with a forceps just as you would a splinter. Be sure to get the entire animal, including the burrowing mouthparts, and spread alcohol over the sore. At campsites in the northeast and the Pantanal, removing *bichos* is a daily, almost communal affair, and helpful Brazilians will sometimes offer to locate and pluck them out from those hard-to-reach spots!

The discovery of **botfly** larvae growing to maturity in a lump beneath your skin is surely one of the tropics' more repulsive surprises. So you'll be glad to know (if you manage to retain your cool, scientific detachment about the whole thing) that there is nothing particularly dangerous about botflies. Because adult botflies are large and slow-moving, they like to lay their eggs via the bite of other flying insects like the *mutuca*. Swelling and minor discomfort accompanies the growth of the larval flies. Some people remove the larvae with forceps, or by smothering them with Bandaids and airplane glue; in either case, you run the risk of infection. It's best to simply wait until your return to civilization, where a doctor can remove the larvae and sterilise the wound.

In Amazônia, watch out for the **toucandeiro**, a black ant about an inch long whose bite is so supernaturally painful that the Amerindians use it for initiation rites. The *toucandeiros* I've seen always seemed to live at the base of trees, swarming out of their hole when disturbed.

There is also a species of biting **termite** (*cupim*) active at night in Amazônia; if you're inclined to wander in the forest barefoot, you probably deserve an occasional nip.

Other health issues
Conjunctivitis
This infectious disease turns the whites of the eyes pinkish, and is accompanied by itching, pain, and a gritty feeling in the eyelids. Conjunctivitis reaches almost epidemic proportions along the coastal areas of Brazil, but fortunately is not serious. Doctors can prescribe antibiotics, but I've never known anyone in Brazil who actually bothered to treat conjunctivitis; it's one of those irritations of travel that goes away on its own within about a week.

AIDS
In late 1988 it was estimated that over one million Brazilians had contracted AIDS, placing it right after the United States and France in total number of cases. Currently, Brazil is one of the sixteen nations hardest-hit by HIV. Outside of the African continent, only two countries are ranked with Brazil in terms of projected AIDS-related deaths: Thailand and Haiti. Any sexual contact, either hetero- or homosexual, puts you at risk, as do blood or plasma transfusions, body piercings, tattoos, acupuncture and injections with unsterilised needles. Brazilian-made condoms (*preservativos*) are available at virtually all pharmacies, of course, but quality-control is lax; you are far safer bringing a supply from home. Incidentally, our favourite Brazilian slang for condom is *camisinha de Venus* – 'Venus' little shirt.' If you expect to receive vaccinations in Brazil, consider taking along a sterile needle pack, available from MASTA in Britain (tel: 0891 224100). These precautions should also safeguard you from hepatitis B, which is contracted in the same way as AIDS.

Sunburn
The equatorial sun can burn right through light cotton clothing and sunshades. Sitting in the shade, we've been burned by sunlight reflected off sand and water. Use a PABA-based sunscreen; don't expect to find sun protection above a number 4 in Brazilian pharmacies, except in Rio and São Paulo.

Traveller's diarrhoea and other intestinal problems
The principal causes of TD are consumption of faecally-contaminated food or water. Some of us have a hunch that all kinds of other things may also come into play: a change in diet, the heat and humidity, the stress of arrival in a strange land. (Witness the fact that visitors from South America frequently get sick when they visit our own spotlessly hygienic nations.) But it is common: sooner or later, you're bound to get a case of TD. Besides

diarrhoea itself, symptoms may include stomach cramps, nausea, bloating, and fever.

To lessen your chances of coming down with the trots, most doctors recommend that you follow a few simple guidelines. Don't drink tap water (*agua de torneira*); even bottled water may not be safe – drink only bottled water, sterilised water, or soft drinks. Likewise, avoid drinks with ice cubes, locally-made popsicles and flavoured ices, which are generally made from tap water. Don't eat cooked food which may have been handled after cooking, avoid cold foods, salads, uncooked fish, fruits you haven't peeled yourself, unboiled dairy products and ice cream. Peel it, boil it, cook it or forget it. Excellent suggestions, every last one of them. Someday I'm going to meet a backcountry traveller who has managed to follow them all, or even most of them, and maintained his or her sanity.

This motto is reasonably easy to stick to, but you may miss a good deal of pleasurable eating and drinking following this regimen. There's no need to get neurotic; just exercise a little caution, particularly in the first week or so of your trip, allowing your digestive system to get acquainted with the new local fauna that will be invading it. Likewise, it is not always possible to avoid tap- or well-water entirely, but don't be drinking tumblers of the stuff if something else is available. When camping in the backcountry, sterilise the water. The prejudice against street vendors' hot food is unwarranted to plenty of us who've travelled extensively in the Third World; their food is freshly cooked, sells quickly, and I've never taken sick after eating it, at least that I'm aware of. On the contrary, my few bouts with stomach ailments in Brazil came after restaurant meals. Similarly, Hilary Bradt got her only dose of Brazilian food poisoning following a meal at Manaus' poshest hotel! As for salads, dairy products, and uncooked vegetables, they're such a welcome treat in Brazil that I prefer to take my chances.

There are perhaps as many remedies for traveller's diarrhoea as there are travellers. The trend nowadays is away from the old 'quick cures' like Lomotil, Kaopectate, Imodium, Enterovioform, Kaolin and the host of other medicines available in South American pharmacies. Most of these simply prolong the problem and may actually make things worse. Tests now show that prophylactic use of the ever-popular Lomotil actually increases the incidence of TD, and it can cause rupture of the bowel. Enterovioform can be responsible for some serious neurological side-effects and has been banned in Britain for years. And Kaolin apparently interferes with the absorption of the commonly-used anti-malarial drug, chloroquine.

Doctors now recommend a simple regimen of rest and liquids. Most sufferers have no problem with the first part, since diarrhoea saps energy. But some people have the notion that if they aren't thirsty, they needn't drink. Nothing could be further from the truth. Thirsty or not, you need to replace the massive amounts of liquids and body salts lost during a bout of

TD; remember that the dehydration associated with diarrhoea is a major killer of infants in Third World countries. The US Center for Disease Control recommends the following drink for sufferers. Mix eight ounces of fruit juice with a teaspoon of sugar or honey and a pinch of salt. In a second glass, dissolve one quarter teaspoon of baking soda in eight ounces of water. Alternate sips from these two glasses, and repeat the ritual; drink two glasses for every bowel movement. Carry plastic sachets or film canisters of baking soda, salt, and sugar just so you're ready.

Drink as much water and/or fruit juice as possible, but avoid alcohol (including beer), caffeine, and foods that are spicy or greasy. Your symptoms should begin to disappear within three or four days; if not, get yourself to a doctor. If a doctor isn't immediately available and you feel very ill, take a three day course of Norfloxacin, Ciprofloxacin or Nalidixic Acid.

Both fever and cramps are normal during a bout of traveller's diarrhoea. Extremely painful cramps, high fever, and/or blood in the stool, however, may mean that you've got one of two forms of dysentery. As with diarrhoea, drink plenty of fluids, but get yourself to a doctor immediately. Dysentery is serious.

The symptoms of food poisoning often resemble those of traveller's diarrhoea, but they are generally more severe and almost invariably involve vomiting. Fortunately, food poisoning is usually much shorter-lived, often disappearing overnight. Treat food poisoning as you would diarrhoea, with plenty of rest and liquids.

Fungal infections

These are common only in Amazônia, where the oppressive humidity creates ideal conditions for fungal growth. The primary symptom is a persistent itchy rash, and the most common infection sites are the crotch, feet, and armpits. Bathe in cool jungle streams as often as possible, and dust yourself with a fungicidal powder such as Tinactin or Tinaderm. Creams containing clotrimazole or miconazole, such as Monistat or Mycelex, are also good. Wear light, loose-fitting clothes made of 100% cotton fabrics, and no underwear. If the insects allow you, wear sandals in camp. We wear the same clothes every day during jungle treks, but save a second set of dry clothing strictly for camp use. (Remember that in the rainforest, 'dry' is a relative term meaning that you can't actually wring a cup of water from it.)

Snakebite

Snakes are not nearly as common in tropical forests as people would have you believe. As an amateur herpetologist, I consider snakes a lucky find even after exhaustive searching. John Harrison (author of *Up the Creek*) spent eleven months in the Brazilian bush and saw only seven snakes, five of which were swimming. Remember too that only a small percentage of snakes are actually venomous, and those that are don't always inject poison with every bite. After feeding, for example, venom sacs are often depleted, and roughly 30% of all snakebites are 'dry', with no venom injected at all. Most snakebites do not cause death in adults even when untreated. Snakes, after all, have evolved their venom systems primarily to stun small mammals and birds.

The most common venomous snake in the Brazilian rainforest is the fer-de-lance (*jararaca* or *jararacussu*). According to the Butantã Institute in São Paulo, fer-de-lances are responsible for 90% of all the snakebites reported in Brazil. Watch your step in the forest, especially near tree-falls, and wear high-topped jungle boots for protection. We've encountered these vipers also in the middle of dirt roads, and on our most recent trip nearly trod upon one at a rural gas station! Be particularly cautious if you're out at night. If bitten, stay calm; most viper snakebite victims recover without any treatment. If symptoms – such as local swelling, redness, tingling in the back, ears, or mouth – do not appear within thirty minutes of the bite, it is likely that no venom was injected. Cleanse the wound and attempt to get to a doctor. Keep the bitten area below the level of the heart. Drink plenty of fluids (but never alcohol), and have the victim walk slowly to reach medical help. Do not try to apply a tourniquet or open the wound with a razor – both can do far more harm than the bite itself. However, a firm crepe bandage may reduce venom absorption.

It is of great help to doctors to be able to identify the snake.

Water sterilisation

David Livingstone, the ultimate backcountry traveller, took pride in drinking water 'swarming with insects, thick with mud, putrid with rhinoceroses' urine and buffalo dung.' Livingstone ended up with dysentery, but he needn't have gone to such extremes to catch it; a crystal-clear, swift-flowing mountain stream could also harbour infectious disease organisms.

Besides dysentery, the most common water-borne maladies in Brazil are hepatitis and giardiasis, and both are present in the backcountry as well as in city tapwater. It's true that many jungle creeks with few people or livestock living upstream are perfectly safe; we've drunk directly from certain Amazonian streams for days without ill effects. Nevertheless, you can never be certain what lies upstream. Don't trust local wisdom on the subject either; in many cases, the inhabitants of small villages are harbouring chronic waterborne parasites such as *Giardia* without even realizing it.

Prevention is clearly the best strategy here. Drinking bottled water is the easiest route although not always absolutely safe, and most tour operators who offer organised camping trips in Brazil provide it. On your own, however, it's rarely possible to pack in enough bottled water to last you more than a day or two. Three general methods of disinfecting water exist: boiling, adding chemicals, and filtering.

Boiling water for over a minute at sea level will destroy all dangerous viruses, bacteria and parasites. Since water boils at lower temperatures with increasing altitude, however, you must remember to increase boiling time at higher elevations. For instance, at 55°C you need to maintain temperature for 10 minutes to kill amoebic cysts.

A second option is chemical treatment. Iodine is one of the oldest and most popular disinfectants, since it destroys almost all waterborne organisms and is sold everywhere. Chlorine, the other popular chemical method and the active ingredient in Halazone tablets, is not as effective as iodine in killing *Giardia* or amoebas. You can buy iodine in three forms: 2% tincture, crystals, and tablets. If you go with 2% tincture, adding five drops of 2% tincture of iodine to each litre (quart) of water will do the trick. Shake well and allow the water to sit for an hour before using. Twenty minutes used to be the recommended waiting period for iodine, but recent tests have shown that the tough cysts of *Giardia* can withstand a half-hour exposure in roughly10% of the tests. Double the waiting time if the water is very cold or cloudy. Iodine tablets such as Coughlan's, Potable-Aqua, and Globaline are a somewhat handier form of iodine, and you'll find instructions on the bottle. Iodine crystals such as Polar Pure are a third option, and perhaps the best if you're travelling for a long time, since crystals don't lose their potency in the same way tablets do with extended exposure to heat and moisture. With both tablets and crystals, as with tincture, you are completely safe if you let the treated water sit for eight hours before drinking; the formerly recommended 20-minute waiting period isn't foolproof against *Giardia*. Iodine has two drawbacks as a disinfectant: persons with thyroid problems may suffer some side effects; and iodine gives an unmistakable taste to treated water. The latter problem can be solved by adding a pinch of sodium thiosulfate (available in pharmacies and photographic equipment shops) to each litre of treated water. Powdered fruit drink also makes treated water palatable.

Water filters have invaded the backpacking market over the past decade, and they're certainly the easiest and fastest way to purify water. Their disadvantage compared to boiling and iodine treatment is that they don't filter out viruses, including those that cause hepatitis A and viral TD. Those filters with a pore size smaller than 0.2 microns, however, are guaranteed to remove all disease-causing bacteria and parasites, including amoebas and *Giardia*. And at least two companies (PUR and Water Tech Purifier) now make filters which incorporate iodine, which destroys viruses. Non-iodine filters which have been recommended by health authorities include the Katadyn, First-Need, and Travel Well systems. Avoid filters such as the Pocket Purifier, which is ineffective against *Giardia*, and remember that even the best filters don't kill viruses unless they contain an iodine matrix too. Filter systems are being improved every year, so visit your backpacking supply store for information on the latest designs.

A word about Brazilian pharmacies

Like most Central and South Americans, Brazilians tend to be pill-crazy. Virtually every city block contains at least one *farmácia*, often more. I once ran across the 'Pope John XXIII Pharmacy', which seemed to epitomize the almost religious faith which Brazilians place in pills and other get-well-quick nostrums. These *farmácias* will be happy to sell you, without a prescription, a whole spectrum of drugs that have been banned as unsafe in North America and Europe. They also advertise injections of everything from antibiotics to vitamins.

For many Brazilians, *farmácias* take the place of doctors; pharmacists regularly diagnose illnesses over the counter and sell the 'cure' in one sitting. In short, don't be expecting the detached sort of professionalism that you've come to expect at home. These people are here to sell drugs, and the more the better. Antibiotics are especially popular, and are prescribed in massive doses for all sorts of ailments (including viruses, for which they are useless).

Following the pharmacist's lead, many Brazilians feel free to offer their own medical advice at the drop of a hat. When Jayne became sick in a small town near the mouth of the Amazon, she was besieged by well-meaning folk, each of whom insisted on donating something from their arsenal of pills and potions for her recovery. We could have opened our own *farmácia* with the spoils. Never mind that Jayne's problem was a high fever and chills; we were given everything from antihistamines to cough remedies to tonics for ailing livers!

NATURAL REMEDIES

Particularly in the backcountry, you'll be offered various natural remedies for your ills. During her bout with the fever, Jayne graciously turned down all the free pills in favour of a herb tea steeped in lemon and garlic. We'll never know whether her subsequent recovery was due to this nauseating brew, but natural remedies such as this have one big advantage over pharmaceuticals: even if they don't actually cure you, they tend to be far more innocuous and a great deal cheaper than pills. Nevertheless, when you have a problem that seems serious, seek bona fide medical advice from a doctor.

Two of the more common natural remedies are *erva sidreira*, a grass that combats insomnia, and *jambu*, a leafy plant which aids digestion. You'll hear Brazilians – especially in Amazônia – sing the praises of energy-restoring *guaraná*, a wild berry-based drink. The source of all that energy turns out to be nothing more exotic than caffeine.

SAFETY

On the eve of our first trip to Brazil over a decade ago, several well-meaning friends tried to persuade us that the place was just too dangerous for travel. Crime statistics seemed to back them up: Rio ranks number ten worldwide in homicides per capita (about 20 per 100,000 residents). São Paulo is close behind at number thirteen. Brazilian newspapers confirmed the fact that lawlessness has risen dramatically with recent downturns in the economy. But a closer look should allay your concerns about safe travel in Brazil. First of all, our friends had forgotten to mention that numbers one through nine on the world homicide rankings were all US cities – one of which happened to be their hometown! (For comparative purposes, Frankfurt ranks number 18, with seven homicides per 100,000 residents; London comes in at number 30, with two deaths per 100,000). Secondly, such figures are relatively meaningless to travellers since victims of homicide in any country are virtually all local residents. Much of the truly violent crime in both Rio and São Paulo has in fact been attributed to the police-vigilante groups, the infamous *Esquadrões da Morte* (Death Squads), known lately as the Polícia Mineira. While certainly regrettable, this violence doesn't extend to foreign travellers. And take comfort in the fact that Brazil, unlike many a South American country, has never had a significant history of political terrorist activity.

In short, the only criminals that you as a foreign traveller need concern yourself with will be purse snatchers, thieves, and pickpockets. Remember too that such crimes are urban phenomena which you'll leave behind, along with the skyscrapers and smog, as you penetrate the backcountry. In our travels throughout Brazil, we have had our belongings lifted only once; the thieves ended up with a cheap plastic men's purse containing an address book, a calculator, and a teletel token.

This doesn't mean that you should throw caution and good sense to the wind; every one of our Brazilian friends living in Rio has been robbed at least once. Yet these were all incidents that could have been avoided by following the usual precautions in large cities:

- Wear a fabric money pouch beneath clothing near your groin, around your neck, or strapped to your leg. Even under the shorts that you'll end up wearing much of the time in Brazil, fabric money pouches are comfortable and very nearly undetectable. Leather money belts worn on the outside are less practical. An alternative to a money pouch is 'tubigrip,' an elasticized tubular bandage. Very comfortable and safe, it can be put round the calf or thigh to hold money and/or passport.
- Keep enough spending money in pockets so that you're not constantly fumbling for cash in the money pouch. In the unlikely event that you're confronted by a robber, this can serve as 'mugger's money'.
- Do not wear expensive jewellery or watches. This is what got our *carioca*

friends in trouble (and perhaps inspired the recent glut of punk jewellery in Rio made with metal washers, nuts, and bolts). Nowadays you can buy a perfectly workable plastic watch for US$5-10, so leave your good one at home. Brazilian thieves have been known to ask couples for the time so that they could assess the best watch!

• Avoid the areas near fancy tourist hotels. Not surprisingly, thieves who prey on rich tourists frequent these spots rather than the residential areas with economy hotels.

• Stay with the crowds at night. In the large Brazilian cities, finding a crowd is rarely a problem.

• At night, take taxis rather than city buses (unless you are certain the bus will be crowded through to your stop and that you won't have far to walk once you're off the bus). Unlike the undergrounds in North America, those in Rio and São Paulo are well-lit, well-patrolled, and quite safe during all working hours (until 23.30 or so).

• Take as little as possible to the beach. Follow the *carioca* example: stuff beer and bus money into your swimsuit, throw on a light cover that can double as a towel and beach mat, and take nothing else. Before going for a swim, bring anything of value to the nearest beachgoers (families and couples are always a safe bet) and ask politely if they might hold it for you. Brazilians themselves do this all the time, and it's a surefire way to meet locals if your Portuguese is at all passable.

• If you must visit a *favela* (slum), go with an experienced local. If you find yourself in one by accident (it happens) don't panic. Ask directions out of the place; their surroundings may be mean, but *favelados* themselves can be quite gracious.

• Don't leave valuables in your hotel room. Even most budget hotels have safes (*cofres*), and the owner will write a receipt for your cash, plane tickets, and passports. It's not unusual for thieves to slip the lock on a hotel room while a single traveller is showering down the hall. We've even heard of this happening to travellers who have taken a room with a bathroom, so take your valuables into the bathroom when showering! (Alternatively, you can buy rubber wedges to push under the door; this prevents entry from outside and keeps your money dry!)

• Don't fall for the trick that is the thief's stock-in-trade: artful distraction. Thieves frequently work in teams, one or two diverting your attention by jostling you, asking questions, or even feigning a fight; meanwhile, a third is whisking your purse away.

• Wear small daypacks in the Brazilian fashion: on your chest rather than on your back. Particularly on buses, thieves have been known to cut daypack straps with a razor, a feat which is made considerably more difficult if the goods are right under your nose.

• If you are robbed of something valuable, report it to the police immediately. It's unlikely that the thieves will be apprehended, and a miracle if your stolen goods are returned, but you'll want written proof

of the incident from the police for insurance purposes.
* Make photocopies (*xerox* in Portuguese) of your passports (including the visa pages) and plane tickets. Although our Brazilian friends are horrified that we go anywhere without our passports, Jayne and I rarely carry them with us during day trips unless we need to change money or buy bus tickets.

Crime in the backcountry is virtually nonexistent. Exceptions to this rule are those areas near goldfields, where prospectors (*garimpeiros*) have been known to fire on people they suspected of claim-jumping. The same caution is advised in remote areas of the Pantanal where *coureiros* (alligator hide poachers) and drug-smugglers operate. In all other backcountry areas, your concerns should be limited to fellow travellers, who do most of the thieving from rented huts, houses, and tents. In these situations, try to have one of the locals watch after your gear while you're off exploring. Usually the person renting the hut to you will be glad to oblige. Keep your money pouch on at all times, even while sleeping. Follow this precaution on river boats as well, although I have never heard of thefts on small cargo boats; travellers on the huge government-run *ENASA* boats sometimes report gear stolen. When beginning bus trips, wait to see that your bags are loaded in the cargo compartment before boarding the bus.

Drugs
Brazil is not the drug haven that some people imagine. Narcotics (*tóxicos*) travel through Brazil from the Andean countries, but few Brazilians actually use them. By North American or European standards, marijuana (*maconha*) and cocaine (*cocaína*) use is uncommon even in the large cities, and nonexistent in the backcountry. Exceptions to this general rule are hip vacation hangouts in the northeast like Canoa Quebrada and Arraial d'Ajuda. Drug laws are severe, with penalties of up to 15 years imprisonment for simple possession of cocaine. Police searches are rare, but undercover federal police routinely check travellers in two backcountry areas: Corumbá near the Bolivian border, and both Benjamin Constant and Tabatinga near the Colombian smuggling centre of Leticia. *Lança perfume*, a mildly euphoric mixture of chloroform and ether that is sniffed through handkerchiefs during Carnaval, is legally a narcotic. While police often turn a blind eye to *lança perfume* use, revellers are occasionally arrested.

Chapter Four

In Brazil

MONEY MATTERS

Cost of living/travelling

Prior to the 1980s, Brazil was one of South America's most expensive countries. Throughout the early and mid-1980s, spiralling inflation made travel in Brazil almost as cheap as in the Andean countries (even if it meant changing money almost daily). Since the late 1980s, however, inflation has decreased – as has the value of the US dollar – and Brazil is once again one of the most expensive countries on the continent. Only in Chile, Argentina, and French Guiana are you likely to find costs as high.

Brazil has gone through five currency changes since 1986, when the venerable cruzeiro was replaced by the cruzado, then the cruzado novo three years later, the cruzeiro (again), the cruzeiro real and, in 1994, the real. If you're wondering how Brazilians keep track of what things are worth, the answer is simple: in many cases, they don't. This can occasionally work to the traveller's advantage – as when a modern hotel with pool, air conditioning, game room and gym ends up costing US$15 for a double – but more often you come out the loser.

Obviously, how much you'll spend depends on your style of travel, so it's risky printing any sort of all-purpose cost-per-day estimate. For food and shelter, however, you probably can't get by on much less than US$25 pp per day, with about US$10 of that spent on food. That estimate assumes double-occupancy hotel rates at the cheaper joints; single travellers will spend a bit more in most places. Add to that basic daily figure your cost estimates for transportation, guided trips, and special activities based on the sections below.

Currency

In July 1994, the real (pronounced hay-ow, plural reais, pronounced hay-AYSH) became Brazil's monetary unit, following almost a decade of monetary chaos (see above). There are 100 centavos per real, and an item costing four reais and forty centavos, for example, is written R$4,40. Note that numbers in Portuguese are always written using this notation, so that a car rental costing seven thousand one hundred and fifty reais would be written R$7.150,00. Often, when you're quoted a price, Brazilians will simply say *Quatro quarenta*, for example, when the item costs R$4,40. Banknotes at this writing are printed in 1, 5,10, 20, 50, and100 real denominations, and there are coins worth 1, 2, 5, 10, 25, and 50 centavos, as well as a coin worth R$1. Although inflation has decreased in recent years, exchange rates still vary considerably over time so that any mention of them here would become meaningless long before our publication date.

Changing money

The US dollar, either cash or travellers cheque, is the only reliable medium of exchange in Brazil. The black market (*o paralelo* or, less frequently, *o mercado negro*) was, until recently, perfectly legal in Brazil and generally gave the best exchange rate for your cash or travellers cheque dollar. The *paralelo* still operates quite brazenly, but these days there is very little difference between the official exchange rate paid at banks and the parallel or black market rate, either for cash or travellers cheques. Even though rates are about the same, there is still an important advantage to changing on the parallel market: it's much quicker. Changing money at banks usually involves long queues and wading through lots of bureaucratic red tape. Some banks add insult to injury by changing at the exact rate as the parallel market, but tacking on ungodly service fees, regardless of the amount changed. The disadvantage of the *paralelo* is that it tends to operate only in the larger cities; finding the black markets becomes increasingly difficult as you move inland, and those in the smaller cities may exchange only cash. But finding the black market is ridiculously simple in most large cities. State or city tourist agencies can usually point you in the right direction, as will most hotels. In downtown Rio de Janeiro, at least eight money and cheque changers (*casas de câmbio*) operate out of prominently-marked offices on the Avenida Rio Branco in the city centre. You'll find a similar concentration of offices near São Paulo's Praça da República. Black market exchange rates in such a situation are generally all within a few cents of each other, so don't waste too much time comparison-shopping. In smaller towns, try enquiring at travel agencies, even if they don't advertise themselves as money-changers (pilots and other travel professionals generally act as conduits for black market currency) or simply ask other gringos. We've changed cash and cheques at furniture stores, hotels, perfume shops, men's clothing stores, veterinarian's offices, and even an undertaker's! Virtually all black marketeers operate openly out of respectable shops; those without a shop will change money in your hotel under the watchful eye of the owners. Don't change money in alleys or cars, and never hand money over to someone who promises to 'be right back.' Accept only cash. Count your reais, although we've never once been shortchanged in literally hundreds of transactions.

When changing on the parallel market we've rarely encountered a difference between the exchange rates for cash and travellers cheques amounting to more than a few percentage points. In short, travellers cheques can buy a lot of peace of mind at very little cost in purchasing power. For this reason, we generally carry about three-quarters of our money in the form of travellers cheques and the remainder in cash.

As you move away from the major cities, black markets will disappear and you'll find yourself having to rely on the banks to change your money. Banco do Brasil, the national bank, is one of only two banks that change either travellers cheques or cash (the other is the Banco Econômico). Banco do Brasil operates branches in most towns with a population over 10,000, but branches in some of the smaller towns may not always change cheques. We generally check the *Guia Quatro Rodas* to determine if a town we're headed to has a Banco do Brasil; if not, we either stock up on reais or hope the town has a black market. Banco do Brasil operates 24-hr câmbios in both the Rio de Janeiro and São Paulo airports.

Travellers cheques are not discounted at banks; they receive exactly the same exchange rate as do cash dollars. But beware service charges on both cash and cheques, which are generally set on a per-transaction basis rather than a percentage of the amount changed. This means that if you must change at a bank, make it worthwhile by changing a large amount. Banks change money only at the official rate (*taxa oficial*). This rate is set by the government and does not vary among banks or localities as it may in other South American countries.

You will be required to show your passport when changing money, either on the black market or at a bank. Sign cheques in front of the buyer, but never date them unless specifically requested – buyers add the date later when they sell the cheques.

Exchange rates vary almost daily in Brazil, but not to the degree they did a few years ago. This new stability means that you needn't change small amounts of money on a daily basis, as travellers once did. Whenever leaving large cities, it's a good idea to stock up on cash. The other time to stock up is before weekends, when it can be extremely difficult to locate a place to change money.

Both official and parallel rates are published daily in many newspapers; *O Jornal do Brasil* and *O Estado de São Paulo* are good bets (look in the section labelled *Câmbio*). Alternatively, watch the national news on TV Globo: both official and *paralelo* rates are announced on a regular basis. Keep in mind that these black market rates reflect the estimated going price for cash in São Paulo or Rio; the rate you receive may vary slightly.

Receiving money from overseas
Receiving money from home used to be a financial and logistic nightmare in Brazil. But in recent years, the advent of cash advances on credit cards has made it easy, quick, and without financial penalty.

Cash advances on international VISA cards can now be had at almost all branches of Banco do Brasil, Banco Econômico, and Bradesco. Moreover, you can get cash on a VISA card at the automatic teller machines (ATMs) of both Bradesco and Banco do Brasil. This process has now become absurdly easy; recently, a friend of ours got a cash advance of US$500 on her VISA card in less time than it took us to change US$100 worth of travellers cheques at the same bank. Likewise, many bank branches in small towns which don't operate a *câmbio* desk will nevertheless give cash advances on VISA. For those with a VISA card, the obvious question then becomes: Why bring cash or cheques to Brazil at all? In fact, you can probably get by just fine on VISA advances, with a small stash of cheques or cash for emergencies.

American Express card-holders may draw on their personal current account at any of the company's five offices in Brazil (Rio, São Paulo, Belo Horizonte, Recife, and Brasília). You must have your American Express card, a personal cheque, and your passport. A fee is charged for this service. Cardholders can also buy American Express travellers cheques at the Brazilian offices.

Credit cards

As mentioned above, the main value of an international VISA card in Brazil is that you can get cash advances easily from banks and ATMs. Credit cards are not nearly as useful for charging goods and services in Brazil. Although the expensive hotels and lodges will often accept credit cards, few budget or mid-rate hotels do, nor do most restaurants or guides. Car rental agencies are one of the few businesses that can be counted on to accept credit cards. Some hotels may attempt to add a surcharge for credit card use, despite the fact that this is not legal; ask before charging. It's also a good idea to keep a record of the exchange rate when making any hefty credit card purchases (tear out and save the daily financial page in the newspaper), because you may return home to find a suspiciously low exchange rate quoted on your bill.

Miscellaneous money problems

When it comes to changing money, always keep an eye on the calendar and your itinerary; make sure you have enough Brazilian currency to get you through the weekends and those periods when you'll be outside the larger cities. Changing money on Sunday in a fishing village isn't impossible, but it's not always easy.

Be sure to liquidate any leftover reais before leaving Brazil; they can rarely be exchanged beyond the border towns of neighbouring countries. If you have changed money on the official market and remembered to save your bank receipts (*recibos*), you may recover up to one-third the sum in foreign currency.

Brazilian law won't allow non-citizens to purchase foreign currency;

even Brazilians must show a plane ticket before they can buy foreign money. This means, for instance, that if you fly to French Guiana, there is no way for you to buy francs prior to your arrival at the Cayenne airport – where, naturally enough, there is no currency exchange booth! To get foreign currency you'll have to find gringos coming the other way with spare cash.

Loose change (*troco*) is a constant problem in Brazil. No matter how many times the currency or national economy has been altered, one thing remains constant: nobody has change. Do as the Brazilians do: when buying something, never relinquish your small bills, nor even admit to having them, unless you absolutely must. Let the seller find change. It gets to be a tiresome game, but one you must play if you want to keep your change for bus rides, snacks etc. This is a constant annoyance, particularly when attempting to pay a taxi fare. Before making a purchase or hopping in a taxi, show the bill you intend to pay with, and notify the seller that you have no smaller bills by saying *Naõ tenho troco*. They'll find a way.

Watch local papers for news of impending bank strikes. Strikes at the Banco do Brasil choke the flow of cash everywhere, including the most reliable black market money changers. At the first rumour of a strike, stock up on reais.

ARRIVAL AND ORIENTATION

Arrival at the airport

Most visitors entering Brazil by air do so via Rio de Janeiro. Galeão International Airport is located on Governor's Island, about 15km north of the city centre. Whether you leave the airport by taxi or bus, you're far better off paying the fare with *reais*; Banco do Brasil, located on the third floor, will change money at a good rate (either cash or travellers cheques), and is open around the clock.

Taxis from the Rio airport to either the city centre or Copacabana are relatively expensive. Transcoopass sells taxi 'tickets' at several counters within the airport, charging about US$15 to Flamengo and the city centre, US$35 to Copacabana. These rates are good for up to four people, so you may as well share a ride. All prices are posted at the Transcoopass booths. Metered taxis are also available, and somewhat cheaper. Much cheaper is the 'Alvorada' bus line, run by the Real company, which leaves from just outside the terminal every half hour between 0520 and 0010. This air-conditioned bus, known colloquially as the *frescão*, charges US$4.50 to the city centre, Santos Dumont airport, Flamengo, Copacabana, and as far as Barra da Tijuca. Along the way are virtually all the hotel districts: cheap, moderate and expensive. See below for directions to the economy hotel districts when taking the Alvorada bus. You can also call the Real company for information on how to catch the bus back to Galeão airport from town. If you're staying in the city centre, Flamengo/Catete, Glória or Lapa, the easiest option is to take a short cab ride to Santos Dumont airport, from where you can catch the Real bus to Galeão.

Porters will approach you within the airport, attempting to change money. There's really no need, since the Banco do Brasil is open upstairs 24 hours a day, seven days a week. Likewise, taxi drivers will try to convince you that there is no bus to town, or that the bus drivers are 'on strike'.

If you need to leave baggage at the airport, there are both key-lock baggage lockers (often full) and a 24-hr baggage security booth (*guarda volumes*).

Accommodation in Rio

Most economy hotels in Rio are located just south of the city centre in the Lapa, Glória, Flamengo, and Botafogo districts. Lapa is a bit on the seedy side, but the other three are all pleasant neighbourhoods close to the Metrô (underground), main bus lines, restaurants, and shops. You'll spend far less and get a much quieter night's sleep here than in the tourist meccas of Leme, Copacabana, Ipanema, and Leblon. *The South American Handbook* gives a number of economy hotels in these districts; I'll confine myself to a brief list of streets in the Glória/Flamengo district with numerous hotels in the US$20–40 range (double occupancy, with breakfast) from which to choose: Cândido Mendes, Silveira Martins, Ferreira Viana, Correia Dutra, and Rua do Catete. All of these streets are within walking distance of the Metrô stations at either Glória or Catete. If coming from the airport on the 'Alvorada' bus line run by the Real company, ask the driver to let you off in Flamengo; alternatively, ask him to to drop you off near Cinelândia, where you can catch the Metrô one stop to the Glória station or two stops to the Catete station.

If you prefer even cheaper lodging – the kind of room where a bare light bulb illuminates a girlie calendar on one wall and a tattered poster of the Virgin Mary on the other – try the Saúde and Mauá districts just north of the city centre. Mauá is full of sailors' dives, and the best thing to be said for staying here is that you're right next door to the Federal Police station where tourist visas are renewed.

The more expensive hotels in Rio are well listed in guides such as *Guia Quatro Rodas* and the *South American Handbook*.

A final word of caution: do not expect to find a room in Rio within three weeks of Carnaval (which falls seven weeks before Easter).

For more information on lodging, see *Accommodation* in this chapter.

TRANSPORT

Interstate buses

Brazilians, like all South Americans, still make the sign of the cross when beginning a long journey by bus. Yet buses (*ônibus* is both the singular and plural) in Brazil are probably the safest and most reliable anywhere in South or Central America. While logging some 50,000km throughout the country, we've experienced only two minor breakdowns, and not a single cliff-hanging nightmare of the type you often hear about. Buses run almost everywhere, most have toilets aboard, fares are still relatively cheap (roughly US$0.04 per kilometre, or US$2–3 per hour of travel), and they are spotlessly clean. Veteran travellers in Spanish-speaking Latin America may already be shaking their heads in disbelief, so prepare for yet another shock: Brazilian buses run on time.

Of course, all this comfort and convenience comes at the expense of some regional colour. You won't be able to regale your friends back home with tales of pigs, chickens, goats, and parrots frolicking down the bus aisles. Nor will you see ornate painted filigree, jewelled crucifixes, or carved Saint Christophers surrounding the driver. Only once, outside Teresina, have I ever seen a pig aboard a Brazilian bus – and it had to ride alongside our luggage in a separate compartment, trussed and squealing.

In most Brazilian cities, the various bus companies are all centralised in a single bus station (*rodoviária*). In large cities the rodoviárias resemble busy airports; restaurants, snack bars, magazine stands, public restrooms (some with showers), information booths, even record stores and movie theatres all vie for space with scores of ticket booths. At least one city – Natal in northeastern Brazil – proudly sells picture postcards of its rodoviária. If you're headed for a small town anywhere within a 500-kilometre radius of the rodoviária, you'll probably find a bus going there.

All bus stations have some sort of facility for storing your baggage while you scout the town for lodging, eat a meal etc. Price per bag per 24-hour period generally runs about US$1 at the *guarda volumes*. Generally you'll check your bags with a clerk, but some of the newer bus stations have installed *guarda volumes* which are nothing more than oversized gym lockers; to unlock and lock them, you'll have to buy a token (*ficha*) at one of the nearby magazine stands. We've never lost anything at a *guarda volumes*, but avoid leaving money or passports with your baggage.

Most bus companies post their schedules and prices inside the ticket booth (*caixa*). Since neither prices nor service vary much between competing bus companies, time schedules will largely determine which bus you choose. Depending on the destination, you can generally buy tickets a day or two in advance. Although there are usually plenty of buses to most destinations, I strongly advise buying tickets at least a day in advance to avoid disappointment. Plan your bus travel around the Brazilian holidays. Don't, for instance, try to buy tickets for the Easter weekend when all of Brazil is standing in line at the rodoviária doing that very thing. The busiest holidays are Easter, Christmas, and Carnaval. Have your passport ready; it'll be required now and then. Virtually all seats on the interstate buses are sold on a numbered, reserved-seat basis, and occasionally you'll be asked for a seat preference. Don't pick seats in the rear or you'll be stuck near the toilet door. Before leaving the booth, check your tickets for accuracy; each ticket should list the destination, departure time and, in large bus stations, the departure gate (*portal*).

Interstate buses are generally classed as either *comun*, *leito*, or *executivo*. *Leito* buses are an option on the longer runs to large cities; they provide extra-large reclining seats for almost double the fare of a regular bus (*comun*). We find that we sleep just as well in the *ônibus comuns*. *Executivos* are generally air-conditioned, with piped music, 'free' snacks served by a *rodomoça* (stewardess), and other luxuries that we can easily do without on a bus trip.

An attendant will tag and load your bags shortly before departure. On the short runs, you may find yourself the only ones with baggage that won't fit in the overhead racks; in this case, simply ask the driver (*motorista*) to stow your bags in the lower luggage compartment. In either case, it's a good idea to watch your baggage until it is safely stowed and the luggage compartment has been shut. Theft is unlikely, but it isn't unheard of for luggage to become mislaid on the crowded medians between departing buses.

Every couple of hours, interstate buses will make a 15-20 minute stop at restaurant/snack bars along the highway. These tend to be clean though somewhat overpriced, so bring your own food if on a tight budget. At some of these roadside restaurants, you'll be given a blank receipt (*ficha*) as you pass the door; even if you end up ordering nothing at all, hold on to the *ficha* because you'll be required to return it on leaving or else pay a set fee of several dollars. At the busier roadside stops, keep an eye on the bus and/or *motorista*; he'll usually count his passengers before pulling out, but don't rely on it.

Buses also make brief stops at smaller rodoviárias along the way. There, you'd be well advised to stay in your seat. Once in a while, new passengers are permitted to board an already full bus, and any empty seat becomes fair game.

On long bus trips, we always take a canteen of purified water or a plastic bottle of mineral water and two bedsheets; nights on the road can get surprisingly chilly in the tropics. Buses are never heated – we once spent a sleepless, shivering overnight journey in Mato Grosso when temperatures plunged to 2°C. Some travellers, who figure they're not missing anything by tuning out that hungry baby or that spirited conversation at two o'clock in the morning, bring earplugs on bus trips.

City buses

Buses are by far the cheapest way to get around town – unless you happen to be in Rio or São Paulo, both of which have excellent underground railways. Stops, unfortunately, are rarely marked, so you'll have to ask locals where to flag down the *ônibus*. City buses can also be insanely crowded; if you're carrying a backpack or other bulky baggage, try to board the bus near the beginning of the line and make a beeline for the seats nearest the front. Once the bus begins to fill, it can become almost impossible to get both yourself and your luggage off if you're seated in the rear (although

passing your bags out the window is an option favoured by many Brazilians).
Enter city buses from the rear door (except in a few cities like Curitiba and
Cuiabá) and pay the *cobrador* before passing through the turnstile. There
will generally be a placard above the *cobrador* announcing the fare. The
cobrador will answer questions, call out your stop to the driver, and make
certain you get off at the proper spot.

Taxis

Although buses run 24 hours a day in most cities, we prefer to play it safe
and take taxis late at night. Many Brazilians do likewise. Taxis are also the
only way to reach the airport in some cities such as Santarém. While taxis
are cheap by European and American standards, many first-time visitors to
Brazil assume they're being cheated when it comes time to pay the fare.
Remember that meters cannot keep pace with inflation, so the cabbie must
refer to a printed table which adjusts the meter price upward. These tables,
authorised by the city government and regularly updated, can usually be
found taped to the left passenger window. If you don't find one prominently
displayed, ask the driver to show you his copy of the *tabela* before the ride
begins. Don't accept a photocopied *tabela*; the official one is printed in
several colours.

   The table also makes adjustments for rides at night (22.00–05.00 in most
cities), when fares increase. Make absolutely sure that the meter is running,
unless you've reached an unambiguous agreement beforehand on the fare.
Airport taxis generally don't fall under these regulations, so make your
fare arrangements with the driver before leaving. Most cabbies are
scrupulously honest, but there's no point in losing your temper with those
who aren't – just ask to see the table.

Hitchhiking

Brazilians generally fall all over themselves to help a traveller in their
country, so it came as a surprise when we learned that thumbing a ride was
next to impossible. Combine big families and little cars with the rising
crime rate and you'll understand why it's usually a waste of time to hitchhike
(*pedir uma corôna*) in Brazil. Even if you manage to catch a lift you may
be asked to contribute money for fuel. In oil-poor Brazil – where fuel
prices are double those in the United States – that can make a large and
unexpected dent in your wallet. If you must hitchhike, try the filling station/
restaurant/hotel complexes (*postos*) that are located on the highways several
miles outside major cities and towns. Truckers (*camioneiros*) stop here
during the day for gas and meals, and can occasionally be talked into taking
you aboard. If you arrive at the *posto* late in the evening, be prepared to
spend the night – that's what most of the truckers are doing.

   Difficult as hitchhiking is in most of Brazil, there are a few notable
exceptions, such as on the Transpantaneira highway (see *Chapter Five*).

Trains

The rail system in Brazil has never been very extensive and backcountry travellers won't be taking the train often. Most of the country's 30,000km of track runs south and west from Rio and São Paulo – nice country at times, but hardly wild. Even many of these lines are being closed by the government. Of the three areas described in this book, only one is served by rail: the RFFSA train runs from Campo Grande in the state of Mato Grosso do Sul westward to Corumbá, a 12-hour journey which leaves you on Brazil's border with Bolivia. Along the way, the train grazes the southern edge of Brazil's vast swampy plain known as the Pantanal. Here, green and yellow parrots flit by the windows, alligators bask along the tracks, and backcountry travellers can revel in the knowledge that they're riding the line known colloquially as the *Trem da Morte*: the Train of Death.

Boats

Particularly in the soggier parts of backcountry Brazil – Amazônia and the Pantanal – boat travel is often the only option from A to B. Even if it weren't, most adventurous travellers wouldn't hesitate to choose a boat over faster but more mundane modes of transport. What traveller can stroll the docks of Santarém, crowded with a riotous assortment of scruffy cargo boats being loaded to the scuppers with bananas, jute, brazil nuts, and Coca-Cola, bound for places with names like Oriximiná, Faro, Nhamundá, and Urucurituba; what real traveller can walk past such a scene and resist racing back to the hotel for a hammock and backpack? Even if Point B turns out to be singularly uninspiring, the trip itself is reward enough for most river vagabonds: nights spent lolling in hammocks, sharing a gourd of *mate* tea with grizzled gold prospectors; days spent gliding past an impenetrable green wall of jungle. Furthermore, your choice of river craft isn't limited to Amazonian cargo boats. Resourceful travellers can find berths (of a sort) aboard cattle boats, cement barges and even Brazilian Army boats bringing fresh troops to jungle outposts. In those cases where public transport can't take you from A to B, or when you simply want to do some fishing, camping, or alligator watching on your own – there are usually local boatmen (*barqueiros*) for hire.

Occasionally, hikers making their way along the beaches of the northeast coast will need to hop on a small ferry to cross the mouth of a river, or perhaps hire a local boatman to make the crossing. There are also several isolated peninsulas which, though accessible by land, are much easier to get to by boat. But with those exceptions, boat travel isn't nearly as common in the northeast as it is in Amazônia and the Pantanal. Coastal villages, however, fairly bristle with the masts of primitive fishing rafts called *jangadas*, and if you can talk yourself aboard one, you'll have savoured a living piece of Brazilian folklore.

Boat travel has more than its share of disadvantages. The food ... well, let's just say that veteran river vagabonds tend to be on the lean side. Travel is slow, and frequently interrupted by everything from engine breakdowns to shallow sand bars. On cargo boats, passengers are a secondary consideration; you may find your hammock wedged tightly between crates of manioc flour and a brand new Volkswagen. But perhaps the most insidious problem with extended boat trips is boredom. Don't expect alligators, toucans, and native rubber-tappers to appear around every bend, even on the best of days. Until you've tried it, don't sign on for a week-long cruise. And bring plenty of books.

More so than any other type of travel, river travel demands a working knowledge of Portuguese. Finding a boat, bartering with the captain, and chewing the fat with your fellow travellers will be a great deal easier if you've taken the time to learn some of the local tongue. The alternative is to travel like the group of four South Africans we met in 1984 on a trip up the mainstem Amazon from Belém; two days into the journey it dawned on them that the word 'Santarém', a word which had been bandied about so much by both passengers and crew, was indeed the name of a city – a city which was not only our boat's final destination but one which was some 700km downriver from the city they had assumed they were heading for!

Specific information on boat travel in the Pantanal and Amazônia can be found in *Chapters Five* and *Six*.

Car Hire

Let me begin this section on how to hire a car in Brazil by recommending that you don't do so. Why, after all, would you want to rent a car in a country where cheap public transportation extends to virtually every backwater, where a litre of fuel costs double its price in the United States, where spare parts may take weeks to arrive and where the roads, traffic and other drivers are abominable? I first pondered this question in 1984 as I coaxed a rented Fiat Uno down the Transpantaneira, 150km of red-dirt highway in the Pantanal. Three days, several headaches and many dollars later (I ripped the car's rear bumper off in a particularly nasty pothole), I was still at a loss for answers. But that didn't stop me from driving a rented Ford Escort some 1,700km down the Brazilian coast from Salvador to Rio while researching this second edition, so apparently I haven't learned my lesson.

To hire a car, you'll need a valid driving licence (domestic or international), your passport, and a major credit card such as American Express or VISA. We once rented a car without a credit card, but had to convince the agency people that our return plane tickets would be adequate collateral. I've never been asked to show the international driving licence, but if you are planning to rent a car in Brazil you should go to the trouble of getting one in advance, since they are officially required.

Car hire prices are roughly the same as in the US or Europe. The absolute cheapest rate I've seen recently was US$70 per day without a mileage charge. This rate was conditional on a week-long rental and was arranged before leaving for Brazil. Call the big international rental companies before leaving home for a quote; in some cases you can save considerable money by reserving from home.

Generally, in addition to the basic daily charge (ranging from US$45 for a Volkswagen bug to US$80 for a VW Golf), you'll pay a mileage charge (anywhere from US$0.30 to US$0.70 per kilometre). Most companies also offer deals where you receive 100 free kilometres (but a higher daily rate), or even mileage-free packages. In many parts of the interior and the northeast, you'll be charged a 'regional tax' (*tarifa regional*) of another 10% or so in view of the poor road conditions. These, of course, are the very areas where a backcountry traveller is most likely to want a rental car. Don't pay extra for insurance, which by law should be included. In most cases, you must return the car to the city where rented; a 'return tax' is charged if you leave the car in another city. As mentioned earlier, you'll be paying for fuel yourself. In late 1996, a litre of gasoline cost US$0.70. And finally, be forewarned that rental agencies frequently won't have the cheap models (VW sedans, Fiats, and Chevettes) advertised in their brochures.

The insurance (*seguro*) you get with your rental will in most cases give you only partial coverage. Be sure you understand exactly how much you would pay and how much the agency would pay were the car to be damaged or stolen. Most agency rental contracts include a clause which specifies that in the event of damage to the car, you will have to pay up to 70% of the daily rental during the time it takes to make the repairs.

If you've taken all these costs into consideration and still feel you're better off renting a car, sign the papers. Someone from the agency will check the car for damage and defects before you drive off. Make sure you note every defect lest you end up paying at the end of your trip.

Before you drive off, find out if your car runs on gasoline or alcohol. Although alcohol cars are less common now than in the past, there's a little trick you need to know should you end up with one. You'll find a small reservoir in the engine compartment filled with real gasoline to get the car started in the morning. Simply press the button on the dashboard labelled with a drawing of a pump, and don't forget to turn it off immediately after the car starts. Always check this reservoir when refuelling; it is damned near impossible to start a cold engine on alcohol alone.

The general word for auto fuel is *combustivel*, and prices for alcohol, gasoline and diesel fuel are fixed by the government. This means that you won't pay any more for fuel in a distant backwater town than you would in the state capital. Check on the availability of fuel as you head out into the backcountry. Ask a truck driver; they're usually the best source of information on this topic.

Drive cautiously in Brazil, but don't expect anyone else to follow your example. Watch out for car-swallowing potholes and gargantuan axle-breaking speed bumps, referred to on signs as *quebra-molas, ondulações,* or *lombadas*. Speed bumps are extremely common on the outskirts of towns, and we've encountered them even on horribly potholed dirt roads. They are often (but not always!) preceded by a *sonorizador*, a textured road surface designed to warn you of the impending bump.

Be especially careful when passing other vehicles. In Brazil, this means slow-moving, heavily laden trucks; it's not likely that you'll ever get the chance to pass a car driven by a Brazilian! Truck drivers will often inform you that it's not safe to pass by blinking their right turn signal. A blinking left turn signal is an invitation to the suicidal.

Internal air travel

The four national airlines – Cruzeiro do Sul, Varig, Transbrasil and Vasp – offer regularly scheduled flights to all state and territorial capitals, as well as a number of other Brazilian cities. While far costlier than bus travel, flying has two advantages for the backcountry traveller: firstly, those on a tight schedule can spend more time in the hinterland and less time on the highways; and secondly, a number of areas in Amazônia are simply not accessible by bus or even boat on a year-round basis. If you plan to strike out into the backcountry from these cities – notably Porto Velho and Rio Branco – you may gain by flying directly from either Rio, Manaus, or São Paulo rather than waste weeks on the road or river.

The Brazil Air Pass offered by Vasp, Varig and Transbrasil airlines is a popular and cheap way to see lots of the country quickly. Each of these airlines sells its own airpass, but they are not interchangeable. For US$330-450, depending on the airline and the season, airpasses allow you virtually unlimited air travel within Brazil for 21 days. You must buy the pass outside Brazil, however, and no city may be visited twice (except at the start and finish of your trip). Depending on which cities within Brazil you plan to visit, and how flights are routed between cities, you will be allowed a certain number of flight 'segments'. These rules are complex enough to warrant a call to the airline selling the pass (rather than a travel agent) in order to unravel them. Also offered is a 14-day version of the airpass, which generally allows you to fly to four cities not including the one you start from. Your travel agent at home will sell you an MCO (Miscellaneous Charges Order) redeemable in Brazil for the pass. At this point, you may, if you wish, confirm reservations from home for all the flights within Brazil you plan to make, but it's important to understand that the MCO is not a ticket. Once in Brazil, you will at some point need to visit the airline office, present your MCO, and have them write up the tickets. Despite the popularity of airpasses with foreign tourists – most of whom want to visit as many Brazilian cities as possible – backcountry travellers should think carefully before purchasing one. Since you'll probably need at least two weeks to really penetrate areas like Amazônia or the Pantanal, a 21-day airpass may not be a wise buy. On the other hand, if you're planning to fly anywhere within Brazil on your trip, be sure to check the current fares for single flights before leaving home, so that you can compare them with the cost of an airpass. Brazil's domestic air fares are outrageously expensive by any standard and it sometimes turns out that it is cheaper to buy an airpass at home, good for many flight segments to many cities, rather than to buy a single flight within Brazil!

Another thing you should know about domestic air travel in Brazil before planning elaborate itineraries is that all the national airlines fly to major cities on circular routes. This means that from city A to city B might involve a nonstop flight in one direction, but in the other direction might require a roundabout itinerary that stops in several cities – wasting your time and using up precious flight 'segments' if you're travelling with an airpass.

If you're anxious to get into the backcountry quickly, don't forget small charter planes. If it's got a runway (or even a reasonably flat pasture) and you've got the money, you can fly there. This is particularly true in Amazônia, where hundreds of pilot-entrepreneurs fly *garimpeiros* in and out of the goldfields daily. The best places to locate small charter flights are in the Manaus and Belém airports. The Brazilian-made Bandeirante, a twelve-seater, is now the most common plane on charter runs.

An airport departure tax is charged on all domestic flights. This varies somewhat depending on the airport, but normally runs at about US$6. You generally have to check in at the main desk, then run across the airport to a second booth which collects the departure tax, then return to the check-in desk to present your departure tax stamp! A few airports don't seem to charge this domestic departure tax, and I've never felt like asking why.

Miscellaneous transport

If there isn't a bus, taxi, plane, or boat going there, don't despair. This is Brazil, after all, where they will *dar um jeitinho* ('find a way'). Four-wheel drive owners often hire their jeep out as a sort of informal collective taxi; you'll pay a flat fee, but you'll also have to wait until the driver has a full load of paying passengers. In the northeast, you can still ride a genuine *pau-de-arara* ('parrot's perch'), a huge flatbed truck designed to carry both passengers and cargo. These tend to operate out of very small towns on loose schedules. Dune buggies (*bugis* or *bugres*) can be hired for trips along the beaches and sand dune country of the northeast. And finally, there is four-legged transport – donkeys, usually – along the northeast coast.

ACCOMMODATION

City lodging

Even the most ardent backpackers end up spending a fair number of nights in hotels. Hotels in Brazil run the gamut from cheap flophouse to four-star palace. Virtually all of them include breakfast (*café da manhã*) in the cost, but be sure to ask before checking in. A room for two in a hotel or *pousada* can cost as little as US$12, and you'll find even cheaper accommodations at *dormitórios, pensões,* or youth hostels. At these prices, bathrooms and showers are often shared. Many hotels feature both *quartos* (simple rooms with a washbasin but shared toilet and bath) and *apartamentos* (rooms with private bath).

Pensões (singular *pensão*) and *pousadas* were originally cheap, simple lodgings with some meals included. Nowadays, few serve anything but breakfast, and the term *pousada* is often applied to quite expensive hotels near the beach. *Hotel familiar* generally refers to a cheap hotel which allows you to wash and dry clothes on the premises, and sometimes provides all meals. Unless your definition of adventure travel is somewhat broader than ours, you won't be staying in *moteis* (singular *motel*); motels in Brazil serve strictly as hideaways for extramarital affairs, complete with circular waterbeds, porn video, and hidden parking.

For hordes of young Brazilians, student residences and youth hostels are a popular and cheap alternative to hotels. These are usually called something like the *casa dos estudantes* or *albergues da juventude*. All state capitals have at least one university, and most have a student residence nearby. I've never heard of one that actually required you to be a student (or asked that you be young, for that matter). Most of the travellers in a student residence or youth hostel do tend to be Brazilians in their twenties on holiday, however. These places are big barracks or dormitory style-affairs, and men and women bunk separately. Don't plan on getting to sleep early; especially during school holidays (January and July), parties can erupt spontaneously in your bunkroom. Unlike a hotel, a hostel or student residence doesn't generally provide breakfast, nor will it be centrally located in most cities. Despite these disadvantages, *albergues da juventude* are popular because they're dirt cheap (most start at about US$6 pp) and because they're a good place to meet other travellers, both Brazilian and foreign. For a list of youth hostels, contact the Federação Brasileira dos Albergues da Juventude, Rua da Assembléia 10, sala 1211, Rio de Janeiro, 2011, RJ, Brasil.

Guidebooks such as the *South American Handbook* and the *Guia Quatro Rodas* are invaluable for locating reasonably-priced rooms (although the latter favours the more expensive hotels, at least in the large cities). Remember, however, that the time lag involved in publication often means that prices can change dramatically. In some cases, hotels listed in a guide may no longer even exist. Rather than following the guidebooks slavishly, we look for patterns in hotel addresses; most budget hotels tend to be concentrated in certain neighbourhoods, so watch for street names that appear often in the guidebooks and head there to begin hotel-shopping. (When arriving in a strange city by bus, we usually check our bags in the rodoviária and then set off to search for lodging). Central bus stations, by the way, are invariably surrounded by cheap hotels, although they are often located in the seedier portions of town.

Some state-run tourist bureaux will have a listing of hotels and may even phone them to check on vacancies and current prices. This service is especially convenient when the information desk is located in the bus station.

The easiest way to locate a good hotel in a strange city, however, is to ask fellow travellers who have been there. In most cases you'll be better off asking foreign travellers; Brazilians themselves will tend to recommend the type of place with four stars and a uniformed doorman.

Insist on looking at hotel rooms before checking in, and be sure to check that the fan, toilet, and shower are in working condition. Test the bed if you have trouble sleeping on a marshmallow-soft mattress. As an alternative, some hotels in northern Brazil have hooks (*ganchos*) installed in the walls from which to hang your hammock. Look for potential irritations such as noisy streets or bars. We once learned, somewhere past midnight, that our budget room in Belo Horizonte faced an all-night *discoteca*. On another occasion, we had to endure the squawking of the family macaw; while perhaps more authentically tropical than disco music, the bird had a smaller repertoire of noises and was equally disturbing.

Many hotels and *pensões*, particularly those in the smaller cities where nightlife is practically nonexistent, close their doors after midnight. If you plan to return late, be sure to ask the staff what the procedure is after-hours. You may be given a pass key, or simply told which window to rap on to get someone's attention.

Most hotel rooms are cooled by fan (*ventilador*); air conditioning costs more, and, once you've acclimatized to the tropics, may give you a nasty cold. If you end up with air conditioning, you may in some hotels have to phone the front desk every time you want it turned on or off. Economy hotels in northern and central Brazil never have hot water – nor will you need it.

Toilets in budget hotels – as well as in many homes – cannot flush toilet paper. Drop used tissue in the box or basket next to the toilet. Unsanitary as it may seem, this practice is much preferable to a plugged and flooding toilet.

Be sure to leave your key at the desk whenever leaving the hotel; otherwise the maid won't change linen and clean the room.

When checking out, we follow the lead of our Brazilian friends and give the maid a 10% tip. Hand it to her personally, since a tip left with the front desk may not always trickle down the chain of command. You may also want to leave a tip with the people at the front desk if they've been of special help.

A final note on hotel security: we have never had anything stolen from a hotel room, and we credit that largely to our preference for small, family-run hotels. A single, well-watched entrance and conscientious owners can make all the difference in the world where security is involved. Most hotels, large and small, also have a safe (*cofre*) where you can store passports, money and airline tickets during your stay. Be sure to fill out a receipt when placing money in the safe; we've never had a problem nor heard of one in this regard.

Lodging in the backcountry

As the pavement begins to run out, so do the well-marked hotels, *pensões*, and *dormitorios*. Don't be discouraged, as long as there are still two bricks stuck together in town there will be a place to stay. Just ask around.

The simplest option is either to take a room or hammock space in a house where the owners will cook meals for you. A breakfast and dinner arrangement allows you to wander off during the day, providing your own lunch. Every small village seems to have a household that can put travellers up in this manner. Feel free to haggle over the price, but in most cases you'll be paying less than US$6 pp, food included. Be sure to ask if there are any special rules of the house you should know about. We learned at one house where we'd decided to rent a room that the owner unleashed her huge watchdog every night at 23.00, and that we'd best be inside by then.

The big advantage to this arrangement is that you'll cease to be a tourist; before long you'll feel like part of a real Brazilian family. Chances are you'll be invited along when the locals go fishing or dancing or firewood collecting. The food will be simple but hearty. We've tasted plenty of unusual, home-made dishes that you'll never see in cafés or restaurants, things like sweet avocado pudding, tapioca cakes, and stingray soup. Living conditions will be simple, often crowded. We once spent several nights in the same room with our host's children – all seven of them. Each night in the dark, I tried manoeuvring silently through an obstacle course of hammocks slung at crazy angles, and each night I managed to wake the whole room. Bathrooms will usually include nothing more than a pit toilet and a hand-operated water pump. Finally, don't expect much peace and quiet; we've been awakened by roosters, pigs, and even on one occasion by a donkey that wandered into our sleeping quarters. And then there was the night we spent with our hammocks slung in the village billiard parlour and dance hall ...

A second option that is particularly popular along the northeast coast is simply to rent a house. These tend to be mud-and-wattle or simple wood houses built by local fishermen. Once again, ask around town and be prepared to bargain a little. Sometimes you'll have a propane stove, a water pump, and a bathroom. In most cases, though, you'll end up with a bare house, no water, and a pit toilet. Ask the locals where you can bathe, wash clothing, and get water. Either cook with a camping stove or make arrangements with someone in town to feed you at breakfast and dinner.

If you don't have a hammock, it's an easy matter to find someone who will rent you one.

CAMPING

Organised campsites are common in Brazil. The most popular are those run by the Camping Clube do Brasil, which has some 50 sites in 13 states. These and other sites are listed in Quatro Rodas' *Guia de Areas de Camping*, an annually updated book on the order of their popular *Guia do Brasil*; you'll find it at most magazine and book stands. Another guidebook available in Brazil which lists campgrounds is Quatro Rodas' *Viajar Bem e Barato*. You can also contact the Camping Clube do Brasil (CCB) at Rua Senador Dantas 75, Rio de Janeiro. At most CCB campsites, you'll pay about US$6 pp, or about US$4 pp if you become a member. Organized campgrounds in Brazil tend to feature far more creature comforts than do their North American counterparts. Some actually have swimming pools, restaurants, electrical hookups and gift shops! A second disadvantage is that the vast majority of campsites are accessible only by car; seldom are they located along a bus route. While they won't put you in the backcountry, organized campgrounds have some advantages if your idea is simply to save some money.

Along the northeast coast, you can feel free to camp just about anywhere on deserted sections of beach. Avoid pitching your tent or hammock directly beneath a coconut palm and be conscious of the high tide mark. In small villages, you'll generally be permitted to set up camp on someone's land for free; ask first, of course. We've even seen people pitching their tents directly in the dirt main streets of small fishing villages. In national parks in Amazônia and the Pantanal, you should check in at the local IBAMA outpost to find out if camping is allowed, and so that you aren't taken as poachers. A number of good, cheap guided camping trips are now available in the Pantanal out of Corumbá; see *Chapter Five* for details. Never camp too close to small creeks in the jungle – they can become raging torrents in a matter of minutes. Remember that much of the jungle and lowland in both these areas is farming or cattle-raising land; ask permission from the local ranchers, and you'll usually be allowed to stay.

Never bring any type of firearm while camping in the Pantanal, lest you be taken for poachers by the IBAMA or army patrols.

We've cooked over both wood and charcoal (*carvão*) in Brazil, but a small backpacking stove is most practical. See *Chapter Two* for stove and fuel recommendations.

As far as I'm concerned, a good hammock (*rede*) is the best way to sleep when camping in the tropics. Hammocks are less bulky and thus more easily carried than either sleeping bags or blankets. Suspended above the ground, you won't be troubled by dampness, ants, snakes, or spiders. It's also a very comfortable way to pass the night; the Amerindians, who were introduced to hammocks by Portuguese and Spanish explorers, claimed that sleeping in one was akin to being wrapped in a mother's arms.

As mentioned in *Chapter Two*, my favourite hammocks for travel are those made in Mexico's Yucatán peninsula. Brazil also produces excellent hammocks at bargain prices and their only real disadvantage is that they are somewhat bulkier and slower to dry than the Yucatecan variety. The best places to buy hammocks in Brazil are the big cities in Amazônia

(Manaus, Belém) and Fortaleza on the northeast coast. Don't bother hammock-shopping in Rio or São Paulo; *cariocas* and paulistas don't sleep in hammocks, so the ones you'll find for sale will be expensive tourist mementos. Be sure to check the size of the hammock against your body before buying – remember that Brazilians tend to be shorter than most gringos.

As long as you're buying a hammock, pick up a mosquito net (*mosquiteiro*). Get the finest mesh available, since some of the coarse meshes allow mosquitoes inside. Have the shop assistant show you how to hang the *mosquiteiro*. You'll also need some rope (*corda*) with which to hang your new hammock. For some reason, stores selling hammocks don't often stock rope, so have the assistant direct you to the nearest hardware store.

Hanging a hammock is relatively easy, but it takes a few moments of practice for the uninitiated to learn the proper way to lie in one. First, put some weight on the hammock to test that both your knots and whatever you've tied to are stable. Then gently climb in at about a 30-degree angle. Beginners commonly try to lie down with their body parallel to the long axis of the hammock, a sure way to spend a sleepless night and stretch the *rede* out of shape.

On the northeast coast, we sleep in our hammocks under a light cotton sheet. In the Amazonian rainforest you'll probably want a light woollen blanket at night (hard to believe, but true!). And in the Pantanal during the months of June, July and August, when cold fronts sweep the area, you should bring woollen blankets and warm clothing to stay warm in your hammock.

When camped near a village, it's always easy to rent a hammock. Just ask around. At the beginning of our first trip to Brazil, this proved so convenient that I wondered why anyone bothered to buy and tote around their own hammock. That was before I spent a nearly sleepless night in a tiny, rented hammock of coarse fibres. The next day, upon closer inspection, it proved to be a trawl net for fishing!

If you're worried about insects creeping into your hammock, spread a film of repellent on the loops at each end.

Store your hammock in a plastic sack, carefully folding the ends so that the small strings don't become tangled. Particularly in Amazônia, be careful that your hammock doesn't get mouldy or mildewy. There is no way to prevent a hammock from soaking up a good deal of that moist rainforest air, but the problem occurs when you pack it for travel. Unless you air-dry the hammock at your next stop, you can wind up with a smelly, mildewed bundle of cotton within a single day. Make a practice of unpacking your hammock immediately upon reaching a new camping site so that it has time to air. When you've left the jungle and returned to civilisation, hang the hammock in your hotel room for as many days as possible before repacking.

STORAGE

Travelling as lightly as possible means that you'll frequently need to store excess gear while you're in the backcountry. This is particularly true if you make numerous short trips into rural Brazil from a central town or city. Assuming that you don't have friends living there, the next best solution in cities is to leave excess baggage at a hotel. I've never been refused, especially since it guarantees that I'll give the hotel my business for at least a day or two upon my return.

The safest bets are small hotels run by families and/or those where you've come to be a regular. Offer to help carry your gear; that way you'll know exactly where it is. Leave a generous tip, both when you stash the gear and upon your return. It's wise to indicate a rough date for your return, but we know one Welshman who cached five different knapsacks (all of which contained money) in hotels throughout Brazil without any idea where his travels would take him. After a year of travelling, he reported no problems claiming his gear. I wouldn't be so cavalier; at least one traveller has reported a bag stolen by someone claiming to be a friend of the owner – complete with note to that effect and a description of the bag. It's easy enough for a thief to claim his own bag and while doing so check out other travellers' luggage. You may avoid this by putting your passport number on the bag and stipulate that it should only be claimed when the passport is presented.

The *guarda volumes* desks at interstate bus stations provide a more formal way to store gear for a small, fixed price. Be careful, though; some have limits on the length of time they'll hold on to your belongings.

FOOD AND DRINK

Eating in restaurants

Food in Brazil tends to be a bland and monotonous combination of white rice, beans, and either fish, chicken, or beef. While gourmet fare can be fashioned from these most prosaic of ingredients (Mexican cooks, after all, have been doing just that for centuries) most Brazilians prefer a simple diet that steers clear of any seasoning other than salt. There are regional exceptions, of course; the African-influenced cuisine of Bahia, rich with palm oil, dried shrimp, okra, nuts and hot peppers, is a celebrated national treasure. Don't expect to see such exotic foods outside the large coastal cities, however.

On the bright side, you won't starve in Brazil. From posh restaurant to seedy riverfront café, the portions are huge – so huge, in fact, that Jayne and I generally split a single plate of food when we eat out.

Brazilians eat three meals a day. Breakfast (*café da manhã*) is a simple affair of French bread, butter, occasionally a piece of fruit and coffee. In the northeast, especially in the countryside, expect chewy tapioca cakes instead of bread. Lunch (*almoço*) is a scaled-down version of supper –

rice, beans, and either fish, chicken or beef – eaten sometime between 11.00 and 14.00. Large, extended lunches aren't as common in Brazil as they are in some other Latin American countries. Supper (*jantar*) is the big meal of the day, and it's eaten any time from 18.00 to 23.00 – earlier in the country, later in the city. *Jantar* is again based on rice, beans, noodles at times, and either fish, chicken, or beef.

Desserts are uncommon, but coffee always follows the meal. Brazil outdistances all other countries in coffee production, but to watch Brazilians down the stuff you would wonder that there's any left to export. The whole country seems to run on *cafezinhos*, thimble-like servings of sweet, syrupy black coffee taken throughout the day until bedtime. Finding an unsweetened *cafezinho* isn't always possible; often it is brewed with copious amounts of sugar mixed in with the grounds. Coffee is something of a national ritual, and we've been offered *cafezinhos* everywhere from posh government offices to tin shanties in the northeast. Unfortunately, backcountry travellers will frequently have to make do with powdered Nescafé.

The cheapest eateries in the towns and cities are the so-called *lanchonettes*. Most serve a variety of *salgadinhos* (deep-fried snack food), sandwiches, and the ubiquitous hamburger. Many *lanchonettes* also whip up excellent fruit juices (*sucos*), freshly-blended from local fruits such as mangoes, papayas, oranges, limes, pineapples, watermelons and passion fruit. *Vitaminas* are juices fortified with milk. *Lanchonettes* generally require that you order and pay first at the cashier where you're given a receipt (*ficha*) to claim your food.

If you're in need of something more substantial, there is no lack of small cafés and restaurants. The most economical meal is the *prato feito* (sometimes known as the *prato commercial* or the *prato do dia*) which features meat, rice, beans and spaghetti for around US$1.50. Brazilians liberally sprinkle such a plate with *farinha* (ground manioc flour), which resembles coarse cracker meal. *Farinha* that has been lightly toasted in butter or oil is known as *farofa*. *Feijoada*, a black bean and smoked meat stew, has a flimsy claim as Brazil's national dish, but the real title should go to *churrasco*, salted beef grilled on a spit. You'll find at least one *churrascaria* in every town big enough to show up on a map. *Rodízios* are specialized *churrascarias* where you can eat your fill of grilled meat for a fixed, reasonable price. The *rodízio* is a vegetarian's worst nightmare: an army of waiters continually parade past the tables, hefting huge slabs of smoky, skewered meat which drip gobbets of fat and blood on the tables as the diners make their choices. One of the most prized cuts is known as *cupim*, the fatty dorsal hump of the zebu steer. Expect to pay anywhere from US$6 to US$25 pp at a rodízio.

Another option which began appearing just a few years ago is the pay-by-the-kilo restaurant (*comida por kilo*). You fill your plate along a buffet line and it's weighed at the end of the line, where you'll pay roughly US$6 per kilo. *Comida por kilo* is a good choice for single travellers who might not want the huge servings which are common in Brazil.

Beer is the national drink at lunch and supper, sharing the spotlight with Coca-Cola. Brazilian beer generally comes in 600ml bottles, with Antárctica, Brahma, Skol and Malt 90 the popular brands. If the waiter pauses before opening your *cerveja*, he's expecting you to test the bottlecap with index and middle finger for the proper icy chill. Draft beer (*choppe*) is particularly common in the larger cities. All restaurants carry bottled water (*agua mineral*) and soft drinks (including *guaraná*, a sweet and mildly stimulating soda made from a native Amazonian berry). Brazil's raw sugarcane rum goes by the name of *cachaça* (or *pinga* in the south); mixed with sugar and limes, it becomes a *caipirinha*. (Some *caipirinha* purists further insist that the limes be crushed with a freshly-cut chunk of sugarcane). Avoid the highly-refined *pingas* such as São Francisco and stick with the cheaper brands (Pitu, Tatuzinho, or Velho Barreiro), all of them redolent of raw cane and a bargain at US$1 a bottle. And finally, there is Brazilian wine. The best thing that can be said about local wine is that it is not actually poisonous. If you must have wine, order Chilean or Argentinian.

Vegetarians won't find much to eat in most restaurants, cafés, or private homes. Green vegetables are virtually non-existent in the Brazilian diet, and I've actually heard locals claim that they were harmful! That attitude is changing somewhat, and at hip resort towns like Canoa Quebrada and Jericoacoara which cater to a youthful crowd you can find vegetarian cafés. All-you-can-eat, buffet-style vegetarian restaurants can also be found in most large cities, but they are generally open only for lunch. Fortunately, the *comida por kilo* restaurants which have sprung up everywhere in recent years usually offer a wide selection of vegetable and pasta dishes. Chinese restaurants (also common in most of the larger cities) can usually serve you a plate of crispy greens. Ironically enough, the restaurants with the best selection of salads, vegetables, and pasta dishes are often the *churrascarias*, so don't turn down a dinner with Brazilian friends on the assumption that they serve nothing but meat. All things considered, a vegetarian's best bet is still the marketplace.

A service charge (*serviço*) of 10% is generally included on a restaurant's bill; leave a tip otherwise. Service can be lackadaisical, and it is not considered at all impolite to call a waiter with a loud hiss (more a *psyoo* than a hiss).

Buying your own food

Food stores in Brazil run the gamut from huge *supermercados* to tiny *mercearias* stocking little more than crackers and Coca-Cola. Shops in the backcountry often specialise: for beef or pork you'll have to locate the *carniceria*, for chicken the *galetaria*, and for fish the *pescaria*.

The best place to lay in stores for camping, however, is the local marketplace (*mercado municipal*). The *mercado* is the focal point, socially speaking, of many small towns, and often occupies the geographical centre of the town as well. Here you'll find a dizzying array of tropical fruits and vegetables that rarely find their way into cafés, restaurants, or middle-class kitchens. Prices for all items are usually displayed per kilogram, but occasionally you'll see fruit put up in small batches called *lotes*. If prices aren't displayed, we usually hang around within earshot until a local buys the product we're interested in; you may find yourself paying a wildly exorbitant price otherwise. Food prices generally aren't haggled over in the marketplace and will vary only slightly from vendor to vendor. Don't be shy about asking for samples; most vendors are eager to prove that they've got the sweetest papayas or mangoes or starfruit and will gladly slice you off a chunk to taste. Bring a large bag or knapsack to carry your produce; there will be children selling large plastic shopping bags if you forget yours.

Bakeries (*padarías*) are often completely sold out of bread by ten o'clock in the morning, so do your shopping early. And if you plan to buy beer, remember that there is a substantial deposit levied on the bottles (*cáscaras*), often as much as a third of the cost of the beer.

FISHING, HUNTING AND FORAGING

My advice to those who plan to eat off the land in Brazil is simple: forget it. Contrary to popular myth, the jungle is not laden with succulent fruits dangling from every tree. Nor is there wild game at every bend in the trail. If you doubt this, reflect for a moment on the lives of the Amazonian Indians, whose daily routine is a constant struggle to find food. Travellers in extremely remote areas for extended periods may have to ignore this advice; John Harrison managed to augment his dried and tinned food during river trips by hunting, fishing, and foraging, all of which he describes in his book *Up the Creek*.

Foraging

Most of the tropical fruits found in the marketplaces are cultivated rather than wild. In some cases these fruits aren't even native to South America; take for instance the banana, originally imported from Southeast Asia. This means that you should think twice before picking that ripe *caju* fruit or that football-sized *jaca* (jack fruit) during your stroll in the 'jungle.' Chances are good they were planted by a local who can ill afford to have his food stolen by wealthy gringos. When in doubt, check the area for any sign of cultivation, fences or nearby huts. Remember that Brazilian orchards are not the neatly manicured affairs that you're used to seeing, and can look a good deal like untamed jungle. If people live nearby, ask politely if you may pick some fruit in the area. You'll rarely be refused. The fruit of the cashew (*caju*) tree is an unexpected delight to those whose only acquaintance is with the nut. Pop the nut off the fruit, squeeze it until soft, and suck out the juices from the hole left by the nut. The nuts can then be roasted in a pan until they pop and sizzle, allowing the husk to be discarded. Other treats include mangoes and coconuts; we've visited areas in the northeast where coconuts and mangoes grew so plentifully that the locals fed them to pigs. Always offer payment.

Fishing

Fishing is, in most cases, a far more rewarding method of supplementing your store-bought foodstuffs than either hunting or fruit-foraging. It's possible to catch saltwater fish with simple hook-and-line gear along the beaches of the northeast, but freshwater generally provides the easiest fishing for novices. Many rivers and creeks in both the Pantanal and Amazônia teem with easily-hooked fish; see *Chapters Five* and *Six* for more detailed information on techniques and local species.

Fishing gear can be hard to come by in Brazil. Don't expect to be able to buy, for example, monofilament line or barbed hooks in most backcountry towns. Local fishermen will be understandably reluctant to part with their gear. *Chapters Five* and *Six* list some suppliers in the large cities like Cuiabá and Manaus. Your best bet is to bring an assortment of line, hooks, and gear from home (see *Chapter Five* for tackle recommendations).

Fishing licences aren't required for beaches along the northeast coast nor for Amazônia. Sport fishing in the Pantanal is controlled by IBAMA (Instituto Brasileiro de Meio Ambiente e Recursos Naturais Renováveis), which sells licences through most branches of the Banco do Brasil. These licences are primarily for big-time sport anglers after prized game fish. Backcountry travellers, most of whom will be filling a modest creel with piranhas and small catfish, will not require a licence.

When in doubt as to the best fishing locations, time of day, or techniques to use, just sidle up to one of the locals and ask politely. Anglers worldwide are a secretive bunch, and while Brazilians are no exception, they'll generally be pleased to let you, the *estrangeiro*, in on a few local secrets. After all, they know you won't be staying long enough to compete with them or drive a species to extinction. They also know that you'll be perfectly happy with the less prized types of fish, such as piranhas. And finally, they know that their fishing secrets are buying a great afternoon's entertainment. On one occasion, local fishermen practically begged Jayne and me to reel in catfish after catfish that they had hooked in the Paraguai River.

TOURIST INFORMATION

Each of the Brazilian states promotes tourism via its own government agency. The larger cities like São Paulo and Rio also fund municipal tourist agencies. Services are free, although sometimes you'll be charged for a map. Sadly, few of these offices provide useful information for the backcountry traveller. In everything from hotel lodging to river travel, you'll be steered toward the expensive and the pre-packaged. Understandably,

Brazilians are proud of their country's technological advances, and they would like to spare you as much discomfort as possible.

In some cases, the staff at these government agencies are enthusiastic but woefully uninformed. We once spent a half hour convincing a young woman at the Paratur office in Belém that we preferred to ascend the Amazon on a small cargo boat rather than the government's *ENASA* ships. She finally shrugged her shoulders and told us how to reach the cargo docks by bus. As we left, an older man with a broom who was apparently the office janitor quietly motioned us over. He'd overheard our conversation and wanted us to know that the young woman had us headed for the wrong bus. And in five minutes, he told us more about boat schedules on the lower Amazon than we'd learned in half an hour with the official.

Despite these misgivings, we always stop off at the government tourist bureaux. They can usually tell you where to change money on the black market and they'll often call hotels for vacancies and current rates. Occasionally, they can help in planning a trip. If they tell us that a particular spot on the map is accessible, we can be certain that it is indeed accessible. And if they tell us that it isn't ... well, we ask someone else.

For information on river travel it's a good idea to check with the local Capitânia do Porto. These are the offices which control commercial river traffic, and they are usually a good source not only of information on cargo boat sailings, but also on river conditions.

Likewise, try the state offices of the IBAMA (Instituto Brasileiro de Meio Ambiente e Recursos Naturais Renováveis), which manage the national parks and biological reserves. These are located in state capitals and, depending on who's sitting behind the desk and how you present yourself, can be either very helpful or a total waste of time. Sometimes these offices are staffed by bureaucrats who've never set foot in territory wilder than the local zoo, but they can usually tell you the rules and regulations regarding the areas you wish to visit.

Several good guidebooks, updated annually, are available at most news stands and bookstores in Brazil. These are all published by Quatro Rodas, and include *Viajar Barato* (Travel Cheaply, a good choice for budget travellers), *Guia do Brasil* (a good all-purpose guide listing hotels, restaurants, and lots of other information), *Guia de Praias* (a guide to some 2,000 beaches throughout Brazil) and *Guia Camping* (a guide to organized campsites).

TELEPHONES

Local calls can be made at the pay phones known colloquially as *orelhões* ('big ears', after the bulbous plastic hemisphere that encloses your head as you speak). Most pay phones now operate on thin plastic cards (*cartões telefônicas*) good for many calls; the old metal tokens (*fichas telefônicas*) are these days used only in the smaller towns, most of which are converting to card-based phones. You can buy a *cartão telefônica* or *ficha* from either news-stands or street vendors nearby. Many small stores also sell them, and they can be used throughout Brazil. They're sold in various denominations, based on how many calling units (*unidades*) the card is good for. If you're calling long-distance, buy a card with at least 20 *unidades*, because they will go fast (you can watch your *unidades* disappearing on the digital display of most phones). You will be disconnected in the middle of a call if your card runs out. Long queues are common at pay phones, probably because two out of every three phones seems to be inoperable.

Long-distance phone calls within Brazil can be made at offices known as Postos Telefônicos DDD. After telling the cashier which city you want to call, you'll be handed a numbered key corresponding to one of the phone booths in the office. Make your call, turn in your key, and the cashier will have a computerised bill waiting for you. The Posto Telefônico generally has phone books encompassing the entire country. In smaller towns in the backcountry, the telephone office, if one exists at all, tends to be a bit more informal: usually one or two phones on a counter top or mounted on the wall; an attendant will dial the number for you and call you over when your party answers. Don't make long-distance phone calls from hotel rooms (in the unlikely event that your room will even *have* a phone) because of the expensive surcharges.

You can phone long-distance overseas from a DDD office as above, or call collect (reverse charge – *ao cobrar*) from most pay phones. To make international calls with operator assistance, dial 000111. Dial 000333 for information on placing overseas calls.

In this book, I've listed all phone numbers within Brazil beginning with their three-digit DDD code (*código*), followed by the phone number itself. Whenever you're calling numbers which are outside the local code – codes are frequently the same for all numbers within a state – it's necessary to dial the code first; if you happen to be within the code area, leave out those first three numbers.

NOTE: Whenever reciting phone numbers (or addresses, for that matter), Brazilians invariably use the word *meia* ('half', as in half a dozen) instead of *seis*, to mean 'six.' This presumably avoids confusion with the word *tres*, but many foreigners who thought they could decipher at least the numbers in Portuguese have been left completely baffled by this custom!

MAIL

In the large Brazilian cities, you'll find a post office (*correio*) in nearly every neighbourhood. Rio, for instance, has at least a dozen small post offices in the city centre alone; simply ask someone in the street. In tiny backcountry towns, the *correio*, if it exists at all, is likely to be a private

home or small store. Our favourite Brazilian post office is located on stilts above the floodwaters of the Paraguai River in Porto Esperança, Mato Grosso do Sul: a casual kind of place, complete with bare-chested postmaster and a parrot on the railing.

Post offices in the cities are generally open from 09.00 to 18.00 with no midday breaks. In small towns, hours vary according to the habits of the postmaster. Post offices are closed on weekends and national holidays.

Don't place mail in public mailboxes in small towns – it may not be picked up for weeks. Wait until you're in a large city or near a post office.

Don't mail anything but letters and postcards from Brazil back to your home. Postal rates are extremely high (letters and even postcards cost upwards of US$1 to mail overseas) and packages have a way of disappearing en route.

To receive mail, have your friends back home address it to you care of the Posta Restante in the town you're visiting (for example: Alex BRADBURY, Posta Restante, Cuiabá, Brasil). Make sure they print or type your last name carefully to avoid confusing the postal officials, who are easily confused by foreign names. Posta Restante mail ends up at the main branch of the post office in cities which have more than one branch. To claim your mail, bring your passport. Postal clerks will often file your mail variously under your first name, last name, or even M for Mr or Mrs, so ask them to check all the possible combinations and permutations. Sometimes you can convince a clerk to let you go through the file of letters yourself. *Posta restantes* will keep mail for 30 days before disposing of it.

You can also have mail sent to any of the five American Express offices in Brazil if you're a cardholder or have their travellers cheques. Some embassies will also hold mail for a limited time. If you're having mail sent to you care of a friend living in Brazil, the notation for 'in care of' is a/c (*ao cuidado*).

It takes about a week for letters to go between Brazil and either the United States or England.

CUSTOMS, ETIQUETTE AND OTHER TOUCHY SUBJECTS

To the traveller accustomed to Spanish-speaking South and Central America, Brazil will come as something of a cultural anomaly. At the risk of some oversimplification, let it be said that Brazilians are a lot more casual than their Latin neighbours. (Brazilians, by the way, often refer to the rest of the continent as *latino*). They are noticeably more gregarious, quicker to begin a conversation with foreigners, more direct in their speech, and more physically expressive. Sexual codes are also more relaxed in Brazil. Brazilians say it best themselves: they are *quente* (hot). All this means that you as a traveller need not be *quite* so concerned with propriety as you might in other South American countries. As in any foreign country, however, recognize that you are a guest and act accordingly. Recognize also that customs do differ throughout Brazil, and what is acceptable in São Paulo may be offensive in the deep *sertão*. Take your cues from the locals before becoming an active participant in their world.

What follows is a random list of dos and don'ts:

- Dress and groom yourself as neatly as possible. Like all South Americans, Brazilians pride themselves on their appearance, and nothing repels them more than an affluent foreigner dressed in tattered, faded jeans, sporting a three-day growth of beard and smelling like the Manaus fish market at noon. Obviously, you and your clothing are going to get pretty rumpled camping along the Transpantaneira; but clean up before you hit the streets of Cuiabá again, or even before visiting that farmhouse to ask permission to pitch your tent. It can't be overemphasised – slovenly dress harkening back to the hippie era is probably the single most common cultural faux pas committed by foreign travellers in Brazil.
- Never enter churches in shorts and/or tee shirts.
- Brazilian women do indeed wear the tiniest bikinis in the world – the *tanga*. And *tangas* are getting smaller, if that's possible; a few years ago the latest version was being called the *fio dental* (dental floss)! Topless bathing, however, is not at all common in Brazil, and nude bathing is unheard of. Unless you are totally and completely secluded, keep your bathing suits on. Keep in mind that villagers along the primitive northeast coast are not nearly as accustomed to seeing the *tanga* as are more cosmopolitan Brazilians; wear a modest cover when returning to the

village. Public beaches near Amazonian river towns are fairly conservative; Rio-style *tangas* are too immodest here and should be avoided.

• Along the northeast coast, dress is extremely casual. Shorts, tee-shirts, and sandals are quite acceptable wear for both men and women at all times of the day and night. In the cities (except at the beach itself) and from Rio south, long trousers and dresses are de rigueur. In general, however, Brazilians are far less offended by beach wear away from the beach than are other South Americans.

• Be especially conscious of your appearance when meeting with government officials for a favour (such as permission to visit a biological reserve). Even in the equatorial zones, wear slacks and a long-sleeved shirt, and clean shoes if you have some. Business cards and/or letters of introduction on letterhead stationery are a real bonus during such meetings. Almost anything official-looking will do.

• Always greet a stranger with a '*bom dia*' or '*boa tarde*' before asking a question. To get someone's attention or to move past them in a crowded bus, say '*licença.*' If you've stepped on their foot, say '*desculpe.*'

• Strangers should be addressed with the formal '*o senhor*' or '*a senhora*' at least in the beginning of a dialogue. As soon as you hear them use the informal '*você*' or '*tu*' feel free to follow suit. Brazilians themselves don't always follow this rule, particularly if they consider the person being addressed as belonging to a lower economic or social class, but you can't go wrong being overly polite. In the same vein, avoid calling waiters and domestic help with the somewhat demeaning '*moço*' (boy), even though Brazilians do it all the time. Professional people are often addressed, even among friends, as '*doutor.*' No knowledge of medicine is required; an architect, a lawyer, an engineer, even a lowly biologist is referred to as '*o doutor*'.

• Brazilian men shake hands on meeting. Once a friendship has been established (and that can happen over a beer in Brazil) the *abraço,* or hug, is used for greeting and taking leave. Take your cues from the Brazilians you meet as to what to do.

• Women and men who are acquainted always kiss upon meeting and taking leave. Kissing is also the standard greeting between women. The Brazilian *beijo* consists of a light hug and a quick peck on first one cheek, then the other, and frequently a third kiss as well. Total strangers often kiss upon being introduced. Once again, just take your cues from the Brazilians. You'll end up doing a lot of kissing in Brazil.

• There are almost never queues (*filas*) for city buses or trains. Push and shove your way like everyone else if you want to make it aboard. I have very rarely seen men give up bus seats to women, even elderly women. Pregnant women are an exception.

• Brazilians are typically late. Let's be honest, they are *always* late. It is considered somewhat rude, in fact, to arrive on time for a dinner or party.

Get used to what is proudly known as the *hora brasileira* (Brazilian time).

- Brazilians never decline invitations to parties, dinners, or other social functions; this is considered rude. If they have other plans or aren't interested, they accept nonetheless and simply don't show up. This isn't considered rude.
- Don't expect Brazilians to understand your occasional desire to be alone for a while. As far as they're concerned, you're either very depressed or very rude to want to be by yourself.
- Our common hand symbol for 'OK' – thumb and index finger forming an 'o' – is an obscene gesture meaning anus in South America. Stick your thumb up instead.
- Politics aren't taken as seriously in Brazil as they are in, say, Argentina. But they are freely discussed throughout the country. Even before the military stepped down, Brazilians were openly derisive of the generals. We heard the military government blamed for everything from potholes to poor fishing. There are no real political tender spots, but foreigners, especially Americans, can expect some ribbing about the FMI (World Monetary Fund) and the debilitating national debt.
- Once in the backcountry you will rarely, if ever, see a beggar; even if the standard of living is dismally low, the rural poor take care of their own here, as in other countries. It is in the cities that begging has become a way of life. Dealing with beggars is obviously a personal decision, but keep one thing in mind: unlike our own societies, Brazil has no government welfare system whatsoever to care for the poor or disabled. We follow a few simple rules: we give money to beggars when we notice other Brazilians doing the same, and we never give money to children; you can be sure that any adult begging for money sincerely needs it to survive, whereas the same is not necessarily true for children.
- Plenty of travellers like to play Santa Claus when they hit a remote town in the backcountry, passing out candies, bubblegum, balloons and trinkets of all kinds to the local children. I suspect that many of these same people balk at giving money to needy beggars in the big city. In any case, it's a detestable practice. Backcountry folk are amazingly self-sufficient; they don't need these gifts – at least until they've been habituated by a string of gift-giving foreigners – and may even resent them. What most rural Brazilians really want from you is an insight into your strange way of life. Sit down and talk with them, show them photographs of your family back home, play a song for them or teach them a dance ... do anything but play Great White Father. Of course, this doesn't mean you shouldn't give presents to people in the same way as you might at home. You can and should give gifts to urban Brazilian friends. Alcohol – especially real Scotch whisky from home – is highly prized.

WOMEN TRAVELLERS

Jayne assures us that Brazil is the easiest country in either South or Central America for the lone female traveller. A number of women we've met on the road agree. It's rare for a woman – even a blonde – to hear the catcalls that are so common in the Spanish-speaking Americas. It's not that *machismo* isn't firmly entrenched in Brazil. It is. Yet Brazilian men, even in the backcountry, seem more sophisticated around single foreign women than do their Spanish-speaking counterparts. I can't explain it; perhaps by acting blasé, they're actually pushing *machismo* to new limits.

Still, if a woman has a choice, she'll have a much easier time of it by travelling with a male friend or with a group of women. In a country where no one would consider vacationing alone, any single traveller of either sex is considered an oddity.

Common sense dictates that women dress modestly in the backcountry.

PHOTOGRAPHY

Supplies

As noted earlier, film is extremely expensive in Brazil. If you find that you've run out, your best bets in terms of availability and price are São Paulo and Rio. Nickel-cadmium batteries for light-meters are tough to find even in the city, so bring extras from home.

Care of equipment and special techniques

The Pantanal presents no unusual challenges for photographers, at least during the dry season. The northeast coast and Amazônia, however, will test both your skill and equipment.

Along the beaches of the northeast, you'll need to protect your gear from the destructive influence of sand and saltwater. Don't underestimate the corrosive power of fine, windblown salt spray on the beach; keep your camera in its case at all times except when actually taking pictures. You may even want to cover the entire camera with a plastic bag, leaving only the lens uncovered. Secure the plastic bag around the lens sleeve with a rubber band. Use an ultraviolet filter to protect the front lens element, and wipe salt spray off frequently with a rag dampened in fresh water or alcohol. Don't change film or open the camera on the beach for any reason; all it takes is a single grain of sand to destroy your film and possibly your camera.

The same clear blue skies and white sand that make deserted beaches so attractive also present some photographic challenges. With the sun overhead, the beach tends to lose all textural detail and photos taken at midday look bland and formless. Avoid this by shooting when the sun is at a low angle – early in the morning or late in the afternoon. Huge expanses of white sand and water reflect so much light that through-the-lens meters and especially automatic-exposure cameras are easily fooled. With all that sun, the ironic result is frequently an underexposed photo. Try increasing the exposure by about one aperture stop; for important pictures, bracket your exposures by two stops on either side. Alternatively, you can use a light-meter that takes incident readings off the subject rather than registering the entire sun-washed scene. A polarizing filter can help restore colour and contrast dulled by the effects of heat haze.

The Amazonian rainforest is perhaps the ultimate challenge for a photographer. Humidity is always above 80%, ever eager to seep into your camera and wreak havoc. The enemy is not only moisture in the air; some jungle photographers have had their gear ruined by fungal growths. There is no drying out a fungus-infested camera, and fungal growth on lenses can actually etch the glass forever. Keep cameras and lenses in two tightly-sealed plastic bags at all times except when actually shooting. And don't try to get away with just one bag! If you have a camera case with a good silicone rubber gasket, so much the better. Whether you've got a case or decide to cheap it out like we do with plastic bags, you'll want to surround your camera with plenty of silica-gel packets to absorb moisture. These can be dried in an oven or even over a campfire when they've become sodden.

Film requires as much protection as do cameras in the rainforest. Never open film canisters until you are ready to load the film. As soon as the roll is exposed, reseal it with some silica gel and keep it as cool as possible. This generally means keeping it in the shade. Do not put exposed film on ice or in cool streams, because you'll run the risk of condensation.

Taking pictures in the rainforest is always difficult. It becomes absolutely impossible unless you've brought that one vital piece of equipment: a tripod. You'll be amazed at how little light actually penetrates below the forest canopy until you consult your light meter. Four-second exposures are not at all uncommon with slow-speed films (ASA 64 and 100), and some situations may require even longer exposures. We favour a lightweight tripod that can easily telescope into a backpack. The disadvantage with lightweight tripods is that you cannot trip the shutter yourself and expect a sharp picture; the forest floor, strewn with leaf litter, assures that your feather-light tripod is going to wiggle. We circumvent this problem by using a cable shutter release. Be forewarned that sunny days actually pose more picture-taking headaches in the rainforest than do overcast days. The contrast between deep shadows and sun-dappled foliage, striking as it may look to your eyes, is far too variable for any film to capture. Neither electronic flashes nor high-speed film will solve the problem. Your best bet is simply to wait until clouds move in creating a more uniform light. In the rainforest, you won't be waiting long. A very similar problem arises when shooting near creeks or rivers in the jungle. The contrast between brightly-lit water and shadowy foliage results in some truly bizarre photographs. Once again, wait for clouds and bracket your exposures.

Some photographers try to outfox the perpetual dark of the rainforest by using high-speed films. If you are satisfied with the inherent graininess of these films, bring some along. Even with ASA 400 film, however, we have had to resort to the tripod on occasion.

We highly recommend an electronic flash for both night photography and for close-ups of insects and plants in the jungle. Let's face it, most of your wildlife photography in the rainforest is going to be confined to small, relatively immobile objects anyway: flowers, butterflies, beetles, snakes, frogs and spiders. With a flash, you can leave the tripod behind and take these sorts of pictures easily. But don't waste your film trying to take wide-angle shots of the jungle with a flash; hand-held flash units don't pack nearly enough punch to light such large areas and they'll leave all but the foreground in deep shadow.

Only trained wildlife photographers are likely to get shots of larger animals in the jungle. Most of your glimpses of large animals will be fleeting. Both the thick jungle foliage and the gloomy light discourage action shots of animals fleeing from you. For the beginner, the wide-open expanses of the Pantanal make a much easier studio for wildlife photos than does the Amazonian rainforest. Even so, you'll need lots of patience, luck, most likely a local guide, and the right equipment. A good telephoto lens is essential for wildlife photography. Even with most zoom lenses, you'll be hardpressed to pick out the animal from the background in the finished photos.

Developing and storing your film

Unless you are staying in Brazil for a long time (over a year) it's probably best to simply hold onto your exposed film and develop it upon your return home. Processing can be shoddy; and mailing film, like mailing anything else from Brazil, is very risky. If you do decide to mail film home, mark the package accordingly to avoid its being x-rayed at customs. Remember that exposed film is more vulnerable than unexposed film to the tropical heat and humidity. Keep your exposed film sealed, dry and as cool as possible without actually chilling it (which can cause condensation). Placing your film on concrete floors will cool it a few degrees, as will burying it in the ground. Unexposed film should be treated with the same respect, although it can be refrigerated safely when you're in the city. Most hotel owners will let you store film in their coolers, even if they cast some quizzical glances your way.

Photographic etiquette

A few words about taking pictures of people, advice that is perhaps just plain common sense and courtesy.

Remember that backcountry folk tend to be fairly shy. Candid shots of what to you is their colourful way of life may make them extremely uncomfortable. Use discretion, and when in doubt don't take out your camera at all. We once came upon a tiny fishing village during a hike along the northeast coast. During our fifteen-minute chat with the villagers, we realized that there was an exceptional photograph staring us right in the face: the sun setting on thatched huts, primitive nets hung up to dry, barefoot children smiling coyly from behind their mothers' skirts, the whole thing framed by coconut palms. But we couldn't do it. We just couldn't whip out the camera and reduce these shy, trusting folk to picturesque curiosities. If we had really wanted that shot – and wanted to retain our self-respect in the bargain – the thing would have been to return the next afternoon, chat some more, invest a bit of ourselves. But we didn't, and consequently we deserved to miss the shot. Too bad ... it would have made one hell of a cover.

Photo opportunities abound in the public markets. Both picturesque vendors and their wares make great travel photos. Once again, however, don't barge in and simply start shooting. Even if what you really want is a shot of the colourful old fishmonger himself, praise first his fine selection of groupers, mullet, and sardines. Ask for a small fillet of his cheapest fish, adding that you'd love to get a picture to remember the moment. You can always give the fish away later. This method ends up costing a little money, but you won't have to sneak furtively through the market, nor will you feel that you're taking advantage of your subjects. Taking shots with a telephoto lens is decidedly sneaky, but sometimes it's the only way to get an unposed picture.

Incidentally, we have never been asked for money by Brazilians whose pictures we've snapped. If you're solicited in this manner, chances are you're not in the backcountry.

JOBS

To work legally in Brazil you must first obtain a work permit. This involves a great deal of time, money and bureaucratic red tape, which probably explains why no one bothers to get one. If you'd like to try, visit the Ministério de Trabalho, Avenida Presidente Antônio Carlos 251 A, ground floor, in Rio.

Most travellers who want to earn money in Brazil become language teachers. It seems as if every Brazilian wants to learn English, although there is also some work for German and French teachers. For professional teachers it's an opportunity to practise the craft under unusual but rewarding circumstances. Unfortunately, virtually all the work is in large and relatively uninspiring cities: São Paulo, Belo Horizonte, and Porto Alegre top the list. Don't bother applying at the established schools such as Yazigi and Cultura Inglesa; they'll probably require a work visa and will pay next to nothing. But smaller schools may be worth trying. Most foreigners simply freelance, advertising locally and eventually drawing students by word of mouth. Average pay for a conversational class runs at about US$5–10 per hour.

Foreign musicians are always in demand in Brazil; a few years ago, American country and western bands were the rage in São Paulo.

VISA RENEWALS

Anyone requiring a tourist visa to enter Brazil (see *Chapter Two*) will need to renew the visa if planning to stay beyond 90 days from the date of arrival (*not* the date of issuance). You'll need to visit one of the larger cities to do this, preferably a state capital, and you should allow at least a half day to deal with the red tape. Visas are renewed at the offices of the Polícia Federal, who will hand you a blank application form. In most cities, you'll then be sent to one of several nearby privately-run offices which, for a small fee, will type your application (handwritten forms are not generally accepted). In some cities, they'll do the typing and charge a fee right at the police office. Next you'll have to go to a bank of the Polícia Federal's choosing – usually the Banco do Brasil – to pay the visa fee (about US$12). The Polícia Federal will then issue your new 90-day visa (sometimes only 60 days) when you present the receipt. Depending on where you renew and who's behind the desk, you may be asked to show a return ticket and/or 'sufficient funds' to continue your stay. I've never been asked.

If you renew your visa for the full 90 days, then leave Brazil, you will have to wait until the 90 days have elapsed before returning. In this case, ask for a shorter-term renewal.

Visas are renewed only once; if you're planning to stay longer than 180 days, you'll have to leave Brazil before the second visa renewal runs out and then re-enter the country. This means that you should plan to be somewhere near a border at the six-month juncture of your trip – the Pantanal, for example, or even portions of Amazônia, but not the northeast coast! Also, check first with the federal police for current rules, because you may not be able to re-enter if you leave before your full 90-day extension has been used. The Brazilian government takes visas very seriously, and the fine for overstaying can be substantial. Once again, be prepared to show a return airline ticket (or photocopy) and 'sufficient funds.'

In theory at least, it is supremely easy to get a fresh visa after a six-month stay in Brazil. You simply step across the border, have your passport stamped, then walk back to Brazil and apply for a visa. That's not quite how it worked for Jayne and me in the Paraguayan border town of Pedro Juan Caballero. Already stamped out of Brazil a few miles up the road, we made the mistake of arriving on a Paraguayan holiday. And there we waited in political limbo for two days and a night while Brazilian bureaucrats argued that we couldn't possibly return to Brazil because, although we had clearly left Brazil, they had no proof that we'd actually been to Paraguay, which was literally across the street!

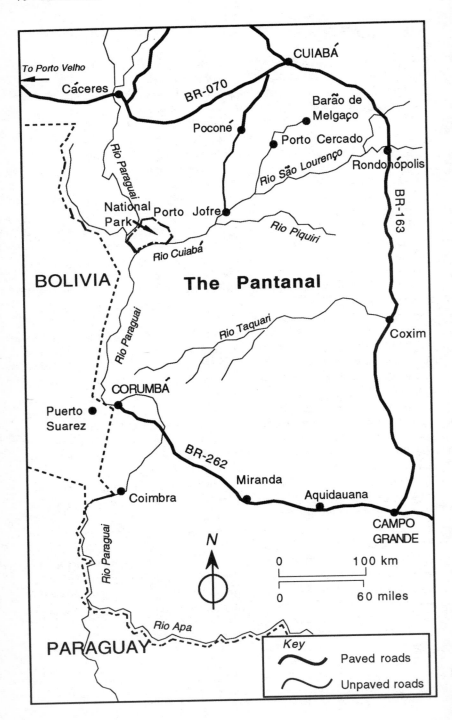

Chapter Five

The Pantanal

Big empty spaces are invariably the most intriguing part of a map for any backcountry traveller. Such a space appears on the *Guia Quatro Rodas* map where the Bolivian and Paraguayan borders touch Brazil. Larger than a hand, this portion of the map is covered entirely by those tiny blue dashes which signify marshy ground. Except around the perimeter, there are no roads, no railway lines, no towns. This is the Pantanal, an immense swampy plain encompassing some 230,000km² along the upper reaches of the Paraguai River.

The chief draw here is wildlife; the Pantanal is home to more than 600 species of birds, 300 species of fish, and a wealth of terrestrial wildlife that includes alligators, monkeys, deer, capybaras, and the flightless, ostrich-like rhea. True, there are other areas – Amazônia, for instance – that are richer in terms of both species and sheer numbers of animals. But unlike the thickly-jungled Amazon, the Pantanal keeps its wildlife largely on display. The terrain is open and veldt-like – the perfect setting for animal-watching. Once a vast inland sea, much of the Pantanal still floods with up to three metres of water during the rainy season. This further concentrates both wildlife and cattle on the remaining dry 'islands'. It is not at all uncommon to see the white, humpbacked steers known as *nelore* sharing an 'island' with a group of basking alligators.

Until recently, the Pantanal's only visitors tended to be wealthy Paulistas on fishing trips and ecotouristic gringos. The 1990 television series *Pantanal*, however, brought the area's natural beauty to national attention, and many Brazilians (for whom a vacation used to mean the beach) are these days grabbing binoculars and heading to Mato Grosso. The Pantanal's increasing popularity within Brazil was really brought home to me on our most recent trip to a fairly secluded outpost deep in Mato Grosso; one afternoon as we lounged along the riverfront, three elderly nuns from the southern state of Santa Catarina arrived in full habits, and within minutes they were shoving off in a canoe to watch alligators and fish for piranhas! This once-forgotten Eden is no longer a secret, but there are tangible compensations: the influx of tourism over the last ten years has made it much easier – and in many cases cheaper – to travel within the Pantanal's watery interior.

The proximity to Bolivia and Paraguay has driven much of the Pantanal's human history over the past five centuries. The entire region was originally ceded to the Spanish following the Treaty of Tordesillas in 1494, but explorers didn't reach the interior until the 1520s. Spurred by tales of gold and silver, groups of hardy fortune-seekers from the São Paulo area cut their way as far west as the Paraguai River. Known as *bandeirantes*, they battled fiercely against both the Spaniards and the Portuguese Jesuits, enslaving Indians captured from the Jesuit missions. (Contrary to popular belief, the Jesuits had no qualms about the institution of slavery itself; they often fought to the death to protect their Amerindian converts but were perfectly willing to see blacks enslaved.) As in the rest of Brazil, only remnant groups of Bororo Indians survive today in the areas bordering the Pantanal. Gold was discovered in the early 1700s. By 1719, Cuiabá had been founded to the north, and the area now known as Mato Grosso and Mato Grosso do Sul was made a royal captaincy by King João V of Portugal in 1748. Within thirty years, strategic forts protecting Portuguese land claims had sprung up on the Paraguai River near present-day Cáceres and Corumbá.

When the gold boom slowed, cattle ranching gradually took its place as the new economic mainstay of the area. That much hasn't changed to this day. Huge ranches, known variously as *fazendas* or *estancias*, make up virtually every square inch of the Pantanal that isn't under water the entire year. Many ranch owners live cosmopolitan lives far from their land and cattle; we visited one *fazendeiro* at his luxurious suburban home in Campo Grande, complete with swimming pool and a bar stocked with Scotch.

Agriculture has played a part in the Pantanal's economy since the 1950s. You'll find rice, soya, sugarcane, and coffee plantations scattered around the perimeter of the Pantanal. Industry has made inroads in the area as well; sugarcane alcohol, cement, and manganese mining may someday vie with cattle-ranching as the prime economic movers in this part of Brazil.

GETTING THERE

The Pantanal – more properly the Pantanal Matogrossense, since it spans the states of Mato Grosso and Mato Grosso do Sul – is accessible via the gateway cities of Campo Grande, Corumbá, Cuiabá, and Cáceres. Corumbá and Cuiabá lie closest to the Pantanal itself and have the most developed infrastructure for travellers. Corumbá is the gateway to what is generally referred to as the southern Pantanal, while Cuiabá gives access to the northern Pantanal.

Domestic airlines (including those with airpasses) schedule daily flights to Cuiabá and Campo Grande from Rio, São Paulo, and all other major cities. Pantanal and TAM have daily flights to Corumbá. Buses run daily to Cuiabá and Campo Grande from most state capitals throughout Brazil. The train from São Paulo to Campo Grande via Bauru, however, has been discontinued.

The cities of Cuiabá, Corumbá, and Cáceres lie on the perimeter of the Pantanal. In the Pantanal itself, there are really only four roads of any length: the Transpantaneira in the northern Pantanal (which runs from near Cuiabá to Porto Jofre); BR-262, the mostly-paved highway running between Corumbá and Miranda; MS-228, a dirt road which heads almost directly east from Corumbá and dead-ends in the middle of Nhecolândia; and MS-184, another dirt road running north-south which connects BR-262 and MS-228. Most travel within the Pantanal relies on these four roads and the many navigable rivers which course through the interior. The roads are rough, muddy, potholed and often covered with up to a foot of water; bridges are in disrepair and sometimes blocked. In short, I don't recommend that you drive these roads with a rental car, even a four-wheel drive vehicle. I've done it and sorely regretted it.

A few of the larger fazendas have airstrips, as do a couple of the lodges, but few travellers rely on flights within the Pantanal.

WHEN TO GO

There is no single 'best time' to visit the Pantanal. The rainy season runs from about late October through to March. During this time the rains which fall in the north of the Pantanal drain to the south, and huge expanses of grassland become completely covered with water. Floods often disrupt travel on the dirt roads around the perimeter of the Pantanal. The floods bring on mosquitoes during January, February and March, with January the worst month. It's also harder to put together group trips during the rainy season due to the dearth of fellow travellers. Despite these problems, there are a couple of advantages to visiting the Pantanal during the rainy season. First, it's warm, generally in the mid-20s. Secondly, as the waters rise, both cattle and wild animals are forced to cluster on the few remaining dry 'islands' (*cordilheiras*), where they are easy to see and photograph. Thirdly, the Pantanal's incredible array of flowering trees, water lilies, and water hyacinths all blossom during the wet season; February and March are best for these species, while orchids flower later (October or November).

But if it's your first visit and you have the choice, you should probably visit the Pantanal during the dry season, which runs generally from late June to early October (August and September are considered ideal by many people). This is the nesting and breeding season for thousands of egrets, storks, herons, cormorants and ibises. Particularly along calm oxbows, you'll see tree after tree swarming with birds returning from their daytime feeding binges. The dry season also makes for better fishing, since gamefish tend to be concentrated in the remaining water. And because the fish are concentrated, so too are their predators; it is during the end of the dry season that you're likely to see literally hundreds of jabiru storks clustered around a tiny pond, snapping up prey with their massive beaks. Fishing for many species is best between May and September, though several of the most important gamefish can be caught as late as December (see *Fish and fishing in the Pantanal* in this chapter).

There are only two disadvantages to visiting during the dry season. One is the temperature; during June, July and August, southerly winds sometimes bring cold Antarctic air to the Pantanal, plunging temperatures to near freezing. (On our most recent camping trip to the Pantanal, I re-read this advice as we huddled in our blankets during a July bout of 2° weather and high winds). September and October, while still dry, usually boast warmer temperatures. A second possible disadvantage to visiting the Pantanal during the dry season is the fact that navigation on the rivers is sometimes impeded by low water. If your itinerary includes river travel, you may want to avoid the driest months (July through to September).

WILDLIFE

Probably the easiest way to see lots of animals is to tour by car the few roads which penetrate the interior of the Pantanal. If you book a stay in either a lodge or organized camp, you'll almost certainly spend several hours on such roads, getting an eyeful of alligators, capybaras, and jabiru storks. For many travellers, the trip in and out of a lodge or campsite provides the best wildlife-viewing opportunities.

A second easy way to see wildlife is to cruise the smaller rivers by canoe. Even with an outboard engine chuffing away, you'll surprise plenty of animals, but insist beforehand that your guide cut the engine every now and then, at least for the trip downriver, so that you can scull silently close to shore. During the bird mating season, a canoe trip to the breeding areas – usually dead-end channels – is a must. My one sight of a South American river otter came while we were navigating a narrow passage of still water in a canoe, moving so slowly and silently that the otter glided within inches of our hull.

A third option is hiking. Unless you get out on foot, you'll miss seeing many species entirely, especially those which live within the forested areas, including howler monkeys, coatis and armadilloes. Walking riverbanks is a great way to see alligators and capybaras, but it's not always possible; you're often cut off by meandering side-channels too deep to wade, or the underbrush gets too thick. You'll also make a good deal of noise thrashing about, noise that can frighten animals a lot more than the unexpected ruckus of a boat approaching from the middle of the stream. Walking the roads, few as they are, is a better way to spot wildlife, as is a hike along the railway. But you're best off hiking with a guide. Most lodges and organized camping trips involve guided day-hikes, and with an experienced *pantaneiro* guide you'll see scores of animals you'd walk right by on your own. On any such nature hike, how much wildlife you see will depend on your guide's ability to locate animals, your ability to keep absolutely quiet, and just plain luck.

Finally, a number of ranches and lodges rent out horses, usually accompanied by a guide; this allows you to cover lots of ground, including marshes that would be difficult on foot. The downside is that horses make a lot of noise, and consequently you won't see quite as much wildlife as you might on foot or in a boat. Still, there are few more thrilling experiences in the Pantanal than fording a swamp, your horse belly-deep in water, surrounded on all sides by dozens of wary alligators.

As a rule of thumb, your best animal-viewing will occur near dusk and near dawn. After dark, a spotlight will pick out the reptilian gleam of alligator eyes on the river; it's also easy at this time to steal up on huge groups of birds dozing in the treetops.

Mammals
Zebu cattle

While a beef steer can't truly be called wildlife, it is the single animal species you'll see most often in the Pantanal. Cattle-ranching is in fact uniquely compatible with much of the Pantanal's wildlife; if traditional agriculture were to replace ranching much of the natural habitat and many of the wild animals would be destroyed. As it is, only the capybara and marsh deer could be considered competitors with cattle for the wild grasses, and this competition is probably minimal.

You'll spot an occasional group of European cattle in the Pantanal, but the white, floppy-eared and humpbacked zebu (Brahma) cattle dominate the landscape. Originally from Asia, they've adapted to life in South America, where they stand up well to both heat and insect pests. There are several varieties of zebu which breed freely with European cattle, but Brazilians call them all *nelóre*. *Nelóre* mingle well with the native wildlife of the region; you'll frequently see white egrets riding atop a steer's back, picking off insects. Some six million *nelóre* inhabit the Pantanal; stockmen also hunt down small herds of 'wild' *nelóre*, runaways which have turned feral.

The meat is noticeably tougher than that of the grain-fed European steers raised in the gaucho country of southern Brazil. Jayne and I once spent an awkward evening at a rancher's home, trying gamely to chew the rubbery steak proffered by our proud host.

Capybara

The name means 'master of the grasses' in the indigenous Guarani language of Brazil and Paraguay. The capybara (*Hydrochoerus hydrochaeris*, *capivara* in Portuguese) earns that title daily, mowing down wild grasses with its four large incisors and grinding them with a set of specialized molars. The incisors identify the capybara as a true rodent – the world's largest, in fact – rather than a pig, as early colonists regarded them. But the capybara might also be termed 'master of the rivers', outfitted as it is with webbed feet and the ability to stay submerged for five minutes at a time.

Capybaras, though closely related to the domestic guinea pig (cavy), weigh in at an impressive 50kg and stand 60cm high. A capybara's eyes, ears and nostrils are located near the top of its head, an adaptation that allows it to see, hear, smell and swim while mostly submerged. They spend a good deal of the day near and in the water, and this is where you are most likely to see them. During the day, they bathe in the river until it is cool enough to begin the afternoon's grazing. (Like all rodents, they have few sweat glands and must rely on the water to avoid a fatal case of overheating.) Grazing and napping occur at intervals throughout the late afternoon and evening. Drift in a boat downstream just before dusk, and you are likely to surprise a group of foraging capybaras on the riverbank. Their first reaction is a series of grunts, snorts and snuffles, followed by a headlong rush for the water or, less likely, into the underbrush.

Capybaras are social animals, living in groups of about 7–15 animals. That number swells during the dry season, when you may see as many as 50 or 100 capybaras in a single group sharing a waterhole. They observe a fairly rigid hierarchy, with a dominant male heading the group. Special male scent glands in the snout produce a sticky white substance used to mark territory and signal mates. The capybara's affinity for water extends to copulation, which occurs in the shallow portions of the river. The young are totally dependent on the adults for protection from marauding dogs, vultures, jacaré and jaguars.

It is difficult to spend much time along the riverbanks without encountering capybaras. Certain waterholes and beaches are especially popular; these will be full of the distinctive webbed-foot tracks and pill-shaped faecal pellets. Find a good vantage point nearby and wait until the sun is high and the capybaras return to cool off. During the heat of the day, we have occasionally surprised capybaras in the forest; don't get too close in such cases because frightened capybaras can deliver a good defensive bite. You'll see them most often, however, along roadsides, particularly along flooded portions of MS-228 in the southern Pantanal, or the last

15km of the Transpantaneira. Leave the engine running and you may be able to approach quietly within a few yards before they dash for the water.

Coati

Unlike other members of the racoon family, the coati (*Nasua nasua*, the name is the same in Portuguese) is active mostly during the day, and you're likely to encounter groups of them in trees during forest walks. At first, you'll notice one animal, generally the dominant male, who will announce his displeasure at your intrusion with a series of sharp snuffling noises. Keep quiet during your walks, because this may be your first indication that coatis are nearby. Once you've run across a male, watch the trees, because coatis rarely live alone, and you'll generally see at least three others scampering close to the male. Like racoons, coatis sport a ringed tail and distinctive 'bandit' markings around the eyes. Their handsome, tawny red coat makes them easy to spot against the forest background, where they root for insects, scorpions, spiders, fruit, lizards and mice. The oft-heard *coatimundi* is a Guarani name meaning 'lone coati', a reference to the solitary males which were once mistakenly believed to be a separate species.

Other mammals

Unfortunately, many other mammals either live secretly or have been decimated by hunting.

You may occasionally see **marsh deer** (*Blastocerus dichotomus*, *veado* in Portuguese), which are listed as endangered by the US government. Illegal hunting still occurs, and some cattlemen insist that deer compete with livestock during the rainy season when all animals are forced onto the remaining dry ground. Diseases contracted from cattle may also be destroying the remaining marsh deer. Only one fawn per doe is born in a season, which further exacerbates the problem. We've seen this species only once; the deer was apparently cooling off in a forested area during the middle of the day when we stumbled into the clearing. Like most deer, they leave the shelter of trees in the late afternoon to seek water; look for tracks in the riverside mud and stake yourself out if you really want to see a marsh deer.

Camping in the Pantanal, you may wake in your tent to the magnificent rolling-thunder roar of **howler monkeys** (*Aluatta* sp., *bugió* in Portuguese). Follow the roars in the early morning or late afternoon – howlers rarely make noise in the middle of the day unless it's raining – and you may get a closer look at a troop of these monkeys high in a tree.

Many travellers mistake the **agouti** (*cutía* in Portuguese) for a juvenile capybara; much smaller rodents, you'll most often see them scampering along flooded roadways.

Two **armadillo** species call the Pantanal home, the common nine-banded armadillo and a stouter, snub-nosed species. Both species of armadillo (*tatu* or *tatuzinho* in Portuguese) are nocturnal, and you will probably see more roadkill armadillos than live specimens. Hiking in forested areas you may happen across them during the day, and their poor eyesight and curiosity make armadillos easy to approach if it's done slowly and cautiously. Often they will pause just outside the safety of their hole in the forest floor to observe you. Consider yourself very lucky if you get a glimpse of **jaguars**, **anteaters** or **river otters**. Hunting and habitat destruction have nearly wiped these animals out. Most guides, however, can take you to waterholes frequented by jaguars and show you their tracks in the mud. Anteaters are easier to find following rains, when insects appear. River otters are a chance sighting on quiet boat trips; don't expect to see them if travelling in a boat with the engine running.

Alligators

These reptiles are variously referred to in English as alligators, crocodiles, and caimans. Since all caimans are members of the family *Alligatoridae*, and since all alligators are members of the order *Crocodilia*, you can probably take your pick without offending herpetologists. Safer yet is the Portuguese term *jacaré*. In any case, *Caiman crocodilus yacaré* is a geographic race or subspecies of the spectacled caiman. The spectacled caiman earned its name owing to the prominent ridge connecting the eyesockets, and various subspecies are found throughout most of South America. *C. crocodilus yacaré* is found only in the Pantanal and nearby areas; it differs from the other spectacled caiman subspecies in having several enlarged teeth in the lower jaw. These teeth generally ride in grooves along the upper jaw but may in some cases actually penetrate the upper jaw. I've never gotten close enough to a jacaré to appreciate this important taxonomic difference.

Jacaré probably grow to a maximum length of about three metres, although

locals invariably have tales of much larger specimens. They eat fish, crabs, snakes and large aquatic snails, along with an occasional duck, bird, capybara, deer, or smaller jacaré. Cattlemen don't regard jacaré as a threat to their livestock, however, and you'll often see alligators basking peacefully within a few feet of a grazing steer. The jacaré's tail is a powerful hunting tool which can stun fish and sweep them into the mouth in a single movement.

When the rivers rise, jacaré sometimes become trapped on the huge mats of water hyacinth and aquatic grasses that break free in the floods and float downstream. Travelling this way, jacaré have drifted as far south as the Tigre Delta near Buenos Aires.

Hide poaching has taken a severe toll, but as one long-time resident told us, there are still *jacaré pra enjoar* – alligators enough to make you sick. Indeed, it is not uncommon to come upon groups of basking jacaré piled one on top of the other along riverbanks.

It is almost impossible to spend a day in the Pantanal without stumbling upon a jacaré. Nevertheless, your chances of seeing these magnificent reptiles are much better in certain locations and at certain times. Probably the best spot to see hundreds of them is along the Transpantaneira highway in the northern Pantanal. Being cold-blooded, jacaré will spend the hottest days submerged up to the eyes, cooling off in the waterways while sun bakes the Pantanal. Just following dawn, and just prior to dusk, they'll emerge to bask along the riverbanks and roadways in an effort to warm up. For the best 'gator-viewing, then, walk the rivers or boat slowly down them during these times. Local boatmen will generally know the haul-out and basking areas preferred by jacaré. If you're wandering on your own, watch during the day for sandy riverbanks scored by tail and belly tracks; these are unmistakable. Returning to these areas prior to dusk or in the cool early-morning hours should yield plenty of sightings. They have excellent eyesight and hearing, so remain as still as possible; they are understandably wary and they'll slither into the water if you approach too closely for photos. If necessary, they can spend at least half an hour completely submerged. During this time, special flaps close over the ear slits and nostrils. Likewise, a throat flap slips into place allowing the jacaré to open its mouth underwater without flooding the lungs; that's important to an animal whose mouth, even closed, is never watertight.

During the cold fronts that occasionally sweep the Pantanal during June, July and August, jacaré become difficult to spot. Since the waterways retain their heat much better than the air, jacaré will spend the bulk of the day submerged except for eyes and nostrils, often foregoing their usual basking periods.

As the morning warms up, but before the heat becomes intolerable, you'll notice basking jacaré with their mouths open, jaws gaping widely. A jacaré's mouth contains a large surface area of moist membrane; when that moisture evaporates, it cools the animal down in much the same way that sweat drying on our own skin keeps us from overheating in the sun. For this reason, you'll rarely see jacaré with their mouths agape at dusk; they'll want to conserve heat for the cool night ahead.

Don't miss a chance to float slowly down the rivers at night with a strong floodlight, illuminating scores or even hundreds of alligator eyes; most guided tours include this as part of the programme. Regular electric torches, by the way, don't work for this except at very close range.

While the black caiman of the Amazon has been reported to attack humans on occasion, none of the spectacled caiman subspecies – which are considerably smaller – share its reputation. Let's face it, humans have lived alongside the jacaré for centuries without spinning any of the usual man-eater yarns; it's a pretty innocuous beast that can boast a record like that.

Birds
Jabiru stork

This stork (*Jabiru mycteria*), a huge bird that has become the region's instantly-recognisable trademark, is the uncontested avian king of the Pantanal. One of the largest flying birds in the western hemisphere, the jabiru (*tuiuíu* in Portuguese, pronounced too-yoo-YOO) may reach 140cm in length. Its white body feathers are offset by a naked black neck ringed at the base with a reddish collar. This featherless collar changes from pink to deep crimson when the bird is excited.

Jabirus feed strictly during the daylight hours, gathering in pairs, families, or sometimes large flocks to pluck fish and frogs from the marshes. Unlike most other wading birds, which feed by sight, the jabiru feeds by touch. Periodically, it dips its huge open bill into the water and waits. When a frog, fish, or snake makes the slightest contact, the jabiru simply snaps its bill shut and swallows. This form of feeding has obvious advantages in the Pantanal, where the water is turbid and prey is plentiful.

The jabiru's nest (*ninho*) is a large, sturdy structure made of sticks and placed high in the treetops. There is no trick to locating jabirus; they are extremely common throughout the Pantanal in open, swampy areas, where their size and vivid colours make them stand out like billboards. If you move quietly, you may approach their nests for a thrilling close-up view of a nesting pair. Walking through forested areas with your concentration at ground level, you may not notice the nest itself, but keep your eyes open for underbrush that is profusely spattered with the white droppings; chances are good that an active nest is overhead. Jabirus also frequent sheltered riverbanks. I remember an afternoon's canoe trip on a small tributary of

PANTANAL
Above: *Cattle drive* (JB)
Below: *Capybara* (JB)

Dusky titi monkey (Callicebus moloch brunneus) (GR)

Above left: *Yellow-banded poison frog* (Dendrobates leucomelas) (GR)
Above right: *Kingfisher, Pantanal* (JB)
Centre: *A lily-trotter or wattled jacana* (Jacana jacana) *among Vitória Régia or Amazon waterlilies* (Victoria amazonica) (GR)
Below left: *Young fer-de-lance* (Bothrops atrox) (GR)
Below right: *Caiman, Rio Negro, Pantanal* (JB)

Above: *Sand dunes, Natal, Northeast coast* (JLA)

Below: *Itatiaia National Park looking over the Paraiba Valley* (RG)

the Capivari River. A wall of reeds hemmed in the meandering waterway on both banks, and we drifted silently, the stillness punctuated only by the dip of the oars. Suddenly, a huge bird took flight from the riverbank alongside us. Looking up, we could see every detail of the naked scarlet neck, could hear the clacking of the huge bill, could even feel the rush of air under massive wings. We had seen literally hundreds of jabirus before, but this single and unexpected close encounter comes to mind every time I think of the Pantanal.

Jacana

The jacana (*Jacana spinosa*) is a small, robin-sized marsh bird sporting black feathers which fade to a gorgeous, rusty tan. This coffee-coloured plumage gave the bird its Portuguese name, *cafezinho*. It is only up close, however, that the jacana's real distinction becomes apparent: its outlandishly long feet and four-inch nails. These ungainly-looking toes allow the cafezinho to walk with confidence upon lilies and other flimsy buoyant plants. (A common English name for these birds – which occasionally find their way to temperate zones – is 'lily-trotter'.) When you approach a mother jacana and her young near water, the mother will frequently fly or hop a short distance away, while the juveniles will submerge, completely out of sight, for many minutes.

Wood ibis

The wood ibis (*Mycteria americana*) is a colonial stork, sporting a black head and neck above a completely white body. Their colonies are impressive, sometimes exceeding tens of thousands of nests within a small area. The nest itself, a platform of sticks built high in the trees, is selected and defended by the male. He then sets about attracting a mate, no mean feat for a bird that has no voice box and is therefore mute. Males and females go through an elaborate series of courtship rituals that include head bobbing and bill gaping. The birds pair up for the breeding season, and both share in incubating the eggs. During this time, you'll often find huge nesting colonies at dead ends or oxbows in small rivers. Here, during the dry season, the storks find a ready food supply of small animals, including snakes, frogs, rodents, and even small birds, concentrated by receding waterways. Like the jabiru stork, the wood ibis feeds primarily by touch rather than by sight, and can snap its bill shut on a fish in 25 milliseconds, one of the fastest vertebrate reflexes. Prey is brought back to the nest and regurgitated for the young to eat. *Cabeça secas*, as they are known in Portuguese, are capable of soaring at extremely high altitudes, winding down in lazy spirals during their return to the nest.

Parakeet

True parakeets (*Myiopsitta monachus*) are among the noisiest birds in the Pantanal. You'll never sleep past dawn if you pitch your hammock or tent anywhere near a parakeet nest. These are huge, ungainly tangles of sticks and twigs built in the crook of a tall tree, often a palm. We've seen these nests house upwards of twenty *periquitos*, as Brazilians call them. The occupants arrive en masse, a chattering chaos of small lime-green and yellow birds, darting in and out of the nest in madcap fashion. By nightfall they'll settle down, but only for a few hours. At first light, or even before, you can count on parakeets for a renewed burst of loud and manic activity.

Rhea

The largest bird in the Pantanal is the rhea (*Rhea americana*, *ema* in Portuguese), which may stand as tall as 1.6m. Rheas are closely related to ostriches, but differ from ostriches in having three toes rather than two. Rhea chicks are raised by the male, and he'll attack any and all potential intruders, including humans. Without this protection, the chicks are vulnerable to a host of predators, *caracaras* in particular. Adult rheas, on the other hand, have virtually no natural enemies. Rheas have been practically exterminated in many parts of South America because they will eat any agricultural crop. This is not a big problem in the Pantanal, where cattle ranching and natural vegetation are the rule. Consequently, rheas are a common sight, often bounding effortlessly across the open spaces in pairs or small groups.

Other birds

A member of the falcon family, the **caracara** feeds primarily on carrion, and you're likely to see it alongside the road picking at the corpse of a capybara or snake.

Kingfishers (*martim pescador* in Portuguese) nest in crevices on earthern river banks, guarding their territorial fishing grounds jealously. They'll sit motionless on a high branch, then suddenly plummet straight down and crash into the water to retrieve their prey.

The **common egret** (*Casmerodius albus*, *garça branca* in Portuguese), its plumage a brilliant white, stands out easily against the Pantanal's green backdrop of vegetation. Egrets take their name from the long, lacy-white specialised feathers called aigrettes. Both males and females begin growing aigrettes just prior to mating in the dry season, and they are among the most beautiful of all bird feathers. Egrets, in fact, were once threatened with extinction because of the millinery trade in aigrettes. During the mating ritual, males will raise these feathers well off their backs, attacking any competitors with their long beaks.

You'll often see **darters** (*Anhinga anhinga*) perched on a log, holding their wings out to dry as do their close relatives the cormorants (*biguá* in Portuguese). Their feathers are water-permeable, allowing them to swim low in the water, sometimes with only the head and neck exposed. Darters hunt their food underwater, being equipped with a bill that is serrated along the front edge, the better to hold prey. Their long, supple necks also contain a special hinge, allowing the neck to dart forward to help impale fish or insects. Upon surfacing, the darter shakes the prey loose, flips it into the air, and gobbles it headfirst.

A bird that you'll hear more often than see is the **curassow**, a large chicken-like bird that lives in the forests. They are poor fliers, spending most of their time on the ground feeding on fruits and leaves. *Mutum*, as currasows are called in Portuguese, will also eat hard-shelled nuts, swallowing pebbles to aid in digestion.

You'll often see the **roseate spoonbill** (*Ajaia ajaja*, *colhereiro* in Portuguese) feeding singly in swampy plains; even more thrilling is the sight of hundreds of these gorgeous pink birds suddenly taking flight.

See the *Further Reading* appendix for a suggested field guide. In Britain, an excellent mail order source of field guides is the Natural History Book Service (tel: 0803 865 913).

Important fish species
Piranha

There are at least a half dozen species of true piranhas in Brazil, and only a few warrant the fierce reputation. The *piranha mafura* and the *piranha encarnada*, for instance, eat only fruits and seeds. Then there is the *piranha mucura* (the 'opossum piranha', owing to its long snout), which feeds almost exclusively on the nipped-off scales and fins of other fish. When foreigners talk piranhas, they have in mind the *piranha preta* and the *piranha caju*, two certifiably voracious carnivores.

Travellers from the northen latitudes have for years been reading adventure stories about razor-toothed fish with a taste for human flesh. It's no wonder, then, that piranhas are probably the most sought-after fish in the Pantanal and Amazon, among non-locals at least. That's fortunate, since locals claim that it's often hard to keep them off the hook. If you can't catch a piranha in Brazilian waters, you should probably consider giving up fishing altogether.

Voracious as they are, their status as man-eaters is overblown. One afternoon Jayne and I came upon a solitary fisherman cleaning a dozen piranhas. Far more intriguing than his catch itself was the fact that he was standing knee-deep in the very same water where he'd hooked the fish only minutes before! Piranhas, he explained, infested nearly all the local waters, yet only a few spots were actually dangerous for bathing. We later heard this same story from a number of other villagers. No one, however, could tell us why; obviously, some painful personal experimentation was involved in mapping the local swimming holes. Piranha stories tend toward wild exaggeration, but a few documented cases of attacks on humans and livestock do exist. Most locals agree that small backwaters cut off from the main rivers and streams during the dry season are dangerous due to the high concentration of piranhas and the lack of prey. Otherwise, the piranha's reputation is largely the stuff of B-grade jungle movies.

Tackle for piranha fishing is embarrassingly simple: thick monofilament line wound around a tin can or tied to a bamboo pole. Four inches of baling wire, however, must be fastened above the hook as a 'leader' to prevent the piranha's teeth from cutting the plastic line.

Almost any piece of meat or fish will do for bait. We've used both strips of cooked beef and live eels. Thrash your bait about the surface for a few seconds before letting it sink. Apparently, this mimics the commotion caused by large prey falling into the water.

Piranhas put up a respectable fight even on hand-held line; on light spinning tackle they would rival the heftiest of trout. Yet the real fun begins once the creature is landed in a boat full of barefooted anglers. It's easy to believe that more piranha 'attacks' occur out of the water than in. The famous triangular cutting teeth snap pencils and plastic pens like so much balsa wood; dispatch piranhas with a sharp whack on the head if you plan to keep your toes.

Pacú

 The fruit-eating *pacú* looks like nothing so much as an overgrown piranha. Pacús sport two sets of teeth in the upper jaw, while piranhas have but one. I can't recommend this test with live fish. Biologists now suspect that pacú and other fish which eat whole fruits and seeds contribute to seed dispersal, and therefore affect the distribution of vegetation along waterways just as birds do on land.

The Pantanal hosts a number of species of pacú, some of which reach 12 to 15kg. The minimum legal catch size is 40cm. Best fishing occurs between October and March, with February especially good. The pacú is generally a herbivore, and the most popular bait is manioc root that has been boiled or roasted just long enough to allow a hook to penetrate. Manioc is easy to buy and store, and may thus be the ideal pacú bait. Some baits owe their success to the pacú's proclivity for snapping up fruits that have fallen from trees overhanging the river bank; *genipapo* fruit, figs, a small wild orange known as *laranjinha* and the so-called *melancia do pacú* are all fruit baits especially popular along the River Paraguai and its tributaries. Fruit and vegetable baits reportedly don't work well in some other waters, however; on the Taquari and Coxim rivers, for example, the preferred baits include chunks of beef heart or fillets cut from other fish such as the *curimbatá*. Whichever bait you choose, it must be very firm or you'll lose it to the pacú's strong teeth. Number 5/0 or 6/0 hooks are ideal, with 20kg test (0.60 or 0.70mm) monofilament line. Spinning reels, baitcasting reels, bamboo poles, and tin cans all work for pacú. Look for spots along the river with overhanging fruit trees which supply pacú with natural food. To keep your chummed bait from going downstream too quickly, try to find a place where the stream widens and forms back-eddies. Chum with manioc chunks or corn kernels before fishing – ideally, a day before.

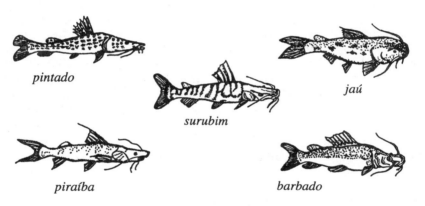

pintado

surubim

jaú

piraíba

barbado

Catfish
Some of the most highly-prized gamefish in the Pantanal are whiskered: *pintado*, *surubim*, *jaú*, *piraíba* and *barbado* are all shovel-nosed catfish, and the first two form the mainstay of all fish restaurants in the Pantanal. Pintado and surubim (the former striped and the latter spotted) can weigh up to 90kg, but generally run from 2 to 15kg. The minimum legal size is 80cm. Best fishing occurs from September through to March, and these species, like all catfish, feed primarily in the hours from dusk to daylight.

You'll need a fishing rod (preferably 2m long and fairly stiff) and a reel if you tie into a pintado of any size; sticks and cans won't do. The bait must be live – eels such as *piramhóia* or small fish such as *lambari* are ideal.

The pintado is a cautious fish; the slightest movements on your part or the smell of gasoline transferred from hands to bait may be enough to spook these giant catfish. If you're really set on catching a pintado, you would be wise to hire a guide.

The jaú is a more cylindrically-shaped catfish than the pintado and surubim, but may reach the same monstrous size and is caught in much the same way. Fishing for jaú is good the year round, and the minimum legal size is 90cm.

The barbado is the smallest (rarely larger than 8kg) of the edible catfish. It also happens to be the easiest to catch without a guide and is every bit as delicious as its heftier brethren. As Jayne can testify, you can haul barbado inshore with the most primitive of equipment – a tin can wrapped with 0.40 monofilament is more than adequate. While live bait helps, it's by no means necessary – any chunk of fish flesh will work. Ask locals for advice on the best locale; you may be invited, as we were, to join villagers for an evening of barbado fishing. Once again, wait for dusk, when the barbado leaves its hiding places to forage.

Dourado

 As its name implies, the *dourado* is a golden yellow-orange, the handsomest fish in the Pantanal. Looking much like a salmon, the dourado is excellent table fare and without a doubt the most sought-after freshwater game fish in South America. The minimum legal size in the Pantanal is 55cm, but dourado can weigh up to 30kg. Fishing is best from August through to December. Unlike the catfish, dourado prefer well-oxygenated, swift-running water, and feed during the day. Use a 24kg test (0.70mm) monofilament line and hook sizes from 5/0 to 9/0, baiting them with live fish or eels. Artificial lures such as Rapalas also work well for dourado.

Fishing in the Pantanal

Until the more or less recent advent of wildlife-oriented travel in the area, sport fishing was the Pantanal's major draw. The lure of a huge, tackle-busting *dourado* or *pintado* still remains the primary attraction for most Brazilian visitors. The Pantanal's rivers, sloughs and backeddies support some 350 species of fish, and only the most adamant non-angler should go there without bringing along a spool of monofilament and a few hooks. Even if you don't plan to wet a line yourself, you'll want to know something about the local fish; 80% of the Pantanal's birds and reptiles survive on a fish diet, as do many of the human inhabitants.

The *piraçema*

The great spawning migration of fish in the Pantanal is known as the *piraçema*. Once a year, the most important game fish – pacú, dourado, curimbatá and pintado, among others – form schools and travel upstream to spawn in the smaller stream margins. Such an arduous trip costs much in terms of energy, and that extra energy comes from the burning of fat reserves that the fish have accumulated over the preceding year. This spawning migration generally takes place between November and February, as the rivers swell with rainfall. Commercial net fishing is prohibited during this time, but angling with sport gear is permitted. For some species, the piraçema provides the best fishing.

Visitors interested in trophy fishing usually wind up at the lodges set aside pretty much exclusively for anglers. In addition to comfortable rooms, sport fishers are provided with bait and tackle, boats, ice, and expert guides. The *Guia Quatro Rodas* lists a number of these; see also the section on *Lodges*.

If, on the other hand, you're like us – perfectly happy reeling in piranhas when nothing else is biting – you'll be able to fish easily and cheaply almost anywhere in the Pantanal.

If you plan to do quite a bit of fishing, bring your own rod and reel. A collapsible 2m rod and spinning reel should do the trick. Five kilogram test monofilament line (0.30mm) will suffice for most species, along with an assortment of hook sizes ranging from 1 to 10 and 3/0 to 9/0. Spinning lures and Rapala-type lures are also a good idea. (Be sure, however, to remove treble hooks from these lures and replace them with single hooks; treble hooks are illegal in the Pantanal.) Lures from home make excellent gifts for local fishermen – especially if they happen to catch fish. You can buy fishing tackle at specialised stores in Cuiabá and Corumbá.

Primitive fishing gear can be made or bought for pennies. A simple fishing rod can be fashioned from any five- to seven-foot length of flexible wooden branch. Fishing tackle stores will sell you, dirt cheap, bamboo poles of varying lengths and flexibilities. A popular Brazilian rod and reel consists of nothing more than a tin can with monofilament wrapped around it; this cuts down on the fishing thrills to be had with a rod, but it does bring in the meat just as efficiently.

Finally, you can usually ask your boatman to provide tackle; if he takes people fishing on a regular basis, this should be no problem. In most cases, however, you'll get the simplest of gear: tree-limb rods or tin cans.

Finding a boat

The easiest way to sport fish in the Pantanal is to book a stay in one of the lodges. Almost all of them offer fishing trips as either part of their package or, more often, as an option which costs extra. Another possibility is to sign on with one of the 'botels' operating out of Corumbá, all of which specialise in fishing.

Putting together your own fishing trip in a tiny backwater town can be quite another matter. For one thing, you'll quickly find that the locals are reluctant to bend their schedule to yours, nor are they as impressed with dollars as their urban counterparts. I once spent an hour in a dirt-floored shack along the Paraguai River, patiently watching all the potential boatmen in town play snooker and drink beer; no one was particularly keen on taking us out on the river, at least not until the snooker champ was crowned. Secondly, you'll be lucky to find a single person with all the gear necessary for a boat trip; Tamires may own a boat, but it's João who has a motor, Vicente sells the only gas in town out of drums behind his house, and Raimundo is the sole outlet for live bait eels ...

My only advice is to be patient, polite and to allow plenty of time for these things to come together. Settle the price beforehand; fuel will be your major expense, but you'll also probably be charged per hour on the river as well as for bait. You'll cut costs considerably if you find other people to go along and share the cost; the price you pay is almost always for the boat, fuel, and guide, regardless of how many people are fishing. Most boats can handle only four anglers and a guide, however. Someone will invariably loan or rent you rustic fishing tackle if you don't have any.

Fishing licences and regulations

Licences are primarily required of trophy anglers at the fancy fishing lodges. Fishing independently in the backcountry, Jayne and I have never once been asked to produce a licence. Still, I recommend you buy one if you plan to do much fishing, and this is why: you'll provide the under-budgeted wildlife agencies with a bit of money and, far more importantly, you'll underscore the fact that foreign travellers are very much interested in resource conservation.

Licences are issued by the Instituto Brasileiro de Meio Ambiente e Recursos Naturais Renováveis (IBAMA) in Cuiabá (tel: 065 644 1511) and Campo Grande (tel: 067 382 1802). The easiest way to purchase a licence is to visit the Banco do Brasil in Cuiabá, Corumbá, Campo Grande or Cuiabá. In other locales, try the city hall (*preifetura municipal*) or ask at travel agencies and tourist bureaux.

Do not fish within 1,000 metres of any dam or natural waterfall, and do not land or transport more than 30kg of fish. Also prohibited is the use of treble hooks (*garatéias*).

NATIONAL PARK OF THE PANTANAL

This 135,000-hectare park, formerly the Cará Cará Biological Reserve, was set aside as a wildlife sanctuary in 1981. (Don't confuse this with the Transpantaneira National Park, which runs alongside the Transpantaneira highway joining Porto Jofre with Poconé.) It lies at the very southernmost part of Mato Grosso where the Paraguai and Cuiabá Rivers branch, midway between Corumbá and Cáceres. This is in fact the only access to the area, and you'll enter the park if you take a cargo boat from either Cáceres or Cuiabá to Corumbá. Porto Jofre on the Cuiabá River is the closest access point, 100km upriver. The western portion of the park is dotted with lakes, oxbows and bays. The Park is primarily for biologists doing research, but permission to camp there can be had by contacting IBAMA in Cuiabá at 065 644 1511. You'll have to provide your own transportation in (hire a boat from Porto Jofre), but check first personally with IBAMA; they may be sending a research crew into the park, with whom you can tag along. There are government camps within the park, but no amenities whatsoever, so you'll be on your own.

CAMPO GRANDE

Campo Grande, the state capital of Mato Grosso do Sul, was founded in 1889 and now boasts 530,000 residents. It doesn't actually border the Pantanal; in fact, the nearest marshy land lies 130km away near Aquidauana. Campo Grande's importance as a gateway city for travellers depended for many years on the daily train which ran west through portions of the Pantanal to Corumbá and the Bolivian border; with improved highways and year-round bus service to Corumbá, that importance has waned considerably. Nevertheless, most travellers headed for the southern Pantanal end up spending a day or two here (especially those with airpasses, since Corumbá's airport isn't served by the airpass companies). Many of the 'eco-lodges' in the southern Pantanal have representatives in town and can be easily accessed via the train or bus from Campo Grande. And finally, the museum and state tourist office are worth visiting prior to a trip in the Pantanal.

Getting there

Travellers can reach Campo Grande by air or bus daily from Rio, São Paulo, and most other Brazilian state capitals. The train service which once linked Campo Grande with Bauru and São Paulo was discontinued in 1994. The train, known locally as the *Trem da Morte* ('Train of Death'), now runs only from Campo Grande to Corumbá, and only twice a week (Wed and Sat at 07.00). The RFFSA train station (tel: 067 383 2762) is located at the corner of Avenida Calógeras and Avenida Mato Grosso. Tickets (US$17 for 1st class, US$12 for 2nd class) should be purchased at least a day in advance. Bring plenty of food and water for this 12-hour trip. Vendors stroll the aisles periodically, selling *cafezinhos*, beer and sandwiches at fairly inflated prices. A good deal of wildlife can be seen from the train following the brief stop in Miranda, but most of the trip is through dry scrub country, and views from the bus are just as good.

Daily buses from Rio to Campo Grande cost US$60 and take 21 hours. From São Paulo, the 14-hour bus trip costs US$45. Buses arrive from Cuiabá daily (10 hours, US$35). There are also daily buses running to and from Ponta Porã on the border with Paraguay; the *executivo* leaving at 08.30 takes 5½ hours to reach the border and costs US$20. To Corumbá, there are 11 buses daily beginning at 05.00 and ending at 24.00; the trip takes 6½ hours and costs US$22. The Campo Grande bus station takes up an entire city block and is located at Rua Joaquim Nabuco 200, an easy two-

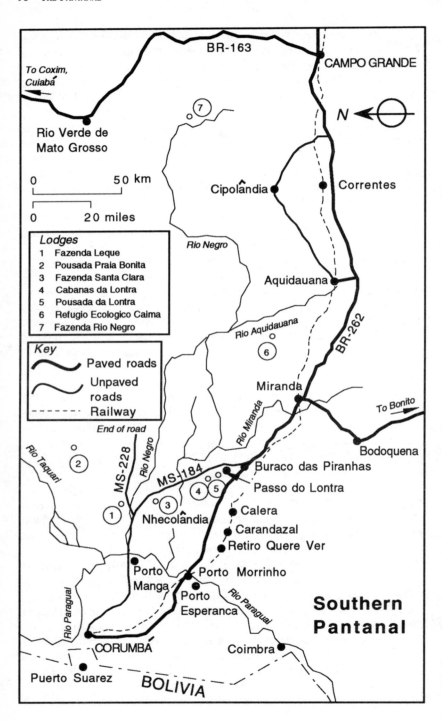

block walk from Avenida Calógeras, the main thoroughfare on which many budget hotels are located. If you prefer to check your baggage while scouting for a hotel, the bus station has a *guarda volumes* desk. It's also a fairly easy walk from the bus station to the train station; just head up either Rua Barão do Rio Branco or Avenida Afonso Peña until you hit Avenida Calógeras, then take a left and walk five or six blocks to the train depot.

Campo Grande is served by daily flights from Rio, São Paulo, Cuiabá, and all the other major hub cities in Brazil. Both Vasp and Varig/Cruzeiro fly here, so travellers with airpasses can arrive in Campo Grande and then take a bus to Corumbá, which is not served by the airpass companies. Antonio João airport lies 7km from the centre, along the BR-262 highway (if coming directly to the Campo Grande airport from Corumbá by bus, there's no need to go into town; just ask the driver to drop you off along the highway next to the airport). Taxis from the airport to downtown cost about US$10 during the day, more at night. The cheap public bus marked *Vila Popular* stops outside the airport on its way into town.

Where to stay and eat

Most hotels in Campo Grande can be reached easily on foot from the bus station. Many cheap-to-moderate choices lie within sight of the bus station, including the Nacional, Novo Hotel, Cosmos, Saigali, Iguaçu, Carandá, and Village Palace. The Hotel Gaspar is opposite the train station, and not nearly as noisy as it used to be in the heyday of rail travel. On the same block are the cheapies: Hotel União, Priape, and Tupí.

Many cheap restaurants and outdoor bars line the Rua Barão do Rio Branco. For *churrasco* and local fish dishes, try the Seriema at Avenida Afonso Pena 1919. Two other good churrasco restaurants offering reasonably-priced *rodízio* (all you can eat barbecue) are the Costelaria do Gaúcho Gastão (Rua Barão do Rio Branco 2192) and the Churrascaría Campo Grande (Avenida Calógeras 2199). Nutri Bem at Rua Pedro Celestino 1696 serves vegetarian lunches by the kilo.

Information and useful addresses

Cash and cheques can be changed at either of two places: the câmbio at Rua Dom Aquino 1682, or the Banco do Brasil, Avenida Afonso Pena 2202. The tourist information bureau Codems staffs a booth at the airport, and also at Avenida Afonso Pena 1897. They can supply maps of the state and information on trips into the Pantanal. Anyone seriously interested in the wildlife of the Pantanal should spend a few hours at the Museo Regional Dom Bosco, Rua Barão do Rio Branco 1843. For natural history buffs, it's one of the best museums in Brazil, featuring several rooms devoted entirely to stuffed birds, mammals, reptiles, and fish of the Pantanal. It's also a great way to learn their local Portuguese names. Along with the regional animal exhibits, there are collections of local Indian artefacts, sea shells, insects and minerals. The museum is open daily, 07.00–11.00 and 13.00–

17.00. Entrance: US$0.75. For shopping, try the Casa do Artesão, Avenida Calógeras 2050, which has a good selection of local handicrafts for sale: carved and painted wooden animals, dried and lacquered river fish, homemade fruit liqueurs, leather, ceramics, Indian headdresses, spears and arrows (open Mon-Fri 08.00–12.00 and 14.00–18.00). Selling similar items, and featuring local foods and music, is Eme-Ene at Avenida Afonso Pena 2303.

Excursions and lodges

Because Campo Grande lies at least 130km from the margins of the Pantanal proper, there are no day-trips to be made from here. However, both the bus and train to Corumbá provide some excellent views of wildlife en route. The bus begins entering marshy areas filled with birds and alligators just after the stop in Miranda, roughly halfway to Corumbá. The train doesn't enter the Pantanal proper until the Carandazal station; from there to just beyond the Paraguai River, a distance of about 40km, many people get their first taste of this magnificent landscape and its wildlife.

A number of lodges within the southeastern Pantanal have offices in Campo Grande and can be got to from there without going all the way to Corumbá. However, most travellers use Corumbá as the hub for exploring the southern Pantanal, and information for all the southern Pantanal lodges is therefore listed under *Lodges near Corumbá* below.

CORUMBÁ

Corumbá lies at the southwestern margin of the Pantanal, a sleepy port of 88,000 people overlooking the Paraguai River. A huge cement factory operates here, as do manganese and iron works. But it is the river that dominates Corumbá. A broad blue-grey ribbon at the north end of the city, the Rio Paraguai flows past so languidly that it is nearly impossible to tell which direction is upriver and which is downriver. The city matches that languid pace.

On our first trip in 1984, we'd expected a bustling port, not unlike Manaus, with scores of boatmen eager to take us into the Pantanal. Corumbá, after all, was the busiest river port in the world during the mid-1800s. We found instead a single row of cargo boats, only one of which was within a week of sailing. The closest that Corumbá's waterfront came to bustling occurred when a solitary fisherman pushed a wheelbarrow of freshly-caught catfish up the the the street.

Corumbá retains that agreeably laid-back air, especially along the waterfront, where you can see the decrepit facades of once-elegant colonial houses. And, fortunately for travellers, these days it is much easier to arrange trips into the Pantanal. Corumbá is still a hub of drug-trafficking and wildlife poaching, however, and foreigners can count on receiving a polite but very thorough search of both clothing and luggage by members of the Polícia

Federal (sometimes plainclothed), especially when entering from Bolivia. These guys are dedicated; I was asked to remove my well-worn and highly pungent tennis shoes during one particularly exhaustive search.

Getting there

You can reach Corumbá by air, bus, or train. Most travellers used to arrive by train from Campo Grande, but with highway improvements over the last decade, the train's importance has faded and it runs only twice a week from Campo Grande, leaving Wed and Sat at 07.00. The trip takes 12 hours and costs US$17 for 1st class, US$12 for 2nd class. The train connections with Bauru and São Paulo have been discontinued since 1994. If you've got the time, want to save some money, or simply love old trains, this may be a good bet, but it takes almost twice as long as the bus and the scenery isn't any better.

Andorinha runs eleven buses daily from Campo Grande to Corumbá, the first at 05.00 and the last at 24.00. The trip takes 6½ hours with stops in Miranda and Aquidauana, and costs US$22. Just past Miranda, you can get some good views of wildlife along the road. At Porto Morrinho, 72km from Corumbá, you'll debark the bus and board a small ferry which takes bus and passengers across the Rio Paraguai. From São Paulo, Andorinha runs one bus a day to Corumbá, leaving at 10.00, while a bus leaves Rio de Janeiro for Corumbá daily at 13.00. Many travel agents in downtown Corumbá, as well as the Vasp airlines office in town, sell Andorinha bus tickets. The price is the same as you'd pay at the rodoviária, and you're saved the walk. The rodoviária is located about seven blocks from the centre of town, an easy 5–10 minute walk.

Only two airlines, Pantanal and TAM, fly to Corumbá, so you can't fly there directly on either the Varig or Vasp airpasses. With these airpasses, the closest you can get is Campo Grande, hopping on either the bus or train to Corumbá from there. Flights on TAM and Pantanal leave Campo Grande daily.

To and from Bolivia

Increasingly, travellers are coming to Corumbá via Bolivia and returning after a brief trip to the Pantanal. The border is about two kilometres outside the Bolivian town of Quijarro and about five kilometres from the centre of Corumbá. There is a Polícia Federal checkpoint on the Brazilian side at which you'll have to stop for border-crossing formalities. To enter Brazil, you'll need an exit stamp out of Bolivia as well as proof of yellow fever vaccination. You and your bags may also be given a thorough search, due to the drug traffic along this frontier. Once on Brazilian soil, you can take a city bus (US$0.30) to the bus depot in the centre of Corumbá, conveniently close to many hotels. Taxi drivers at the border will undoubtedly try to convince you that this cheap bus does not exist, is not operating, or is on strike, and they'll stick to this unlikely story right up to the moment the bus arrives. The bus depot in Corumbá, incidentally, is for local city buses only; the rodoviária, from which all the long-distance buses leave, is about eight blocks away.

To reach Bolivia from Corumbá, take the Linea Canarinho city bus marked *Fronteira* from the depot at Rua Antônio Maria Coelho to the border (US$0.25). Buses leave every half hour or so, and the Brazilian Polícia Federal will stamp your passport at the depot; the police station opens at 08.00 every morning. Cross the small bridge into Bolivia, go through formalities, then catch one of the collective taxis (be sure to bargain, prices range anywhere from US$1–4 pp) or walk the two kilometres into Quijarro. Visa requirements are constantly changing; for current information, stop in at the Bolivian consulate in Corumbá, Rua Antônio Maria Coelho 881.

Where to stay and eat

Corumbá has plenty of cheap hotels and a handful of more upmarket options. Virtually all of the hotels lie within about eight blocks of the bus and train depots, and most of them are concentrated along Ruas Delamare and Antônio Maria Coelho. Of the cheapies, the Brasil, Salette, Condor and Moderno are all worth checking out, and all within a few doors of each other on Rua Delamare. A bit further up the scale but still good are the Santa Rita at Rua Dom Aquino Corrêa 860 and the relatively new Laura Vicuña at Rua Cuiabá 775. Closer to the rodoviária and train depot are two other cheapies along Rua Frei Mariano, the Pousada Pantaneira (run by a Swiss woman and her Brazilian husband) and the somewhat decrepit Londres. Just off Rua Frei Mariano on Rua Cuiabá is the budget Hotel Copacabana. The Pousada Pantaneira at Rua Ladario 271 is a sort of bed-and-breakfast in very pleasant surroundings, and it is consistently recommended. The Albergue da Juventude (youth hostel) is located at Rua Antônio Maria Coelho 677.

You'll find plenty of restaurants along Rua Frei Mariano, including Tarantella (Italian) and the excellent Churrascaria do Gaúcho. For local fish dishes, like *surubim na brasa* or *piranha ensopada*, try either of two places that have been doing business in Corumbá for many years: Peixaria do Lulu, tucked away at Rua Antônio João 410, or Bar El Pacu, run by 'Hermann the German' on Rua Cabral. Veteran travellers may miss the original Bar El Pacu in its venerable waterfront building, but the food is still excellent at Hermann's new location.

Information and useful addresses

There are two *casas de câmbio* in town, both located on Rua 15 de Novembro between Avenida 13 de Junho and Rua Delamare. Both change American Express travellers cheques as well as cash, and are open Mon-Fri during regular business hours and on Saturday until noon. Banco do Brasil (Rua 13 de Junho 914) also changes cheques and cash at their second floor câmbio, which opens on weekdays at 11.00. Cheques can also be changed, even on weekends, at the Hotel Pousada Pantaneira, Rua Frei Mariano 1335 (the base for Colibri Pantanal Safari tours, see below).

The staff at EMCOTUR, an official tourist office at Rua America 963, across from the National Palace Hotel, are friendly but not terribly helpful. There are many travel agencies in town selling tours and tickets. Plane and train tickets to Bolivia can also be reserved through the Hotel Pousada Pantaneira, Rua Frei Mariano 1335.

If you happen to be in Corumbá during the latter part of June, don't miss the festival of São Joao and São Pedro, which the citizenry celebrate with music, local foods, and dancing along the waterfront. Children dress festively as cowboys and cowgirls, complete with painted moustaches. You can lounge at rustic outdoor booths on the waterfront, eating cheap barbecued meats and drinking *quentão*, the hot spiced beverage that Brazilians love in the wintertime.

Excursions
Near town

Many hotels and boat operators in Corumbá offer day excursions on the River Paraguai. Travellers are often tempted by these trips because they are easy to arrange, require but a day, are relatively cheap, and run on a dependable schedule. The flip side of all this convenience is that you won't really see much wildlife. Travellers usually return from such boat trips with nothing more than a sunburn. They will have taken a snapshot or two of the Vitória Regias (giant water lilies), but the chances of actually seeing an alligator or a capybara are slim indeed. Few wild animals, after all, opt to live within earshot of a city of nearly 90,000 people. If you're still tempted, the boats *Pérola do Pantanal*, *Labarca* and *Sairu* can all be found along the waterfront, and run 3–5 hours tours costing between US$10–20.

Further afield
Organized camping trips in the Pantanal

For most travellers, this is the best and most economical way to really experience the Pantanal. In the mid-1980s, such trips were unknown. Until recently, the only option for land-based travel within the Pantanal – besides the handful of relatively expensive lodges and fishing resorts – was to find your own guide, transportation and fellow travellers to share costs. By the time you'd done this sort of legwork, you'd often have spent more time in town than in the Pantanal itself. As more and more travellers learned of the Pantanal, tour operators of every stripe began springing up in Corumbá to handle the boom. In the scramble for business, some of these ersatz guides ran hasty, disorganized forays into the Pantanal in which animals were harassed and camps were pitched illegally on ranches. Not surprisingly, most of these characters have since gone out of business, and Corumbá currently hosts just two operators running camping trips, both recommended.

You'll probably be approached by someone working for one or both of these tour operators as soon as you step off the bus or train. My advice is to first find out exactly what they're offering: the number of days you'll be camping, the location of the camp or camps, the sort of camping equipment provided and what you'll need to bring, the usual daily activities, the experience and background of the guide, the maximum number of travellers that they would take to the camp, the sort of food you'll be eating. You'll probably be shown a book of photographs of frequently-spotted animals, the camp, and the trusty four-wheel drive vehicle that will get you there. Secondly, ask to meet the guide who would actually be with you on the trip. You could also ask the tour operator to introduce you to someone who's just returned from a trip, or ask around town on your own; chances are that most travellers in town are either just returned from such a trip, or waiting like you for one to happen. And thirdly, try to meet some of the other travellers who've signed up – a good guide and plenty of wildlife don't always compensate for obnoxious camp mates.

In any case, find out as much as you can about the trip specifics before signing on. Ideally you'll have a day in Corumbá to suss all this out and buy supplies for your trip. On the other hand, if you're like us you'll end up arriving in Corumbá late at night, only to find out that a group is leaving the very next morning. This requires some quick and decisive action without all the information; the alternative is sometimes spending a few days in Corumbá cooling your heels – and in Corumbá there's little else to do – while another group forms. If time is important, then go ahead and sign up for a next-day departure; you can't really go too far wrong with the tour operators currently running camping trips.

Gil's Tours (Rua Delamare 895-B, tel/fax: 067 231 1777, 231 6558) is probably the most popular, owing at least in part to the charismatic salesmanship of owner Gilberto Magalhães. Gil could pass in both appearance and manner for a California surf bum, but in fact he's a native of Corumbá and an enthusiastic promoter of responsible travel in the Pantanal. He learned English as a soccer coach in Florida and Michigan, and is keenly aware of the kind of wilderness experience that foreigners desire. When we visited, Gil's camp sat alongside a bend in the Rio Negro in the Nhecolândia region of the Pantanal, about 4–5 hours by truck from Corumbá. The cost for three days is US$70 pp, with each additional day US$10. These costs include round-trip transportation by truck, tent, blankets, guided day-hikes and three hot meals a day. Distilled drinking water in huge plastic jugs is provided in the camp. We were camped with about ten other travellers. Tubing on the river among alligators is an option. One of Gil's best guides at this writing is Johnny Indiano, who was trained by the near-legendary Katu, who's given up land-based guiding for sport fishing.

Colibri Pantanal Safari operates from the Hotel Pousada Pantaneira, Rua Frei Mariano 1335, tel/fax: 067 231 3934. Both the guide service and hotel are run by Claudine Roth, a personable Swiss woman who speaks good English, and her Brazilian husband Jose Paraguaio. Cost is identical to Gil's Tours and includes round-trip transportation, three hot meals per day, tents and blankets, all at their riverside camp in Nhecolândia along the Rio Negro.

Regardless of whom you book a trip with, most of the first day is typically spent on the dirt road which penetrates Nhecolândia. You'll also spend part of the morning buying supplies at the local supermarket. Although three filling hot meals are provided each day, you'd be wise to bring snacks (biscuits, chocolate, cookies etc). If you bring liquor to the camp, pass it around sparingly until you've decided if your guides will be in shape for guiding in the morning. To be fair, I never saw either guides or cooks take a drink, except when offered one by fellow campers.

The trip to the campsite may well be one of the trip highlights. You're bound to see scores of capybaras alongside the road, sometimes hundreds. Where the road is flooded, capybaras may be reluctant to move out of the way for the truck, and at times they are so abundant that it's almost impossible to avoid hitting one in order to avoid another. Many of the larger capybaras sport ugly wounds, the result of territorial battles. Agoutis, much smaller rodent cousins of the capybara, scurry alongside the road as the trucks pass. You're also likely to see huge flocks of jabiru storks (*tuiuíu*) along portions of the road. Once you've veered off the dirt highway, rheas are a common sight on the grassy ranchland.

Guests generally make a guided day hike during the morning, returning to camp for lunch and possibly a nap, followed by an afternoon hike. Hikes generally last several hours and invariably require that you ford rivers and creeks. Bring a hat, sunscreen, insect repellent, drinking water, binoculars and snacks in a daypack. You'll tramp through open grassland, forest clearings, and along riverbanks.

Commercial boat trips from Corumbá

The cement barges that used to ply the Rio Paraguai as far as Porto Jofre no longer make the run. A host of smaller commercial boats still head into the Pantanal's waterways, however, supplying cattle ranches with food, machinery and other supplies. Remember that these aren't tour boats, so they're not about to bring you in close for photos of alligators or jabiru storks. You'll see lots of alligators and birdlife along the riverbank on such trips, but not nearly the variety of animals you'd see on guided camping trips. But if you want relative solitude and the feeling that you're far from the gringo crowd, this may be the trip for you. Just be ready for some inconvenience, cramped quarters, and the constant drone and stink of a diesel engine.

You're also likely to find yourself stuck in Corumbá for several days while you find a boat. One option is to talk to the Capitânia dos Portos on Rua Delamare next to the Post Office for information on which boats are leaving. Just as easy (maybe easier, considering the fact that the Capitânia office is frequently closed) is to walk Corumbá's tiny waterfront yourself and ask around. Most boats keep irregular schedules, but there are exceptions. For example, the small cargo boat *Flor de Yayá* leaves every Monday for Porto Fundão on the Rio Taquari. They'll take passengers on the five-day journey (three days upriver and two days back down) for US$30 pp.

Passenger fares always include simple meals, but be sure to bring plenty of snacks (and if you're squeamish about drinking river water, bring bottled water or a water purifier; the crew will think you're crazy). You'll need your own hammock, and plan on slinging it between tractors, bags of rice and assorted farm machinery.

Lodges

Although obviously more expensive than camping or buying passage on a boat, lodges are the most comfortable option, and one that will get you close to lots of wildlife. They're also the best choice for families with young children. Lodges in the Pantanal used to be structured exclusively toward fishing, and the guests tended to be wealthy Paulistas. Over the last ten years or so, new lodges have sprung up within the Pantanal which cater to 'eco-tourists', and many of the fishing lodges have re-structured themselves for non-fishing guests. Be sure to check with lodges on just what is covered in the daily price; in many cases, you'll be paying extra for guided tours, horses, boats, etc. The price almost invariably includes three meals, but drinks are generally not included in the base price.

The following lodges are a sampling of those currently operating, and are most easily accessed via Corumbá and/or Campo Grande (for lodges in the northern portion of the Pantanal, see the sections describing the Transpantaneira, Cáceres and Barão de Melgaço below).

Pousada da Lontra (tel: 067 231 6569 in Corumbá). Note: don't confuse this lodge with the nearby Cabanas do Lontra (see below). About 115km from Corumbá and 7km off BR-262, at Passo da Lontra. You can sling hammocks under cover here for US$35 (the *barracas* can sleep up to five people for that price), while cabins for up to six people go for US$120. Guided boat trips for fishing and 'photographic safaris'. If coming by bus from either Corumbá or Campo Grande, you can have the owners pick you up at the junction of BR-262 and MS-184.

Refúgio Ecológico Caimã (tel: 067 242 1102 in Corumbá, 067 5267 in Campo Grande, or São Paulo 246 9934).This is actually a complex of five different lodges, all within a single huge working fazenda. A stay usually consists of 4–5 days, in which guests move from one lodge to another. Numerous other options are available, depending on your particular interests. English-speaking guides lead guests on horseback, on foot, in jeeps and by boat. At roughly US$200 pp per day (the cost includes all meals, land transport, and all tours), this is undoubtedly the most expensive lodge in the Pantanal, but is highly recommended.

Cabanas da Lontra (tel: 067 383 4532 in Corumbá). Located in Passo da Lontra,

about 120km from Corumbá (roughly 2 hours by truck) and easy to confuse with
the similarly-named Pousada da Lontra. They charge US$50 pp per day with all
meals included. Guided boat tours cost extra, US$150 for 4 hours, up to 10 people.
Highly recommended, but they have no horses. The owners can arrange to pick
you up at the junction of BR-262 and MS-184 if you tell them what bus you'll be
taking; ask the bus driver to let you off at the junction, known locally as Buraco
das Piranhas.

Fazenda Rio Negro (tel: 067 725 7853 in Campo Grande). This working fazenda
and eco-lodge became famous in 1990 – and spurred Brazilian interest in the
region – when television crews descended upon it to film the popular
telenovela *Pantanal*. Owned by the Rondon family since 1895, the fazenda
charges US$180 pp per day, including full board and all guided tours by boat,
horse, or on foot.

Fazenda Santa Clara (*aka* Pousada do Pantanal, tel: 067 231 5797 in Corumbá).
One of the longest-established non-fishing lodges in the southern Pantanal, and
still very popular. Located in Nhecolândia just off MS-184, about 125km from
Corumbá. They charge US$110 pp for a three-day stay, and other options are
available. The food when we visited was excellent. Tours by boat, horse, horse-
drawn carriage cost extra. They have an office in downtown Corumbá at Rua Frei
Mariano 502.

Fazenda Leque (tel: 067 231 1598 in Corumbá). Located in Nhecolândia, not far
from the Fazenda Santa Clara on the other side of MS-184.

Hotel Fazenda Xaraes (tel: 067 231 6777 in Corumbá). Located on the banks of
the Rio Abobral in Nhecolândia, about 130km from Corumbá, this lodge is fairly
new and well-appointed. They have an office in the centre of Corumbá at Rua
America 969.

Pousada Baia Bonita (tel: 067 231 4009 in Corumbá). Deep in Nhecolândia,
roughly 200 km from Corumbá, this lodge offers 3–4 guided programmes, with
horseback, jeep, and hiking tours.

Other land trips from Corumbá

The very cheapest and easiest way to see a slice of the Pantanal, albeit a
very tiny slice, is to simply ride the bus to Campo Grande. Only a portion
of the 6½ hour trip, however, actually passes through swampy areas filled
with wildlife, and there is one other obvious problem: you can't stop. Your
bus driver will be hell-bent on reaching Campo Grande before dinner, and no
amount of alligators, jabiru storks or capybaras is going to slow him down.
    There are two options, then, if you want a relatively quick road tour
within the Pantanal that allows for stopping and taking pictures: either rent
a car or hire one with a driver ... The two car rental agencies in Corumbá
are Localiza, Rua América 482 (tel: 067 231 6379) and Nobre, Rua Cabral
1373 (tel: 067 231 5566). Both will rent cars for round-trip excursions into
the Pantanal on BR-262 and MS-228. Be sure, however, to read about
Brazilian car rentals in *Chapter Three*. I wouldn't advise attempting the
round-trip from Corumbá via MS-184, even in the 'dry season'. Make sure
you ask about road conditions before setting out. If you prefer to let someone

else worry about the car and driving, guides can be found through any of the tour agencies in town (eg Corumbátur at Rua Antonio Maria 852, tel: 067 231 1260). All things considered, this usually turns out cheaper in most cases than renting a car yourself.

If you want more than a whirlwind 'Pantanal-through-the-windscreen' tour, but don't feel you have the time to spend a few days camping with the tour operators listed above, you'll need to disembark somewhere along the highway. One possibility is Porto Morrinho, the point at which buses stop to catch the ferry across the Rio Paraguai, 72km from Corumbá. Simple lodging is available. Much more wildlife, however, can be seen in the vicinity of Porto da Manga, 61km east from Corumbá on MS-228. The bus to Campo Grande used to travel this route before BR-262 was improved, but your only option now would be to hitch a ride with one of the tour operators who head out this way almost daily on the way to their camps in Nhecolândia. There's a small ferry at Porto da Manga and also a hotel, the Pesqueiro São Cosme e Damião, which rents doubles for US$40. From here, you could catch a boat downriver to Porto Esperança, about 15 min away, and which lies close to the rail line linking Corumbá and Campo Grande. Early morning or late afternoon walks east from Porto da Manga usually turn up hundreds of jabiru storks (known locally as *tuiuíus*) and basking alligators.

Finally, you can always disembark from the Corumbá–Campo Grande train, which makes five stops that put you off within the Pantanal proper. Running east from Corumbá, these are: Porto Esperança, Retiro Quere Ver, Carandazal, Calera, and Bodoquena. The most intriguing of these from the train (and the only one we've actually sampled) is Porto Esperança. To reach this tiny riverside settlement, you must debark at Posto Agente Inocêncio, which is nothing more than a crude station house and platform set in seasonally-flooded scrub forest above the Paraguai River. The small train which used to run down the spur track from here to Porto Esperança no longer operates, so you will have to walk the tracks down to the river. A couple of small pensoes operate there, mostly catering to sport fishermen. From this lethargic little outpost, you can walk the riverbanks, where we've seen alligators within a half kilometre of the village. You can also walk the train tracks toward Corumbá, passing through hyacinth-studded waterways filled with bitterns, hawks, finches, cormorants and spoonbills. From Porto Esperança, there are occasional ferries down the Rio Paragaui to Forte Coimbra.

CUIABÁ

Cuiabá sits in the exact geodesic centre of South America. There are probably some metaphysical implications to this, and if you're so inclined there is a plaque marking the precise spot in Praça Moreira Cabral downtown. For most travellers, however, Cuiabá's importance is that of the northern gateway to the Pantanal. Just a few hours from this bustling state capital begin the vast watery expanses which continue south for some 400km.

A modern, noisy metropolis of over 800,000 people, Cuiabá is no sleepy backwater like Corumbá. You can't walk to the rodoviária from the centre, nor check out all the city's hotels within a six-block radius, nor stroll to the waterfront for a quiet afternoon beer. Neither does it perch on the perimeter of the Pantanal like Corumbá; for that, you have to travel to much smaller towns like Poconé, Cáceres, and Barão de Melgaço, all about two to three hours away by bus. For these reasons, I prefer Corumbá to Cuiabá as a base for exploring the Pantanal. But Cuiabá, for all its big-city bustle, is a friendly place, and is home to some of the Pantanal's best guides. In addition, it's more convenient than Corumbá for travellers with airpasses and those on tight schedules, since it is served directly by all the major airlines. And sooner or later, aficionados of this soggy paradise called the Pantanal will want to see its northern reaches – which means a stay in Cuiabá.

Getting there

Cuiabá is served by daily flights from Rio, São Paulo, and all the other major Brazilian cities. Varig/Cruzeiro, Transbrasil and Vasp fly here, so travellers with airpasses can reach Cuiabá directly. Marechal Rondon airport is in Varzea Grande, some 12km southwest of Cuiabá proper. Taxis to the centre are metered, but you'll end up paying US$18–23 depending on your destination and whether it's day or night. City buses leave from the covered bus stop across the highway, near the Hotel Las Velas, and cost US$0.50. From the centre to the airport, take the bus marked *Aeroporto* from the Praça Ipiranga; the bus stop itself is on the side of the praça facing Avenida Tenente Cel. Duarte.

Daily bus services are available from all the state capitals. Local buses to Poconé, Cáceres and Barão de Melgaço, which sit on the perimeter of the Pantanal, leave frequently from the rodoviária. There are plenty of city buses from the rodoviária to the city centre. To reach the rodoviária from the centre, catch bus route number 202 from the corner of Avenida Getúlio Vargas and Rua Joaquim Murtinho.

Where to stay and eat

Cuiabá does not have a wealth of budget hotels, nor do you get good value here in any price range. We've never quite figured out why. The Hotel Mato Grosso at Rua Comandante Costa 2522 has raised its prices considerably over the years but is still reliable. Another reasonable choice is the Real Palace Hotel at Praça Ipiranga 102. Other hotels popular with budget travellers include the now very overpriced Hotel Samara at Rua Joaquim Murtinho 270, and the Hotel Presidente at Avenida Getúlio Vargas 345. If you need to stay near the airport (flights often leave Cuiabá at ungodly hours), the cheapest hotel in the area is the Globo. Tour guides can often arrange cheaper rates with certain hotels if you've already signed on for an excursion with them.

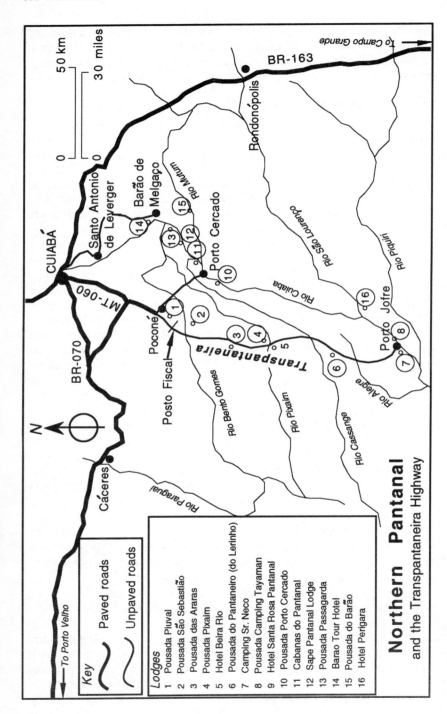

Northern Pantanal
and the Transpantaneira Highway

Key
Paved roads
Unpaved roads

Lodges
1 Pousada Piuval
2 Pousada São Sebastião
3 Pousada das Araras
4 Pousada Pixaim
5 Hotel Beira Rio
6 Pousada do Pantaneiro (do Lerinho)
7 Camping Sr. Neco
8 Pousada Camping Tayaman
9 Hotel Santa Rosa Pantanal
10 Pousada Porto Cercado
11 Cabanas do Pantanal
12 Sape Pantanal Lodge
13 Pousada Passagarda
14 Barao Tour Hotel
15 Pousada do Barão
16 Hotel Perigara

If you have to wait for a trip to form in Cuiabá you might consider hopping on a bus for Poconé and have your tour group meet you there; all tours on the Transpantaneira have to pass through Poconé, and the town is quiet and relatively cheap.

Information and useful addresses

Unfortunately, there are no simple câmbios in Cuiabá, nor was I able to change cheques at hotels. BEMAT (Banco do Estado de Mato Grosso), located in the city centre near the corner of Avenida Getúlio Vargas and Rua Joaquim Murtinho, has a câmbio desk open Mon-Fri 10.00–15.00. They give a good rate on American Express travellers cheques, but charge US$5 as a commission regardless of the amount changed. Banco do Brasil, also on Avenida Vargas near Rua Barão de Melgaço, has a câmbio desk on the third floor. Both banks take forever to process cheques.

Funcetur, located in the Praça da República next to the main post office, provides helpful information on guided tours and lodges in the northern Pantanal. They're open Mon-Fri 08.00–18.00.

Excursions

Most travellers come to Cuiabá in order to tour the Transpantaneira, the 150km dirt highway which winds through the heart of the northern Pantanal. Cuiabá, although it lies about 100km from the start of the Transpantaneira, is the best place to arrange a tour of this kind. Guides and tour outfits, as well as lodging and alternative transportation are described in the section below on *The Transpantaneira*.

The towns actually bordering the Pantanal, all of them much smaller than Cuiabá, include Poconé, Cáceres and Barão de Melgaço. These towns, pleasant in their own right, serve primarily as jumping-off spots for the tours and lodges deep within the Pantanal. Lodging and transportation are described below for Poconé, Cáceres and Barão de Melgaço, as well as the 'eco-lodges' which are accessed via them. But remember that in most cases you are best off arranging trips and lodging first in Cuiabá.

The other excursion option from Cuiabá is Chapada dos Guimarães, a mountainous plateau which boasts waterfalls, forests and commanding views. This is not the Pantanal, however, and foreign tourists from temperate zones are often not as impressed with the landscape as Brazilian tourists might be.

POCONÉ

A fine paved highway (MT-060) runs south from Cuiabá for 98km to the town of Poconé, where the Transpantaneira actually starts. TUT Transportes runs six buses daily to Poconé, from 06.00 to 19.00, and six return buses. The fare is US$7 and the trip takes two hours. My first impression of Poconé as I stepped off the bus in 1984 was that it was not particularly enticing; the dusty streets were littered with hundreds of flying cockroaches, each the size of a golf ball. But I've since come to like this quiet, hospitable little town on the edge of the Pantanal. It's the ideal place to escape the bustle and expense of Cuiabá for a few days, particularly if you're waiting for a tour group to form in Cuiabá; just let potential guides know where you are, and they'll be able to pick you up in Poconé on their way to the Transpantaneira.

To reach Poconé's main plaza from the small rodoviária, walk two blocks to Rua Antonio João, take a right, and walk 5–10 minutes. The Hotel Skala is to your right about a block away, but for cheap lodging I prefer the hotels just outside town, near the beginning of the Transpantaneira. To reach these, walk straight out of town, past the church on your left, to the Texaco gas station. Turn right, follow the signs to the Transpantaneira, and you'll quickly come to three rustic hotels: Pousada Pantaneira on the right, owned by a friendly family from the southern state of Paraná; the Santa Cruz, also on the right; and the Pousada Aurora do Pantanal, on the left. Doubles at these hotels run US$15–30. All three places serve good food, as do a number of small restaurants in the main square. Just outside town on the way to the Transpantaneira are a couple of rustic souvenir shops which sell wood carvings, honey, preserved fruits, and locally-produced fruit liqueurs.

Poconé is where cheap, regularly-scheduled public transportation ends. If you plan to continue south on the Transpantaneira, you'll need to hire a guide, rent a car, hitchhike, cycle, or walk.

THE TRANSPANTANEIRA

Most excursions in the northern Pantanal focus on the Rodovía Transpantaneira, a long ribbon of red-dirt highway which winds through 150km of formerly pristine swampy plain, crossing 114 rickety wooden bridges. Mercedes trucks now share the landscape with jabiru storks, alligators, capybaras and ibises. Any environmentalist worthy of the name – myself included – has to feel more than a little uneasy about the Transpantaneira. We can wag our heads self-righteously, but the uncomfortable fact is that the Transpantaneira has made the Pantanal far more accessible to low-budget travellers and amateur naturalists.

The Transpantaneira was originally envisioned as a major highway connecting Cuiabá and Corumbá. Construction began in September 1973 but has been halted for at least twelve years. This is precisely the kind of project that vote-hungry Brazilian governors love to tackle, but for now at least, the Transpantaneira has bogged down scarcely half-way to Corumbá. It now seems unlikely that the Transpantaneira will ever expand beyond Porto Jofre, a tiny settlement along the banks of the Rio Cuiabá. Merely maintaining the existing roadway following a rainy season has proved too ambitious for the government, and local ranchers have reluctantly begun rebuilding the crumbling bridges at their own expense.

During the dry season, you'll come upon the first water just 10km outside Poconé. Here also, on your left, is the first of the lodges along the Transpantaneira, the Pousada Piuval. Beyond this, at km19, you'll reach IBAMA's Posto Fiscal, a small barracks on the left side, and an attractive portal announcing in several languages that you are entering the Pantanal. A brief stop to chat with the IBAMA guard is obligatory here.

At km27 (about 1½ hours from Poconé if making a leisurely tour), the Pousada São Sebastião (aka Fazenda Curicaca) offers lodging and full board for US$95 for two people. You can rent a canoe for US$30 per day and explore the Reserva Ecologica Curicaca (no fishing is allowed). Tel: 065 322 0178 for reservations and information.

At km32, another 15 minutes down the road, you'll come to Pousada das Araras (tel: 065 381 4959, or through Expeditours in Cuiabá at 065 682 2800). A four day tour (by boat and on horseback) for two people costs US$400, including lodging in comfortable rooms with private bath and hot showers, plus full board.

Pixaim (km60), is a major fuelling stop for truckers, selling gasoline (US$0.68 per litre), diesel and alcohol. Leaving Poconé in the morning, this is about as far as you're likely to get in a single day of leisurely sightseeing along the Transpantaneira. If you're driving, fill up here because your next chance is at Porto Jofre, where the pumps are often empty. Flat tyres are almost as common as alligators along the Transpantaneira, and there's a tiny *borracharia* here to mend them. You'll also find two lodges. The venerable Pousada Pixaim (tel: 065 721 1899) has been here for many years, and its simple rooms along a wooden boardwalk on stilts have had a recent facelift, now featuring air conditioning. Lodging for a couple costs US$78, with private bath, hot shower and three excellent buffet-style meals. Drinks cost extra. Long-time owner Miguel José Ourives and his friendly staff can arrange guided boat tours, birdwatching, or fishing trips on the Rio Pixaim, and will rent you a canoe for US$20 per day. They're happy to cook whatever fish you catch, including piranhas. You can often arrange for free transport out here if you call ahead and arrange to ride back with Miguel or his staff from Poconé. We've stayed here on several occasions, and have always enjoyed the rustic ambience and good spirits.

Just across the concrete bridge (built in 1995 after the old wooden bridge was swept away during floods) is the new, upscale Hotel Beira Rio (tel: 065 321 9445). Doubles cost US$100 with full board. The hotel runs package programmes in conjunction with Anaconda Tours, and is very popular with hordes of Paulistas; thanks to this new hotel, you'll see boatload after boatload of them on the Rio Pixaim, buzzing downstream at high speed and scaring much of the wildlife that could just as easily be seen by paddling silently with the current. To be fair, the place seems very comfortable and I've been told that the food is excellent. They also rent out horses.

At about km100 you'll reach the Pousada do Pantaneiro do Lerinho (tel: 065 721 1545), one of the newest and, at this writing, the cheapest of the lodges along the Transpantaneira. It's a friendly, rustic, place run by Lerinho, son Eduardo and his family. They charge US$35 pp per day with full board. The food is tasty, particularly the ample breakfasts of *pao de queijo*, several homemade breads, fruit, eggs with *farofa*, coffee and herb tea. There are a number of trails on the fazenda, all of which can be hiked on foot, and some of which you can explore on horseback. Birding is excellent, and tour groups specializing in birding are increasingly booking the place. The owners will take you to one nearby field of *coqueiros* (coconut palms) where we saw upwards of 40 blue macaws in a single tree.

Continuing south from the Pousado do Pantaneiro, tall trees begin to disappear and the countryside opens up near the Rio Alegre, providing watery vistas stretching all the way south to the distant, forested banks of the Rio Cuiabá. Capybaras, seldom seen along the roadway further north, scamper in hordes along this stretch. This area is known as Campo Jofre, not to be confused with Porto Jofre, still about 12km ahead.

The Transpantaneira dead-ends 145km south of Poconé at **Porto Jofre** on the banks of the Cuiabá River. Porto Jofre consists of a couple of petrol pumps (frequently empty), two hotels (one currently closed), and two places to camp. Sr Neco, whose campsite is located along the riverbank, charges US$5 to sling your hammock under cover; restrooms and cooking facilities are provided. There's an electricity generator. He also rents out a house with two rooms and kitchen, sleeping up to eight people, for US$80. Boats and limited fishing gear are available for rent. Since Sr Neco caters for fishermen, his place closes during the *piraçema* (spawning period), from November to February. Camping is also available on the grounds of the Pousada Tayaman, for US$4 pp. There's a restaurant on site. The upscale Hotel Fazenda Santa Rosa Pantanal (tel: 065 322 0948), a few kilometres upriver, was closed during our last visit, but may re-open by the time you read this. The Santa Rosa is one of the oldest lodges within the Pantanal, and also one of the most expensive.

From Porto Jofre, it's possible to catch a cargo boat down the Cuiabá River to Corumbá, a journey of 3–4 days. For more information, see the section on *Cargo Boats* below.

Other lodges nearby

Besides the lodges listed above which are actually located along the Transpantaneira, there are two others which lie to the west and are best accessed via Poconé. The more luxurious of the two is the Hotel Cabanas do Pantanal (tel: Confianca Tours, 065 321 4142 in Cuiabá for reservations), 42km southeast of Poconé near the Rio Piraim. Three-day fishing and photographic safari tours, including horse riding, run to US$350 pp with full board. The second option is the Pousada Porto Cercado (tel: 065 322 0178 in Cuiabá), 47km from Poconé along the banks of the Rio Cuiabá.

Lodging and full board is US$50 pp.
See also the lodges listed below under *Barão de Melgaço*.

Guided tours along the Transpantaneira

What can you expect to see on a trip down the Transpantaneira? Unless the weather turns frosty, you are virtually guaranteed close views of hundreds of alligators (*jacaré*). At times, you'll encounter them stacked atop each other like cordwood, basking in the ditches alongside the road. You will almost certainly see lots of birdlife, including jabiru storks, ibises, kingfishers, egrets, and possibly roseate spoonbills. Beyond this, what you see will depend on your exact itinerary, the skill of your guide, seasonal and weather conditions, how observant and quiet you are, and just plain luck. Capybaras are quite common, especially as you get within 20km of Porto Jofre, but there are travellers who've spent days in the Pantanal without seeing one. We never saw a river otter until our most recent trip, and have yet to see a jaguar. Deer, macaws, peccaries, toucans, boa constrictors, anteaters, monkeys and armadillos are all common sights in the Pantanal, but you can't count on seeing them during any one particular visit.

There are two excellent and well-known guides currently working out of Cuiabá: Laércio Sá and Joel Souza. If you arrive at the airport, you're likely to be approached by one or both. Unless you're in a big hurry, I'd make it a point to search out both and talk to them about their tours. Quite frankly, you can't go wrong with either of these guys. Their prices are competitive, both speak English, they're real professionals with extensive knowledge of the flora and fauna, they're personable, and both have lots of recommendations in the travel guidebooks.

Laércio Sa's outfit is called Faunatours, and works out of the Real Palace Hotel (tel: 065 321 5375). **Joel Souza** can be reached at 065 624 1386, and his office is at Avenida Getúlio Vargas 155A, next to the Hotel Presidente. They were both offering three-day trips for US$190 pp; this includes all transportation, lodging, meals, and guided tours. You'll travel along the Transpantaneira by van, staying overnight at some of the more rustic lodges listed in the section above, and make detours along the way by boat, on foot and on horseback. These side trips generally involve some piranha fishing and drifing downriver at night to spot alligators. How far down the Transpantaneira you'll travel depends on the guide; neither Laércio nor Joel were going all the way to Porto Jofre, but most travellers don't need to go all the way to Jofre for a real taste of the Pantanal. They like to go with about four or five people, so you may have to wait a day or two for a group to form, or make up the difference yourself. As always, ask for specifics on where you'll be going and what you'll be doing. Do remember, however, that weather and other factors can force a change in your schedule, so be flexible.

I like the personalised treatment and small group size you get with independent guides like Laércio and Joel. The other option involves bigger tour companies like **Anaconda Tours** (tel: 065 624 4142 or 624 5128). They have an office at Rua Comandante Costa 649, next to the Hotel Mato Grosso, and were offering three-day trips for US$210; once again, that price includes all transportation, lodging, meals, and guided tours by boat, on foot and on horseback. These tours take place in big four-wheel drive rigs painted in camouflage colours, and you'll stay at the upscale Hotel Beira Rio in Pixaim, which might explain the slightly higher price. The general programme is roughly the same as outlined above, but once again, ask for a detailed itinerary before putting your money down.

Still another option is a specialized tour for birders offered by the **Soletur** company in São Paulo. Groups are led by expert guides well-versed in local ornithology and fluent in English. You'll travel by van and stay at the rustic lodges listed above. These trips are for serious birders, folks willing to get up well before dawn, sit motionless in clouds of mosquitoes, in pursuit of another tick on their lifelist. Soletur advertises in major birding magazines.

When you sign on with a guide or tour group, you'll be provided with a list of things to bring. Most important on this list should be: binoculars, camera, insect repellent, sunscreen, warm clothing, long-sleeved shirt and long trousers, snacks and bottled water. This last item is seldom mentioned by the guides (who are accustomed to the heat), but unless you bring your own water, you'll end up paying exorbitant prices for bottled water at the lodges. Remember, food is included in the tour price, but not beverages. This can really add up on a three-day trip, so I recommend buying several large jugs or even a case of mineral water in Cuiabá before setting out.

Touring the Transpantaneira by hired car
By car and driver

This isn't the ideal way to see the Transpantaneira, but it may be your only option if you have but a single day to spare or can't afford the price of a two- or three-day tour. In Cuiabá and Poconé you can find taxi drivers who will take you all the way to Porto Jofre and back in a single day. Try Adelmar, who works at the Mato Grosso Palace Hotel in Cuiabá, or one of the *taxistas* who hang around the plaza in Poconé. You'll have to bargain, and expect to pay around US$200–250 for three or four people. (You'll end up paying about the same even if you're travelling alone). To see anything at all you'll have to leave at the crack of dawn, returning to Cuiabá or Poconé long after dark. At this pace, you can't be stopping for pictures of every alligator, capybara or jabiru stork, nor can you expect your driver to be an expert on the natural history of the Pantanal and its creatures. Of course, you can hire a driver for two or more days, but then you'll be expected to pay his room and board, and at that point you might as well go with a qualified guide.

By hire car

I've done this only once, and I don't recommend it.You'll end up spending more than you would hiring a guide, far more if you damage the car, which is all too easy to do. The cheapest car rental you're bound to find in Brazil will run about US$70 per day, and it's very doubtful you'll find such a rate in Mato Grosso, which is generally socked with a *tarifa regional* by the rental companies. Arriving in Cuiabá and renting a VW Golf will probably cost, at the very least, US$235 per day with free mileage, or as much as US$90 per day plus US$0.60 per kilometre. The round trip from Cuiabá to Porto Jofre involves about 500km, so the bill could amount to US$375 before fuel costs. And all of this assumes that you'll be able to make the trip in a single day (or want to, for that matter). In any case, by the time you figure in food and lodging, you're paying far more than a three-day guided tour. Moreover, you'll spend much of your time watching for potholes and manoeuvring your way over narrow bridges, rather than gazing at wildlife. And you'll miss the information that a local guide can provide, as well as his sharply-attuned senses. Be forewarned that the Transpantaneira, due to lack of maintenance, is deteriorating with each passing year, and the bridges are getting trickier to navigate in small cars. I have driven the Transpantaneira in a Fiat Uno, but the vehicle of choice is the VW Golf, or better yet, a VW van, which has greater clearance. Four-wheel drive isn't much of an advantage. Make sure your spare tyre is in good shape before setting out.

In Cuiabá, try Atlântida Rent A Car, Avenida Isaac Póvoas 547 (tel: 065 623 0700) or Localiza, Avenida Dom Bosco 963 (tel: 065 321 0846). With any car rental company, it's best to phone ahead for reservations, but this is never a guarantee that they'll actually have a car available.

Hitchhiking the Transpantaneira

The Transpantaneira is one of the few places in Brazil where you can successfully thumb a ride. There's usually a steady stream of commercial truck traffic, fishermen, Brazilian tourists, fazendeiros, and foreigners in rental cars. Truck drivers will often stop for you, but you'll usually have to stand in the back – there's rarely room in the cab – and you'll often be asked for a small fee. But besides eating dust, there's a big disadvantage to hitching with truck drivers: you won't be able to stop to admire the wildlife. You'll enjoy your ride far more if you can wrangle a ride with fellow travellers who aren't hellbent on reaching Porto Jofre by nightfall. Try hitching on the weekends, when other tourists and sport anglers are more likely to be on the road.

Other options for touring the Transpantaneira

In several trips up and down the Transpantaneira, I have never seen a single foreign cyclist, but it would seem an ideal way to tour the area on the cheap. Roads don't get much flatter than this, and there are now plenty of lodging options conveniently spaced along the way. Everyone in Poconé rides bicycles, and you'll see plenty of sturdy mountain bikes. I have asked locals why someone doesn't set up a rental shop; this notion is invariably greeted with polite but baffled silence. Still, I would think that the dedicated cyclist could scare up a cheap bike rental without much trouble in Poconé.

Another option is hiking a portion or all of the Transpantaneira. Camping is not allowed, nor is it easy to find a spot from which to sling a hammock, but there are now enough lodges along the way to make this feasible.

Finally, you could do the trip on motorcycle. I've only met one traveller who's actually done this, but he recommended it highly. He loaded his motorbike aboard a commercial cargo vessel in Corumbá, disembarked at Porto Jofre four days later, and was in Poconé the next evening.

Cargo boats

Although Cuiabá overlooks the upper reaches of its namesake river, the city is still some 110km north of the Pantanal proper. The closest ports of call for cargo boats plying the lower Cuiabá River are Porto Jofre and Porto Cercado. Both these towns are reached via Poconé. River traffic to Corumbá has decreased markedly with the completion of the all-weather highway in Mato Grosso do Sul. During the dry season, cargo boats rarely operate out of these towns; indeed, the Cuiabá River is often unnavigable during this time, so plan accordingly.

Boats leave from Porto Cercado irregularly during the wet season, heading downstream for Corumbá. During the dry season – assuming that the river isn't blocked by exposed sandbars – a boat leaves about once every month or so. Be prepared to wait; there is no schedule.

If you have plenty of time to hang around Porto Jofre, you might be able to pay for passage downriver on a small (roughly ten metres long) cargo boat bound for Corumbá. These boats make periodic trips up and down the Rio Cuiabá, supplying fazendas along the way. Boats leave Porto Jofre roughly twice a month, but schedules are erratic, and they generally take about 3–4 days to reach Corumbá. You'll see lots of wildlife if your boat happens to take one of the side routes, but virtually nothing if you stick to the centre channel of the immense Rio Cuiabá. Expect to pay about US$30 pp (very simple food is usually provided), but rates vary considerably because the skippers aren't in the habit of taking passengers.

CÁCERES

Cáceres has the agreeably sleepy air of all tropical river ports. Ice-cream salesmen gather to chat under the mango trees in the main plaza; an occasional fisherman ambles by, balancing *pintado* catfish on a pole above his shoulders; and along the riverfront stevedores lounge in the shade of double-decked boats being loaded for the trip downstream. These days, with the advent of more reliable ground transport in Mato Grosso do Sul, there are far fewer boats making this trip. Be prepared to wait for a very long time if planning to catch a cargo boat bound for Corumbá on the Paraguai River.

Colibri and Cascavel each run nine buses daily from Cuiabá to Cáceres beginning at 06.30. The fare costs US$12 and the trip takes 3½ hours with a single stop at Posto 120 to eat. Passengers arriving at Posto 120 from Poconé can board the bus for Cáceres here. You'll be dropped off in Cáceres at the open bus station in the centre of town, on the Avenida 7 de Setembro. Buses to and from Cáceres are very crowded, so book early.

You'll find many cheap hotels in Cáceres, including the Comodoro, the Fénix, the Capri, and the Avenida; these are all located within a few blocks of the rodoviária. There is but one lodge currently operating outside Cáceres, the Hotel Barranquinho, located 72km from Cáceres along the banks of the Rio Jaurú. For reservations, contact Ametur at Rua Joaquim Murtinho 242 in Cuiabá (tel: 065 624 1000). Cash and cheques can be changed during the week at both Banco do Brasil and a câmbio on the main square.

Cáceres lies along the eastern bank of the Paraguai River. It's an easy walk from the bus station to the waterfront; ask directions to the main square (Praça Barão do Rio Branco), then head left on Rua Celso Faria, which runs parallel to the river.

In the rainy season, you may be lucky enough to find a boat or two leaving every month for Corumbá, but there is no set schedule. Speak directly to the captains aboard the vessels. The trip downriver from Cáceres to Corumbá takes about four days in the rainy season.

In the dry season, the Paraguai River often becomes impassable near Taimã. Before you spend the time and money travelling to Cáceres, try calling the Capitânia dos Portos there at 065 221 1266 for information on the river and the availability of boats. In Cáceres, the office is located at Rua Professor Rizzo 1. Facing the river from the Praça Barão do Rio Branco, turn right and look for a pastel yellow building.

BARÃO DE MELGAÇO

Yet another access point for the Pantanal, Barão de Melgaço lies roughly 100km southeast from Cuiabá, depending on which road you take. Both roads are mostly unpaved, one from Santo Antonio de Leverger and the other from São Vicente on the main highway. TUT Transportes runs two buses a day from Cuiabá, leaving at 07.30 and 15.00. The trip takes three hours and costs US$12. Lodging options in town consist of the cheapie Nossa Senhora do Carmo and the more upscale Hotel Tuiuíu and Barão Tour Hotel.

Numerous lodges within the Pantanal are accessed by boat from Barão de Melgaço. Highly recommended is the Sapé Pantanal Lodge (tel: 065 322 3426 and 065 361 4069 in Cuiabá). The lodge is located on the right bank of the Rio Cuiabá, roughly midway between Barão de Melgaço and

Porto Cercado further downstream, about two hours by boat in either case. Multilingual guides lead boat and land tours for birding and nature photography. They currently charge US$90 pp per day for lodging and full board; more complete tour packages are also available.

Upstream from the Sapé Lodge, along the Rio Piraim, lies the Pousada Passárgada (tel: 065 322 0178 in Cuiabá). Boat transport downriver from Barão de Melgaço (about 1½ hours) is included in the tour packages, which include full board and multilingual guides. Also highly recommended.

Much further downriver, near the confluence of the Rio São Lourenço and about six hours by boat from Porto Cercado (dry season only), is the Acampamento Pirigara (tel: 065 322 8961 in Cuiabá). You can also fly in from Poconé by arrangement with the owners. Rooms accommodate up to four people, and they charge US$40 pp with full board.

WILL THE PANTANAL SURVIVE?

Environmentally speaking, the Pantanal's future is on much more solid footing than that of the Amazonian rainforest. The huge cattle ranches that dominate the area lie on naturally open and fertile grasslands, not the thin jungle soil being cleared daily in northern Brazil. Ironically, as long as beef production remains lucrative, much habitat will undoubtedly remain in its present, relatively pristine state. But whether or not there will be wildlife to fill that habitat is still uncertain. Poaching, commercial fishing, waterway expansion, erosion due to farming and mining all pose serious threats to the Pantanal's future.

Poaching has taken a severe toll in the Pantanal, and no single species has been more devastated than the alligator (*Caiman crocodilus yacaré*). Valued for its hide, the jacaré has for decades been pursued by *coureiros* (leather hunters) from both Brazil and nearby Bolivia. Each year, they butcher an estimated one to two million alligators in the Pantanal. The economic crisis in Brazil has only worsened the problem; one local resident admitted to us that a ranch hand could make more in a single night of alligator poaching than his entire monthly salary. The poachers, of whom there are perhaps as many as 5000 in the Pantanal, hunt primarily at night, using flashlights and lanterns to spot the reflective eyes of their sluggish prey. It is not uncommon for a single *coureiro* to shoot 200 jacaré in a single night. Poachers flay only two small strips of leathery hide from the jacaré's flanks and leave the rest, including the tail meat, to rot.

While alligators lead the list of poaching targets, the *coureiros* regularly shoot a number of other species for their pelts or feathers: river otters, blue macaws, pacas (another oversized rodent) and monkeys. Jaguars, which poachers hunt with the aid of trained dogs, are now extremely rare within the Pantanal.

It's true that the Brazilian government has made recent strides in coming to grips with the poaching problem. Army troops, for instance, are now combining jungle-combat training with anti-poaching patrols. Yet the problem is not likely to go away, and may actually get worse if Brazil's economy continues to stagnate. A staggeringly huge chunk of real estate, the Pantanal is almost impossible to patrol effectively: a dozen IBAMA agents have responsibility for all 230,000km². And poachers, like the drug cartels, are becoming increasingly sophisticated; some now use radios to warn their cohorts of an approaching patrol. Eliminating the demand for these goods (the market is primarily European) seems far more likely to succeed than on-site surveillance. Strict import controls and certification of farm-origin furs and hides will help stem the flow of these animal goods; this is one of the few arenas where non-Brazilians can truly effect change.

Mechanized mining, concentrated near Poconé and Nossa Senhora do Livramento in Mato Grosso, is permanently scarring huge tracts of land. The resulting runoff clogs streams and smothers fish eggs for miles. Meanwhile, the mining industry burns some 40 tons of mercury each year in Mato Grosso alone. This toxic metal ends up a permanent and deadly part of the Pantanal's earth and water supply.

Because the Pantanal depends on rivers as its lifeblood, development outside the Pantanal itself can have huge consequences downstream. For instance, the Taquari River in the southern Pantanal has experienced major siltation due to reckless farming practices on the plateaux bordering the Pantanal's eastern perimeter. Siltation clogs the waterways and precludes successful spawning of many fish species.

Commercial fishing goes on largely unrestricted. Fishing with illegal nets and traps, even during the *piraçema* (spawning migration), is a flagrant commonplace.

Perhaps the biggest single threat to the Pantanal is the Hidrovia, the ambitious commercial inland waterway which has been proposed to link Brazil, Paraguay, Bolivia, Uruguay, and Argentina. The InterAmerican Development Bank (IDB) and the United Nations Development Program have already begun planning and environmental-impact work clearing the way for the project, which would involve dredging, dynamiting and straightening the upper Paraguai River to more efficiently link it with the Paraná River. If completed, the multi-billion dollar project would expand and ease commerce all the way to the Atlantic Ocean. Hydrologists warn, however, that such a dredged and straightened river channel would seriously disrupt the water cycle within the Pantanal, possibly draining a third of the region's water – 15 billion cubic metres – and flushing it downriver.

Finally, chemical spills are no longer unheard of in the Pantanal. Just before one of our visits, hundreds of thousands of fish washed ashore near Miranda in the wake of a massive fertilizer spill.

There are few environmental groups devoted strictly to preserving the Pantanal, but interest has grown considerably over the last decade. One is Ecology and Action (ECOA). Wildlife Conservation International (a branch of the New York Zoological Society, Bronx, New York 10460 USA), however, has been involved in a great deal of research in the region and deserves your support. World Wildlife Fund (Worldwide Fund for Nature), International Rivers Network, and Wetlands for the Americas are also involved with protecting the Pantanal, particularly in regard to the huge Hidrovia proposal. Likewise, take every opportunity while in Brazil to talk to the state tourist-agency personnel; let them know that you are there to observe wildlife in a relatively undisturbed state, and that you'll spend money to do so. Tell them – and anyone else who'll listen – that what the Pantanal needs isn't fancy hotels but more protection. And urge your own politicians to ban the sale of non-farmed alligator hides and animal furs.

Caracara

Chapter Six

The Amazon

Geoffrey Roy

The Amazon – its name alone conjures up
great things from within the imagination.
Almost everyone on the planet has heard
of it, but few have any idea just how vast
the region truly is. The entire Amazon basin
or water-catchment area, including the
great river itself, all the tributaries and the
entire area known as the rainforest, covers
parts of nine South American countries.
Brazil's share is by far the largest and the
basin covers almost half the country.

A journey through the Amazon region
of Brazil is an unforgettable experience, yet some people come away a
little disappointed. These are the people who come for the jungle encounter
but only allow themselves a few short days to sample this probably once-
in-a-lifetime event. The jungle appears to them as a vast green carpet from
the window of an aeroplane or as a thin green line from the deck of a cruise
ship sailing mid-stream up the Amazon. Any excursion they take into the
forest is along trails so well worn that the wildlife check their filofaxes for
arrival times.

The truth about a real rainforest is that it can never match its popular
image – it looks nothing like you might have seen in some Tarzan movie
(lions and tigers don't exist here). In reality there aren't snakes behind
every bush, nor are there monkeys hanging from all the trees. If you are
likely to see anything at all in the forest on one of these flying visits it will
be a fleeting glimpse of a disappearing animal hundreds of feet up in the
canopy. A mere spot vanishing out of harm's way.

If you free yourself of all expectations, switch off that vivid imagination,
and give yourself a bit of time, a journey into the Amazon Basin will prove
to be extremely rewarding – full of excitement and challenge.

Loren McIntyre, the photojournalist who discovered the true source of the

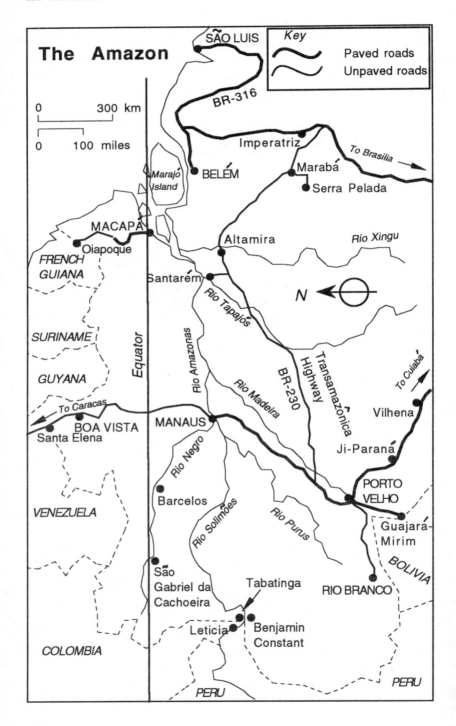

Amazon River high up in the Peruvian Andes Mountains, once said, 'How do I convey the scent of the wet forest, as ineffable as a mixture of crushed herbs?' Poetical? Yes of course, but exploring the Amazon is about tantalising your mind and all your physical senses – sight, hearing, touch, taste, and above all, smell. Travelling through the rainforest is an exercise in acute observation. Shut off one sense and you might – no, you *will* – miss something.

Travelling through backcountry Brazil you'll meet the locals who eke the most meagre of livings from the forest: *Caboclos*, the mixed race descendants of the original Indian, African and European settlers of the forest who live in houses built on stilts along the banks of the rivers; gold prospectors, farmers and fishermen; people who have fled the over-polluted slums of the big cities, escaping violence, smog and noise for a poorer but more peaceful existence in the forest. You might see fresh-water dolphins frolicking in the rivers chasing piranha as your cargo boat heads up stream. If you spend a couple of days camped in the forest, given patience and good observation, you might see some of the region's elusive wildlife. Life in the forest will become more active at night if you take the trouble to strap on a headlamp and poke around. Everyone you meet, everything you see, hear, smell, touch and taste will add to your understanding of what the Amazon rainforest is all about, and how unique an ecosystem and how fragile and delicate a paradise it truly is.

HISTORY

Christopher Columbus opened a Pandora's box when he proved the existence of a great land to the west. By the beginning of the 16th century, Europeans were marching throughout South America 'with eyes wide open, the conquistadors lived in a lucid and endless delirium'. In 1493 a papal decree divided up the New World between Spain and Portugal. Portugal received all territories east of the longitudinal line running through Cape Verde Island. Spain got all that was west. Less than a year later the Treaty of Tordesillas moved this line 370 leagues to the west, giving Portugal even more land to play with, and had little to do with the King of Portugal's claims in the South Atlantic. At this time there were some six million native peoples living in Brazil and probably nine million throughout South America.

It was a myth, pure and simple, that sent the conquistadors on their merry way across the continent raping, conquering, pillaging and subjugating native peoples while raising forts, churches and missions along the numerous rivers and tributaries of the hot and humid tropical forest. *El Dorado*, the Golden Man, was the myth based on a rumour that a certain tribal chief was so wealthy that he covered his body in gold dust daily. It inspired the conquistadors to go to enormous lengths risking famine, disease and even death for a mere glimpse of this immense wealth.

The Amazon delta was first sighted in 1500 by Vicente Yáñez Pinzón (who had commanded the *Niña* on Columbus' first voyage), but the land beyond it, the interior or the 'Green Hell', never came to an explorer's notice until 40 years later, and not from the Atlantic but from the unforgiving land of the Andean Altiplano, at a place called Quito in what is now Ecuador.

On December 1 1540 Gonzalo Pizarro, younger brother of the conquistador and wrecker of the Inca Empire, Francisco Pizarro, arrived at the gates of Quito after a 1,600 kilometre journey from the then Peruvian capital of Cuzco. He had been made the *gobernador* of Quito and was met by his cousin, the brilliant lieutenant-general Francisco de Orellana, who immediately put himself and his troops at Gonzalo's disposal. Orellana had founded Guayaquil and knew that there was about to be a great expedition mounted, and he wanted to be on it. In those days spices were as important as gold, and it was rumoured that the expedition was going in search of cinnamon, or rather a country carpeted in cinnamon: La Canela. Cinnamon not only improved the taste of food, but was used as an antiseptic, a powerful digestive and a respiratory stimulant. The magic that surrounded it and the quest for El Dorado would have been an incredible incentive and an absolutely irresistible temptation for those conquistadors to go exploring.

The expedition, when it left Quito on February 21, 1541, was an unbelievable sight: 350 armoured Hidalgos (200 on horseback), 2,000 ferocious dogs trained to attack Indians, 4,000 porters laden with weapons and provisions, 2,000 llamas equally laden and 2,000 pigs bringing up the rear. The weather was terrible with much rain and snow, they were constantly attacked by Indians, and after 70 days found only a few cinnamon trees. Pizarro was so disappointed that he threw half his guides to his dogs and burnt the other half at the stake. The party then headed north and after 100 kilometres reached a huge wide river at a place we now call Coca (Puerto Francisco de Orellana). They built a brigantine and sailed on (with most of the expedition walking – there was no room in the boat). By the beginning of December 1541 the expedition ran out of food, and Orellana suggested to Pizarro that he take the brigantine and 60 men and go downstream in search of food. Pizarro reluctantly agreed and Orellana set off. He was never to see Pizarro again. Pizarro regretted his consent, and after eating all his dogs and the remaining hundred horses he returned to Quito. It took him six months of hard struggle. It took Orellana only slightly longer to discover the mightiest river in the world.

Orellana sailed along 'a current so strong that we covered twenty-five leagues (about 120 kilometres) a day'. On February 11 1542, Orellana and his men sailed out of the Napo and into the Amazon. So big was the river that they called it El Rio Mar – the River Sea. The party finally reached the Atlantic Ocean on August 26, 1542. It had taken eight months to get from Coca to the Atlantic (it took ten months to get from Quito to Coca). Eleven men had died along the way; battles had claimed only three of them. The first journey down the Amazon had been accomplished.

And the name *Amazon*? Orellana and his men fought many battles along the way, but one seemed all the more important. On June 5 1542, they landed at a village that his chronicler, the Friar Gaspar de Carvajal, believed to be the land of the Amazons. He takes up the story:

> 'In this village there is a very large public square, and in the centre was a hewn tree trunk three metres in girth, there being represented and carved in relief a walled city with its enclosure and gate. At this gate were two towers, very tall and having windows, and each tower had a door, the two facing each other, and at each door were two columns. Two very fierce lions, which turned their glances backward, held between their forepaws and claws the entire structure, in the middle of which there was a hole through which they offered and poured out *chicha* for the sun, for this is the wine which they drink'.

When he asked the Indian chief what all this meant, he answered that they were the subjects of 'the Amazons'. And on June 24th there was a battle with the Amazons 'so fierce we all came close to perishing ... the Amazons go about naked but with their privy parts covered, with their bows and arrows in their hands, doing as much fighting as ten Indian men'.

Fierce women warriors, with their right breasts removed to facilitate the shooting of bows and arrows, was the stuff of legend, and for some reason Carvajal felt the need to include this fanciful episode in his otherwise supposedly realistic account of the journey. Yet the stuff of legends has a way of becoming fact, and in 1544 Orellana was sent back to South America as the *gobernador* of the Amazon territory, by then officially known as the province of New Andalusia. He had four ships and 400 men. He tried twice to build a brigantine and sail back up the Amazon, and twice he failed. He eventually succumbed to fever and died. Although he was determined to call the river he had discovered Rio de las Amazonas, it was known for a while (and under protest from Orellana himself) as Rio de Orellana.

By the turn of the century the Spanish conquistadors had lost interest in the search for El Dorado and had gone home, but the Portuguese hadn't. Slaves were on the agenda. The Jesuit priests tried to stop the trade but they were thrown out by the Portuguese Crown. By the middle of the 18th century the Jesuits, the slavers and the adventurer/explorers had gone, and the jungle was left to its own devices.

By 1800 a new kind of adventurer arrived in the Amazon – the amateur scientist: Alexander von Humboldt, Alfred Russel Wallace, Henry Walter Bates and the botanist Richard Spruce. These commercial plant and bug collectors threw incredible light on the Amazon rainforest. Bates alone collected 14,712 species, of which over 8,000 were at that time unknown to science, and Wallace's studies led him to solving the problem of evolution at about the same time as the more famous Darwin.

Then rubber came into its own. In 1823 a Scotsman, Charles MacIntosh, won instant fame with his rubber-coated fabric. Charles Goodyear discovered vulcanisation in 1839, which led to an Irishman, John Boyd Dunlop, developing the pneumatic rubber tyre for his ten-year old son's tricycle. The patent revolutionised the budding car industry. The so called 'rubber boom' created untold wealth for the traders in Manaus. It all came to a dramatic end when an Englishman called Henry Wickham nicked some seeds of the *Hevea* tree in 1870, smuggled them to England and they became what formed the basis for the great rubber plantations of Malaysia. Asian production readily outstripped the Amazonian market, which collapsed in 1923 and everybody left town.

Gold came back onto the scene for a while, but the last twenty years have seen open conflict with all the inhabitants of the forest and the international environmental lobby at crosspurposes. Somewhere along the line, planners, policy-makers and environmentalists must get together and decide whether the world's largest remaining rainforest should go the way of its African and Asian counterparts toward irreversible destruction, or if the massive resources of the region can be harnessed for the benefit not only of Brazilians but of the rest of the world.

INDIGENOUS PEOPLES

When Europeans first arrived in the Amazon region it was estimated that there were somewhere between six and nine million indigenous peoples; now there are probably less than 150,000. Disease, destruction of natural habitats and something akin to genocide has led to their demise.

There is a huge amount of controversy over the 'Indian question'. Your chances of seeing real indigenous people living by traditional means in the forest – unless it is created for the tourist – are zero. FUNAI (Fundação Nacional do Indio) prevents all contact with westerners unless they are bona fide anthropologists doing research. This prevents several things: firstly, it prevents us spreading our diseases to these people who have never come in contact with, for example, the common cold. These diseases would have a debilitating effect on the Indians themselves who have no resistance to these illnesses. Secondly, it prevents the loss of any form of cultural identity. Thirdly, it allows the government total control over the Indian areas without interfering western eyes. They have had some bad press lately and it's probably well deserved.

Someone once wrote that the fate of the Amazonian Indian is trapped somewhere between a rock and a very hard place. Despite the positive work by activist groups, ill-intentioned rock stars and well-intentioned Westerners generally, the future of the Amazonian Indian populations will probably depend on how well they can push themselves and span the centuries from their unique but stone-age existence and arrive in the 20th century.

What the native population of the Amazonian forest is most likely to lose in the push for civilization is lost on dimmed Western eyes. This is best illustrated by quoting a statement made by an Amerindian chief called Taxapuh of the Waura tribe, who sums up all that we Westerners strive for and demand from our world so perfectly through his enlightened eyes. He had been flown to São Paulo for a hernia operation and was asked how he could return to the forest after seeing the wonders of the big city. His reply came with staggering confidence!: 'How can you breathe this foul air (pollution) or sleep with these noises (traffic)? How can you eat this food made to taste not its own? Why would men want to have intercourse with these women who are afraid to be women and hide themselves and cover their eyes? Who are these men with guns that stand in the paths of the village?'

NATURAL HISTORY

Geology

In the beginning – some 4,600 million years ago, give or take a thousand million years – the Earth formed. There was no land or sea and certainly no Amazon – just a hot, fiery, throbbing mass of rock and gas. But the Earth grew and developed. It moved further away from the sun, thus cooling, and subsequently it developed a hydrosphere (the seas) around the taller land masses. This led to the limited creation of the biosphere (algae, bacteria and some plants) that in turn led to the development of the atmosphere that led to a more expanded biosphere and, far down the trail of geological history, the creation of birds, animals and finally man. As simply put as this is, the process was actually immensely complex, complicated and slow.

About 250 million years ago the earth had only one land mass, called by geologists *Pangaea*, which slowly but surely began to break up and create continental masses. As these masses began to move apart, they too began to break up with what we now know as South America breaking away from Africa. This split, some 150 million years ago, created the Atlantic Ocean and the Amazon river flowed east to west towards the Pacific Ocean. Somewhere between two and four million years ago, the Andes Mountains heaved and pushed themselves upward between the Brazilian and Guianan shields, at that time the two highest points of land on the continent, and the Amazon began to flow in the opposite direction, toward the Atlantic.

About 1.6 million years ago tall trees, tangled canopy and undergrowth and a soil that derived its nutrients from leaf-litter emerged as the dominant form of vegetation, and the Amazon rainforest was truly born.

Amazon statistics

The statistics are staggering, but vital to a full understanding of just how vast the Amazon basin truly is. The river itself is the second longest in the world, but its true length is still a matter of definition as the river has several mouths that all widen into the Atlantic Ocean. The problem is that no-one is certain where the river actually ends. At the most distant mouth on the Pará estuary, the river is approximately 6,740km or 4,195 miles long. Sadly, the accepted length is taken from the river source to the Canal do Norte and the Ilha Bailique, and is 6,489km or 4,030 miles, giving the Nile the title as the world's longest river (at 6,670km or 4,145 miles). Other than this, the Amazon wins the stats competition hands down.

The basin itself covers 7,045,000km^2, or 30 degrees of longitude (1/12th of the earth's circumference) and passes through or fringes nine countries or dependencies: Brazil, Bolivia, Peru, Colombia, Ecuador, Venezuela, Guyana, Suriname and French Guiana. There are 15,000 tributaries, of which twelve exceed 1,600km in length. One, the Madeira, is the world's longest tributary and has a world rating as the 14th longest river at 3,200km. Another, the Rio Purus, is classified as the world's most meandering at 3,100km.

It is estimated that the basin contains a fifth of all the freshwater in the world, and its average flow at the mouth is 120 million litres per second (maximum flow in full flood is 200 million litres per second) which is four times larger than its nearest rival, the Congo, and sixty times greater than the Nile. This relates to the entire annual water consumption of Greater London passing through the river's mouth each second.

The river begins it journey high in the Peruvian Andes some 35km south of Cailloma as a trickle in the Quebrada Carthuasanta. This small trickle becomes the Hornillos River, which flows on to become the Apurimac, then the Ené, Tambo, Ucayali, Marañón and finally the Amazonas. At Iquitos in Peru, the river has travelled only a third of its length, yet it has dropped down to 106 metres above sea level and is now almost four kilometres wide. At Tabatinga, the triple frontier of Brazil, Peru and Colombia where its name changes to the Solimões, the river is only 96 metres above sea level. When the river reaches its confluence with the Rio Negro at Manaus, it once again becomes the Amazon. It is now only 48 metres above sea level and is almost six kilometres wide. There are still 1,600km to go.

At certain places the river exceeds a width of seven kilometres and achieves a depth of 124 metres (407 feet). The Amazon is navigable all the way to Iquitos, Peru, for ocean-going vessels and there are 48,000km of navigable waters throughout the basin. When the river finally reaches the Atlantic Ocean, its estuary is more than 80km wide and fresh water can be found 40 nautical miles out to sea.

Plant life of the rainforest

Even before Europeans arrived in Brazil, Amerindian tribes had discovered the great paradox of the rainforest: when the trees and underbrush were cleared for farming, the soil produced only one or two years worth of crops before giving out completely. How could the greatest forest on earth grow from this poorest and most infertile of soils?

The forest, as it turns out, doesn't depend much on soil. In fact, soil as we know it hardly exists in the Amazon. Kick the ground and you'll find an extremely thin layer of topsoil, with virtually none of the humus and leaf litter we might expect from our own temperate lands. In a sense, the rainforest vegetation is its own 'soil' – virtually all the nutrients of the Amazon are tied up in the trees, plants, and vines themselves. These are constantly and quickly recycled, bypassing the soil stage. And when that vegetation is cut, burned and washed away, those nutrients are lost forever.

This notion takes some getting used to, especially for those of us from temperate lands where soils are the great reservoirs of nutrients. How is it, for instance, that nutrients can bypass the soil stage? Look at that chunk of rainforest land you've turned over with your boot for the answer. Fine white filaments of fungi called mycorrhizae form a complicated web just below the topsoil. This mycorrhizal network quickly sops up decomposing nutrients and feeds them back to the forest via a whole series of shallow, intertwining rootlets. Aiding this process is the tropical heat, the humidity, and the action of microbes, ants and termites, all of which speed the breakdown. Unlike our own temperate forests, there is no build-up of nutrients; what isn't reabsorbed quickly is washed away by the constant

WHAT IS A RAINFOREST?

The Oxford dictionary defines a rainforest as 'dense forest found in tropical areas of heavy rainfall'. The trees are broad-leaved and evergreen, and the vegetation tends to grow in three layers (undergrowth, intermediate trees and scrubs, and very tall trees, forming the canopy).

Alexander von Humboldt was the first botanist to describe the tropical rainforest. He called it *hylaea*, from the Greek meaning 'forest'. Technically speaking, a true rainforest is a nonseasonal forest, where rainfall is both abundant and constant. A tropical moist forest, which the Amazon rainforest actually is, has seasonal variations in rainfall which are both necessary and vital to the profusion of ecosystems that make up the forest. It is defined as: an evergreen or partly evergreen (some trees may be deciduous) forest receiving not less than 100mm precipitation in any month for two out of three years, frost-free, and with an average annual temperature of 24°C or more.

The Amazonian rainforest is found in three distinct types: the *várzea*, or flood plain, where the seasonal rising of the rivers floods the forest floor to a depth of several metres and expands the river's limits, in some places up to 75 km; the *igarapés* are the channels and streams that are the back roads and tree-lined avenues of the forest but disappear with the seasonal flooding that occurs along some of the Amazon's major tributaries; and, finally, the *terra firma*, the usually unflooded forest with tall stands of trees that make up the majority of the forest.

The forest itself comes in three distinctive layers with the intermediary layer being divided up into two further parts:

Situated between 33m and 45m above the ground, the canopy is the only part of the forest with unlimited access to the sun – that vital ingredient necessary for the growth of plants. Here everything competes to gain crucial access to the warming and life-giving rays. The majority of the animals and birds live here. The tallest trees poke above the canopy and define the highest limits of the forest.

The divided intermediary layer merges both with the canopy and the forest floor. At the top level is found a form of vegetation known as *epiphytes,* or air plants. These plants are not parasitic as such, but claim a space on a branch and trap soil and dust particles, set out roots, catch rainfall and vie for that essential sun to photosynthesise as other canopy plants do. Then there are the shorter trees struggling to reach the canopy. With these are the lianas, climbers and stranglers – nature's hitch-hikers – who impose on a tree's natural vertical stairway to heaven, clinging to their host as they grow toward the canopy. Quite often they literally strangle the life out of their host tree and are sometimes so thick, numerous and tangled about the host tree that they support it long after it has died and should have fallen over. At the bottom level are the scrubs and herbaceous plants that share the floor with the saplings and seedling trees, ferns and palms that survive on perhaps 2% of the available sunlight that manages to finally reach the ground.

The forest floor is the final layer. Ants and termites are in abundance, assisting in the breakdown of vegetable matter, along with the fungi, snakes, small rodents and large land-based mammals. Here everything returns to the soil to form the nutrients needed to begin the cycle all over again.

rains. It is a rapid recycling system that works admirably – so long as things aren't disrupted.

Nowhere else on earth has plant life reached such levels of diversity. The Amazon basin boasts more than twenty times the tree species found in Europe – and that includes only the species thus far discovered. Unlike trees in our temperate forests, rainforest trees rarely grow in stands of the same species; this is an adaptation to the poor soil, preventing groups of trees with identical nutrient requirements from depleting the earth around them. This also makes logging difficult and wasteful – loggers must sometimes cut down ten trees to reach a species with marketable wood. Most of the large trees you'll see in the forest support themselves on thin topsoil with flange-like buttress roots.

Plant life in the forest involves a manic competition for sun. To this end, creepers and lianas (the first soft, the second woody) wind their way up to the canopy, where they provide convenient 'highways' for monkeys and other arboreal animals. A number of plants – the epiphytes (or 'air plants') – have simplified matters by cutting all contact with the earth, growing in moist crooks and hollows high in the trees.

Palms dominate the *igapó* and even much of the *terra firma* forest. A number of these have evolved long, needle-like spines encircling their stems, so watch what you grab for support.

Probably the signature plant of Amazônia is the giant water lily *Vitória Régia (V. amazonica)*. You'll see these in the *igapó*, where they grow to 1.80m in diameter. Their huge flowers (30cm in diameter) last only three days, and the plants themselves are scarce during the rainy season. These lilies sport a set of spines on their undersides, presumably for protection.

Animals of the rainforest

No single habitat on earth contains as many animal species as does the Amazonian rainforest. And unlike our own temperate forests, which contain large numbers of relatively few species, the rainforest is home to a bewildering array of species, none of which exist in particularly great numbers in any one area. As one rainforest biologist puts it, 'common species are rare and rare species are common'. The following section is therefore intended to highlight just a few of the more interesting and/or easily seen animals in Amazônia.

Spiders and insects

Tiny green or blue eyes reflected in your headlamp at night often indicate a spider nearby. Tarantulas (a number of species exist, often referred to as *caranguejeiros* by locals) are primarily nocturnal, preying on small insects near their burrows. You can locate these burrows at the base of trees, and they may be as wide as 15cm. Tarantulas can often be enticed out of their den – they live singly – by scraping a small stick near the entrance. This trick doesn't work during the daytime. I've been told by a Brazilian biologist that tarantulas attack only objects weighing less than 30g – someone has actually tested this – so that placing your finger near the den will elicit no response. You can be sure I would have tried this, except that we had no scales in camp for accurately weighing fingers.

Ants and especially termites perform one of the most important tasks in the forest: reducing fallen vegetable matter into humus.

Phyllomedusa

Frogs

It's not surprising to find plenty of frogs inhabiting one of the wettest places on earth. Still, the variety of frogs in Amazônia is astounding. A well-studied biological reserve north of Manaus, for example, contains 42 frog species in less than 13,000 hectares of land, while the entire North American continent boasts only 81 frog species. Most of the rainforest frogs are nocturnal, and you'll find them everywhere, especially on wet evenings: on tree branches, under leaves, in streams, in hollowed-out trees. Some croak in the familiar fashion, but others 'bark', and still others trill like a bird. Most frogs will leap or climb to safety as you approach; and the ones that don't flee have protection of another kind from the predators they normally face. *Phyllomedusa*, for example, is a bright green, fist-sized frog which stands out in the forest like a neon sign. It allows itself to be plucked off a branch and will wander complacently up your arm and around your shoulders until replaced on a tree. *Phyllomedusa's* complacency is well-warranted; its mucus coating contains a poison which potential predators have come to associate with the frog's neon-green coloration. I paid only a slight price for handling *Phyllomedusa*: a mild rash on my hands and wrists which itched for a few hours.

Besides *Phyllomedusa*, a number of frogs have developed toxic defences to make up for their obvious lack of shell, claws, teeth and speed. Perhaps best known are the 'poison-arrow' frogs of the genus *Dendrobates*. Their bright yellow, blue, red or orange colouration has evolved as advertisement rather than camouflage, and their toxic secretions can enter and kill through simple cuts in the skin. In 1985, *Dendrobates* figured in a Brazilian news story which blended science, witch doctors, presidential politics and Indian land rights. Famed Brazilian hummingbird biologist Dr Augusto Ruschii became seriously ill, and after numerous and inconclusive medical tests he called in Amerindian chief and political activist Raoni, along with Raoni's *pajé* ('witch doctor') to diagnose the problem. Raoni announced that Ruschii's liver was failing due to his handling of *Dendrobates* specimens years before in Amazônia. According to Raoni, Ruschii had actually taken on the appearance of his amphibian tormentors. He would cure the beloved scientist, but he called on then-president José Sarney to pay for the cure by guaranteeing a boundary around certain Amerindian lands. Ruschii (who was in his eighties), died after an extended illness despite Raoni's cure.

Reptiles
Although Amazônia is rich in snake species, populations aren't huge, and you may spend a great deal of time searching before you actually find a snake. Most species are nocturnal, so night walks provide the best opportunity.

PROJETO PIABA
We've all seen a tropical fish aquarium full of beautifully coloured little fish swimming about. Ever wondered where they come from? About 30% of the world's species come from the Amazon basin. The most popular tropical fish, the cardinal tetra, comes from the middle Rio Negro area around Barcelos, some 450km northwest of Manaus. Some 20 million fish are exported from the Amazon each year to destinations throughout the world. Barcelos is a small 200 year old riverine town with a local population of some 12,000 people. About 60% of them are directly engaged in one way or another in the collection and sale of ornamental fish.

Dr Ning Labbish Chao, an ichthyologist at the University of Amazonas in Manaus is in charge of Projeto Piaba (*piaba* is the local *caboclo* name for ornamental fish). His purpose is to study the sustainable use of the ornamental fish industry as a resource, yet conserving the fish population for future generations. You can visit the Dr HR Axelrod Laboratory of Ornamental Fishes at Barcelos and if you come at the right time of the year (January and August) it is possible to join one of Dr Chao's research trips as an assistant. The project is fully involved in the socio-economic environment of the area with school projects and lectures, licensing of *piabeiros* (fishermen), advice on fish management and transportation, educational programmes and many other regional activities.

Each year during the last weekend in January is the Festa de Peixes Ornamentais (Festival of Ornamental Fish). There are parades, games, a beauty contest and a procession. To get involved or find out more information about the project, write to Dr Ning Labbish Chao, Bio-Amazonia Conservation International, Caixa Postal 2310.69.061, Manaus, Amazonas, Brazil, or look him up on the Internet home page at http://www.cr-rnp.br/inpahome.htm

Note: Of the 1,500 known but 2,000 estimated species of ornamental fish only 177 are permitted for export. The remaining species grow to a large enough size to be considered a food source in Brazil and so their export is prohibited. This rule doesn't apply to other South American countries.

Look not only on the ground but in trees (a great many rainforest species never touch ground) and even in streams and temporary ponds. Remember that very few species are venomous, although many will bite if you attempt to handle them. The one you're most likely to see on night walks in Amazônia – indeed anywhere in the South American forest – is the fer-de-lance, *Bothrops atrox*. Fer-de-lances (called *jararacas* or *jararacussus* locally) often congregate near recent tree falls, feeding on the wide variety of smaller animals found there. Like all pit vipers – a group which includes rattlesnakes – fer-de-lances possess a tiny heat-sensing pit below their eyes which allows them to detect and strike at body warmth even in total darkness. You'd be wise to stay out of striking distance, although I have inched to within 30cm of a lethargic specimen. I'd seen this particular animal on a low-lying tree branch, and the next day retraced my steps; not surprisingly, it was gone. That night, however, I returned with Jayne, and the same fer-de-lance (or one just like it) had draped itself over the exact same branch, practically begging to be photographed.

The black alligator (*jacaré uassus*), now nearly wiped out, was one of South America's largest reptiles. On the other end of the size spectrum – and

---

DOLPHINS

On every journey I took on the waterways of the Amazon I saw dolphins. Sometimes only once a day and only one dolphin – sometimes only once during a voyage; other days I would have several sightings of lone dolphins or dolphins in pairs. Once whilst helping the crew to manhandle a boat stuck fast on a sandbar, we were surrounded by twenty or more dolphins feeding intensively on the same sandbar. The animals would come to within a foot or so of us, appearing to be totally oblivious to our presence. They weren't, but it is a nice thought. It was a wonderful feeling and although the animals weren't paying us as much attention as their ocean-bound relatives would have been, I wasn't sure if I should push or just stand up to my neck in water and buzz.

There are two species prevalent in the river system: the larger Amazonian River dolphin (*Inia geoffrensis*) or *bôto,* and its smaller cousin, the grey dolphin (*Sotalia fluviatilis*) or *tucuxi* (pronounced too-coo-SHEE) as it is known locally. The bôto is a true river dolphin and can reach 2.5 metres in length and weigh as much as 150kg. They often turn a bright pinkish colour as they get older. The tucuxi, on the other hand, is considered an estuarine species, indicating that it doesn't mind a bit of salt with its dinner. In the muddy waters of the Amazon these aquatic mammals have become almost totally blind, finding their prey almost exclusively by echolocation. They are the most voracious feeders in Amazonian waters and will eat as much as twenty times more fish than a catfish or pirarucú of the same or similar size. The bôto with its longer snout and more flexible neck will readily leave the channels and streams during high water and feed in the flooded forest. Bôtos are virtually the only river animals not extensively hunted. Their meat is thought to be relatively tasteless, although some are occasionally caught in fishing nets. They are believed to have very high intelligence and mermaid-like qualities causing them much superstitious veneration.

All South American river dolphins are on the CITES Appendix 1 Endangered Species list.

apparently still thriving – are the so-called 'dwarf alligators'. We stayed briefly at one jungle camp with an Australian researcher who for years has been radio-collaring and tracking the *jacaré coroa* (*Paleosuchus trigonatus*) deep in the forest. Until Bill Magnusson's work began, even Indians and local hunters weren't aware that the *jacaré coroa* rambled so extensively throughout the forest, often more than 100m from the nearest creek. They invariably make their nest beside a termite hill, allowing the rotting vegetation to warm the eggs. Spurned by hunters because of its unmarketable leather, the *jacaré coroa* seems to be far more abundant than anyone guessed a few years ago.

Fish

The Amazon and its tributaries play home to more species of fish than are found in the Atlantic Ocean. Fishing for the game species is best from September through to November, before the rivers swell. You'll find many Amazonian species, including piranhas, *pacú* and catfish, along with fishing tips that work equally well in the Amazon. Interestingly, one of the more highly-prized catfish in the Pantanal, the *jaú*, is despised as a trash fish throughout much of Amazônia. A variety of other delicious species, however, are pretty much limited to Amazonian rivers: the gorgeously-coloured cichlid called the *tucunaré*, the *curimatā*, the *acari-bosó*, *cará-açu, jaraqui*, and my own favourite, the *tambaqui*. Most spectacular of the basin's fish is the *pirarucú*, at 115kg the world's largest freshwater fish.

Besides the much-maligned piranha, the Amazon and its tributaries contain several other fish that deserve caution. *Candirus* have by now eclipsed piranhas in the field of gruesome fish lore; they comprise a family of mostly tiny parasitic catfish which enjoy swimming up swimmers' urethras, anuses, vaginas and nostrils, lodging themselves painfully with a pair of sharp pectoral spines. Although we've never been warned to stay out of the water on account of them, I wouldn't bathe nude in the Amazon. On several occasions we've been told by locals that the waters were swarming with *arraias* – freshwater stingrays. Supposedly these won't sink their barb into your ankle if you shuffle your feet along the bottom, as opposed to stomping on top of the animal.

Mammals

People generally think of monkeys, tapirs, peccaries, otters and jaguars as the dominant rainforest mammals. Yet none of these animals outweigh the **bats** in terms of sheer biomass. This becomes more apparent at dusk, when more than 100 known species take to the air. While most rainforest bats eat insects, as do our familiar temperate-zone species, Amazônia has some surprises: some species hunt birds and lizards, another prefers frogs, still others eat fruit, and there are even species that sip nectar from flowers, pollinating them as would a bee. Brazil possesses true vampire bats (*Desmodus*), but they are found primarily near cattle or horses and rarely in the rainforest itself.

One nocturnal mammal you're sure to see, particularly if you're camped near a stream, is the **spiny rat** *Proechimys*. Spiny rats spend their day in burrows or under logs, creeping about the underbrush at night in search of food. Indeed, they creep in a curious cat-like fashion that's quite unlike anything I've ever seen in temperate zone mice or rats. Spiny rats don't grow much longer than 5cm, yet they are closely related to the giant capybara.

At least thirty species of **monkeys** live in Amazônia. Active during the day and extremely wary, many species will be difficult to see simply because they live in the forest canopy. Most of our own monkey sightings have been but fleeting glimpses, such as the characteristic twitching black tail of the *macaco prego*. Unless you are more patient than we are, you will hear far more monkeys than you will ever actually see. And the monkey heard most easily in the rainforest is unquestionably the howler, or *guaríba*. Two of the six howler monkey species – the red howler and the black howler – inhabit the areas near Manaus. The 'howl' of these animals is one of the rainforest's most unforgettable experiences, a thundering roar which shakes most travellers out of their hammocks during the first night. Howlers usually live in troops of 10–20 individuals, but a single dominant male does most of the troop's howling. An enlarged bone in the howler's throat serves as sounding box for the call, which can be heard for over 3km through dense forest. You'll hear the roar throughout the night, but especially at dawn. Howlers call to warn other troops of their presence. While troops don't actually claim a particular part of the forest, they roam over areas as large as 75 hectares and they don't like other troops getting too close. The cascading quality to the roars results when the call of one male is answered by another troop's male, and then another, even more distant male. Despite the howler's strident roar, it is a gentle creature which eats leaves and

---

AMAZON BASIN NATURAL HISTORY STATISTICS

- The Amazon Basin contains 30% of all known plant and animal species.
- There are 80,000 species of trees; 3,000 of land vertebrates; and 2,000 species of freshwater fish. Brazil alone has 55,000 species of flowering plants.
- The most deadly animals are the poison arrow frogs of the genus *Dendrobates* and *Phyllobates*. The Golden poison arrow frog (*Phyllobates terribilis*) of western Colombia is the most dangerous.
- The world's largest rodent is the capybara (*Hydrochoerus hydrochaeris*).
- The sleepiest mammals are the three species of three-toed sloths (*Bradypus*).
- The bird with the fastest wing beat is the horned sungem (*Heliactin cornuta*) at 90 beats per second.
- The heaviest snake is the anaconda (*Eunectas murimus*).
- The Goliath bird-eating spider (*Thesaphosa lebloud*) found in the coastal rainforest near the border of Guyana and Brazil is thought to be the largest. The family is also the longest living (25 years).
- The deadliest spiders are the Brazilian wandering spiders of the genus *Phoneutria*. The Brazilian Huntsman (*P. fera*) is the deadliest with a neurotoxic venom.

fruits. Although Brazilian law prohibits commercial export of howlers, they are threatened with habitat destruction as jungle is cleared.

The only mammal that I've heard *caboclos* mention with anything resembling fear is the **collared peccary** (*porco da mata*). Peccaries are pig-like animals which feed largely on roots, seeds, insects and fruits, but they can turn nasty if threatened. Since herds generally run from 15 to 50 animals strong, it's not a good idea to give peccaries the idea they're being cornered. Peccaries feed almost exclusively during the daytime. Like most of the larger rainforest mammals, they've always been hunted for their meat; it is habitat destruction rather than hunting that threatens peccaries.

Unfortunately, you will probably see more dead **armadillos** (*tatús*) than live ones; they are the most common road-kill in Amazônia. Almost entirely nocturnal, the nine-banded armadillo trots about the forest, sniffing for its steady diet of larval and adult insects. Armadillos dig their burrows near streambanks, padding the insides with soft carpets of forest vegetation. *Caboclos* have long prized the white, succulent meat of the armadillo, but this is one animal that can probably withstand not only hunting pressure but some habitat loss.

GETTING THERE

The two gateway cities to the Brazilian Amazon are Belém and Manaus. Both are serviced daily from all Brazilian capital cities by Varig, Vasp, and Transbrasil, all of which offer airpasses. The flights, however, tend to arrive in the wee hours of the morning. Both Belém and Manaus are also accessible from the US and other South American countries via international airlines. Belém is easily accessed by interstate bus on a good highway from most major Brazilian cities, but Manaus remains virtually inaccessible by all but a few interstate buses.

Everyone travels around Brazil's Amazonas state in boats. As every town that is of any importance is on a river, it is the perfect way to wander. The boats, called *gaiolas*, cost between US$10–12 pp per day, including food and hammock space. They're crowded, the food isn't brilliant and the journeys are slow, but, if you speak some Portuguese, it's a great way to mix with the locals. Approximate journey times are: Belém to Manaus, six days (US$90); Manaus to Porto Velho, five days (US$60); Manaus to Tabatinga and Peru/Colombia, ten days (US$80); Manaus to São Gabriel da Cachoeira, seven days (US$70).

Major roads now cut a swathe across the Amazon but overland transport remains difficult if not impossible, particularly when it rains. Buses must wait to cross the rivers on ferries. An accumulation of traffic and broken-down ferries slow things down even more. Travelling by road is a nightmare – it's slow, crowded, dusty and you have nowhere to stretch your legs whilst travelling. Having said this, there are regular buses from Manaus to Boa Vista and on to Venezuela (about US$60). The bus service from Manaus to Porto Velho in the state of Roraima was no longer operating at the time of this writing, and the gruelling two-day Manaus-Santarém bus remains very hit-or-miss depending on road conditions. For those in a hurry, river boat and bus travel is too slow and undependable. To meet the needs of these people, there are charter airlines and air taxis flying all over the basin. All the bigger towns, and many of the smaller ones, have airfields and these aircraft are a quick and easy method of transport. Many spend a lot of their time flying *garimpeiros* (gold prospectors) into the bush. They are expensive (eg: a 1½-hour flight from Manaus to Barcelos costs about US$120), and there are often too few seats.

WHEN TO GO

The Amazon rainforest is wet – it is one of the wettest places on the planet. As with all tropical moist forest areas, it has a dry season and a wet one. The dry season is July to November, and it is during this period that the flooded forest recedes; some of the rivers change into deep channels, and beaches suddenly appear along the river's edges. This time of year the

---

LEGENDS

No matter where you go throughout the Amazon, there are legends and superstitions about every plant and animal that inhabits the jungle. Spirits abound everywhere, day and night, and there are stories concerning everything from the creation to the afterworld. Here are a couple to get you started.

Dolphins or *bôtos* have almost enchanted status in jungle legends. It is said that they can leave the rivers, transforming themselves into gentlemen in white suits and then seducing unwary young virgins. It is also said that bôtos are attracted to the scent of menstruating women and have been known to overturn canoes to get the women into the water and work their seductive magic on them. This folk belief is so strong that some women and, particularly young girls, refuse to bathe during their periods. Dolphins have also been known to disguise themselves as a husband and seduce unsuspecting but normally loyal wives; a handy way of explaining away an inconvenient pregnancy.

There is a bird in the Amazon called a *japiim* which has a notorious reputation. It seems that once upon a long time ago the japiim had a wonderful voice and a place at the right hand of God in heaven. One day he came to earth and tried imitating all the other birds, thus attracting all the females. The males told him where to get off or else, so the japiim turned to the bees for help. They allowed him to nest near them. Which is why where you find the japiim singing songs, you'll find also a bee hive.

One of the most beautiful plants in the Amazon is the *Vitória amazonica* (formerly *V. regia*) water lily. Legend has it that a beautiful maiden called Arari wanted to be just like the moon. She tried everything to achieve that magical status, including climbing a great mountain to reach it. In despair she leaped to her death and fell into a shining lake. The moon, who was a very kind person, took pity on the girl and transformed her into a part of the forest – a lily pad. This lily pad is formed when a dying blossom sinks to the bottom of the lake only to resurface again as another lily.

rainforest is spectacular. There are, of course, plenty of torrential downpours but they are less frequent, tend to be of shorter duration and are more unpredictable. Thunder storms seem to be more visible, filling the skies with many superb and violent displays of lightning. During this so-called summer, the temperatures range from 26–37°C.

The rainy season, or as the locals call it *o inverno* – winter – occurs between December and June. This isn't a period of one long continual downpour, but the rain does come most days. Toward the end of this season, in May and June, the water levels in the rivers and tributaries rise dramatically, overflowing the banks and flooding the surrounding land, creating the flooded forest or *várzea*. Mosquitoes and other more annoying insects are more predominant at this time, but the humidity hasn't changed too much – it is still around 80%. Temperatures are slightly lower, ranging somewhere between 22 and 30°C.

July through to September is the vacation season for Brazilians and, particularly for Manaus, it is the peak tourist season for Westerners coming to Brazil in search of that jungle experience. This won't usually affect your travel plans, though hotels tend to be more expensive at this time and are often full.

HOW TO EXPERIENCE THE RAINFOREST

Brazilian Amazônia comprises the states of Pará, Amazonas, Rondônia, Acre, Amapá and Roraima. Although not all this land is covered in dense rainforest, it is the rainforest that attracts the most visitors. This chapter deals with travel along the river and the true *mata* or jungle surrounding it. The following suggestions will be your gateway to the Amazon, seeing both the river and the forest. The time you have available will dictate how much you can see, but I hope these few guidelines will help you gain the most from your Amazonian rainforest experience.

A true appreciation of the rainforest is only gained by being comfortable, relaxed, observant and yet having the curiosity of a fascinated child.

Firstly I would suggest that you get an overview of the river itself and travel by boat up (not down) the mainstream Amazon. It's the lifeline of the region, the highway along which everyone travels, and the source of all things Amazonian. Boats travelling downstream always appear to be in a hurry and so stay in the middle of the river. Here the current is stronger and flows more swiftly. Subsequently, it takes less time for them to reach their destination. Boats travelling upstream sail closer to the banks, taking advantage of the weaker currents and allowing a better glimpse of that thin green line that is the forest. As far as wildlife viewing goes, you may only see the disappearing flight of a toucan or macaw, although there should be regular sightings of both species of river dolphins. On all my journeys along numerous Amazonian rivers, I never failed to see dolphins every day frolicking and feeding in the various rivers. Sadly, these beautiful creatures don't seem to like bow-riding like their sea-going cousins do. Being at the very edge of the forest also allows you a more intimate peek into the lives of the *caboclos,* the forest settlers that make a paltry living from along the river's banks.

Next, from one of the major towns along the river, take a journey into the *igarapés*. This is the classic jungle boat trip and the stuff of movies. You won't see Tarzan and Jane, lions or tigers, but you will get a real feel for the forest, its sights, its smells and its sounds.

Lastly, spend some time in the *terra firma* or, to give it its local name, the *mata fechada* (closed forest). Plan to camp out and spend several days and one or two nights walking, exploring and just being at one with the forest. Using the services of a good guide will open your eyes to a whole new world that for many people only appears on a 14-inch TV screen in the comfort of their living room.

If you can manage all this you should develop a true appreciation of the forest and be aware of her beauty and sense her strength. You will have taken a journey into one of nature's true Gardens of Eden.

BOAT TRIPS

This section provides a general description only. Boats trips are generally the same, no matter where you are going, as far as what you need to bring, finding the boat in the first place and life on board. The relevant city sections will include any specific information such as from which port the boats depart for the various destinations throughout the Amazon.

Since I've been back in the modern world, I have often been asked if I had any problems with Portuguese. Simply put – No! I speak none whatsoever. I am conversational in French and Spanish and from all my travels I have learnt bits of several other languages – certainly enough to make myself understood. So I was rather brazen about having to learn another language, especially as English is so widely spoken.

I regretted this! Few people if any speak English in Brazil. I once got flak for not understanding Portuguese on one of my boat trips. My shipboard companions were a Swiss chap (we spoke French), two South Africans (we spoke English) and a Peruvian (we spoke Spanish), with me quite happily swapping between all three languages. When I pointed out that I could be understood in several languages and was curious as to why they didn't speak English or another European language besides Portuguese, all I got in return was a shrug of the shoulders or 'You are in Brazil now'. It was frustrating!

In general, Brazilians can understand some Spanish (though, contrary to popular belief, I found written Portuguese difficult to decipher). Their version of Portuguese with its slang or, as I put it, a 'Brazilian twist' sometimes puzzles even good Portuguese speakers. Unfortunately, life in Brazil without a little Portuguese means you can't tell anyone what you do, find out about their life, get directions or discuss the weather. Luckily most good tour guides in Brazil do speak English – it comes with the territory.

On boats it's different. The Brazilians are very affable, pleasant, delightful people who are as curious about you as you are about them. Social intercourse between you and ship-board companions is a vital part of the backcountry experience. Brazilians also love to party. Someone once said ' If the end of the world was nigh it wouldn't occur until they [the Brazilians] had thrown a party first ... and what a party that would be!' I suggest you make at least some effort to learn to speak and understand even the most basic of Portuguese. You will be rewarded in the long-term.

Finding a boat

A stroll through any backcountry port will tell you that the place is bedlam. There are covered stalls selling boat tickets and cold drinks; food stalls selling barbecued meat on skewers, chicken and, of course, Amazonian fish; boys cleaning shoes and selling rope for securing hammocks; women jostling with children, passengers struggling with baggage, onlookers and idle passers-by standing in the way. Mix this altogether with smoke, exhaust fumes, engine noises, voices and foghorns and all the ports are bustling, vibrant, throbbing swarms of activity and, to the uninitiated, a nightmare.

There will be dozens of boats to choose from. Some are just cargo; some are cargo and passengers; others just for passengers. There are tourist boats, family boats, and fishing boats. So which one is for you? Generally, if boats are taking passengers, there will be a sign on the front of the boat indicating the destination, all the ports of call, and the day and time of sailing. It's just a matter of deciphering the sign.

The boats are generally of wooden and steel construction. They are flat-bottomed river boats designed to be beached and easily refloated along the river banks. By their very nature, they are inherently unstable, being long, thin and top heavy. In the late 1980s a *gaiola* called the *Cisne Branco* overturned during a New Year's Eve cruise when all the passengers crowded to one side to see the lights of Manaus. The ship sank, drowning everyone on board. Whilst I was in Manaus researching this chapter, another *gaiola* overturned when the deck load shifted. The boat had been loaded unbalanced and sailed with quite a heavy list. Three people died, although the boat was in only ten feet of water. Since the *Cisne Branco* incident, safety throughout the Amazon has improved, with lifejackets and liferafts on board all boats. But accidents do happen.

The most common and popular way to travel the waters of the Amazon basin is on the two- or three-decked vessels called *gaiolas* or *barcos de linha* ('water-buses'). They look like something straight out of the *African Queen*. The bigger boats are rather impersonal, are packed far beyond what I would consider comfortable, and you have to queue for everything. They also ply the more popular routes. The smaller boats are usually family-run, have fewer people on board, but take a lot longer to get anywhere as they travel much more slowly and often stop at night. They all cost about the same for the same journey – about US$10–12 pp per day, including meals and hammock space. Cabins are about 50% more expensive for the same journey, and are usually for two people sharing. I heard in Manaus that the prices were fixed by the port authorities but that they could be undercut by boat owners. It is apparently designed to stop boat owners overcharging unsuspecting, unknowing first-time passengers on the popular routes. I was often quizzed as to how much I was paying, to ensure, as I didn't speak Portuguese, that I wasn't being cheated (or getting a better deal).

The government-run ENASA (Empresa de Navegacão de Amazônia) company plies the major routes in large steel ferries. They carry about 600 passengers and cargo as well. I never bothered to catch one. They look far too impersonal for me, too crowded. I'd heard that thefts are common and that the food is inedible. Their only advantage is that they leave and arrive on time. Sailing up the middle of the river, all you have to do is buy a ticket, get on, get bored and get off at your destination. No fun at all.

Once you have decided on your destination and found a boat heading in the right direction, go on board and ask for the captain. Don't concern yourself with anyone else, just the captain. You will know him – he'll be the busiest man on board and everyone will be paying him attention. Check out the boat. It might be your home for quite a few days. If you're not happy with the boat for any reason find another one. There are usually several boats sailing on the same day. If not, you will only have to wait one or two days at most. Your comfort is important and it makes your voyage more enjoyable. Don't pay for your passage until you have moved on board. Certainly don't pay for a cabin until the captain gives you the key and you are sure it works. On most of the boats you will get an official receipt; on others the captain will come around and just collect the money at some point during the voyage. Confirm the sailing day and time with the captain and try to arrive three hours before that time (it improves your chances of securing a good hammock position).

None of the cargo/passenger boats I caught left on time, but they did leave on the right day. Cargo is loaded by hand and is very time consuming though quite entertaining. Cargo boats don't leave until the loading is finished. Transporting cargo is where the money is, and often passengers appear to be only an afterthought.

Once on board, life becomes a lesson in patience. Most boats try to leave by 18.00 hours. In general the port authorities demand this for safety reasons. You won't be fed on the first night so be prepared for this. Passenger boats, on the other hand, leave earlier, at about 16.00 hours, and as they have little or no cargo tend to be away on time.

If you want to save on hotel bills, most captains will let you come on board early and sling your hammock. Beware – your kit will be insecure unless you are literally sitting on top of it. Most theft on boats occurs whilst they are still in port and, as loading goes on all night, there are people coming and going all the time. Being tired before your journey begins because you've been awake all night watching your kit is not a good way to see the Amazon.

Hammocks versus cabins

These are the two accommodation choices you have on boats, and much of it is about personal preference and availability. Cabins are often booked well in advance of sailing day. If you want one, it is advisable to get in early. I only once took a cabin and it was on my last journey in Brazil on river boats. I chose it for two reasons. Firstly, although I am a light sleeper, this voyage was going to be for ten days and I was concerned that one night whilst the boat was in a port loading and unloading somewhere I would shut out the sounds and sleep quite heavily. Secondly, and this is mainly a fear of being robbed, is that I normally carry a large amount of photographic equipment with me. I had been on assignment in South America for three months and had several hundred rolls of completed magazine work with me. It was something I couldn't afford to lose. Thieves aren't fussy about what they take if it's contained in a bag. They just take the bag and dump the useless stuff afterwards. To a thief my exposed film is worthless. On that particular journey there happened to be several thefts during the passage up river. By the end of the voyage I was pleased that I took a cabin.

Cabins are more expensive – by about 50% per person – and they usually sleep two people. They are cramped, hot, smelly and I wouldn't consider the bedding too clean, although the sheets are washed. They have only a fan for ventilation and I also think, on reflection, that they aren't that secure. Still, they are better than nothing. There are sometimes air-conditioned cabins but these are usually reserved for special guests. Personally I can't imagine why anyone would want to spend their time in an air-conditioned cabin – the nights are generally cool enough. A word of warning: after the heat of the day, cabins, because they are part of the boat's superstructure, do take several hours to cool down.

Hammock space, on the other hand, is rough, crowded, cramped and fun. You can't get any closer to your fellow travellers without sharing their hammock. Together with grandmothers, babies, soldiers and travelling salesmen, you might share your space with kids, baggage, boxes, produce, chickens, dogs and cats (I never managed to travel with pigs and goats). Everything brought by the passengers on-board is stored underneath the swinging hammocks. It is a great way to meet the local people.

The best place on board is towards the front. It's cooler, getting more of any breeze that occurs during the day, and it's generally the furthest point away from the engine. In the quiet hours of night, the engine can sound like a jack-hammer next to your ear if you are too close to it. The toilets are also towards the rear, so the front may also prove to be sweeter smelling.

What to take

First thing you need is a hammock. All the markets in Belém, Santarém and Manaus sell them, and there is a huge variety to choose from. They vary in price from US$10–25 and they come in a plain style or with frills. Some are embroidered, others are multi-coloured. There are thick cotton ones and lacy string ones. The choice is endless. I personally like the thick cotton ones at about US$15. They help to keep you warm when the night air cools down. Next thing you'll need is a thick sheet or a light cotton sheet and a light blanket. It does get cold at night. Some people recommend sleeping bags, but it is awkward to get into a hammock with one, and if you aren't experienced, falling out of a hammock is not only embarrassing, it totally amuses the locals. Sleeping bags also mean you can't extract yourself quickly from your hammock if for some reason you are in a hurry.

T-shirts and shorts are quite adequate for daytime wear, but beware of the sun – it's quite fierce so close to the equator and you burn quickly, so bring plenty of suncream or blockout, a decent hat and sunglasses. When it gets cold at night I layer up the T-shirts, put on cotton track suit bottoms, and wear a long-sleeved sweat shirt; that way I can put more (or less) on depending on the temperature.

All the boats I travelled on had a water fountain on board, but some people prefer to bring their own bottled water. I carry sterilisation tabs just in case. Binoculars are a must and help to get you closer to your fellow passengers, as does a collection of photos from home. For decent photographs, a telephoto lens will bring the shore line a little closer. Don't forget a Swiss army knife, plenty of reading matter, a deck of playing cards, a Portuguese dictionary, insect repellent and malaria pills, a flashlight to find your way around after dark, fruit, snacks, biscuits and choky-bars. Meals are fairly bland and I have a passion for chilli, so I also take along a bottle of chilli sauce (*molho de pimenta*) and Worcestershire sauce (*molho inglese*) plus salt and black pepper – anything you fancy to improve the taste.

Keep your passport, cheques, cash, plane tickets and other important documents on your person at all times – preferably in a concealed pouch. Thieves can be a problem, especially at night while the boat is in port. On two boats I was on thieves were caught. One was thrown overboard in the middle of the river, bags and all; the other one was handed over to the police in handcuffs at Santo Antônio do Içá with more lumps on his face than he came on board with. No-one likes a thief, but with so many people crowded into such a small place, the pickings are worth the effort. Fortunately, everyone on board watches everybody else's kit; yet thefts still do occur.

Life on board

What I want to describe here is a typical day on the usual cargo/passenger boats that ply the major rivers of the Amazon basin. Where I feel that it is appropriate, I have included the basic differences found on the smaller family-run cargo or fishing boats. I spent some time in and around the Rio Negro region researching an article on tropical fish. I travelled with *piabeiros* – the fishermen who catch the tiny tropical fish, such as the angelfish and cardinal tetras we all find in our aquariums at home – and experienced a different way of looking at backcountry Brazil.

The day begins at dawn, and on a boat it warms up slowly. People struggle out of their nightly cocoon bumping into one another as they negotiate the tangled mess of hammocks strung so close together that they touch. There is a long queue for the showers and toilets, and at some point one of the crew will roll up the plastic tarpaulin that has sheltered the decks and passengers from the river all night.

Breakfast occurs somewhere between 06.30 and 07.00 and consists of bread or dry biscuits, margarine and sweet milky coffee. On most boats with a large complement of passengers, feeding them all becomes a matter of doing it in shifts with the dining area seating perhaps twenty or thirty people. Some of the folk will take their portion and return to their hammocks or the benches that line the decks and sides of the boat. On the smaller cargo/family boats, breakfast is a small cosy affair, with the boat usually tied up to the bank.

Nothing much happens after breakfast until lunchtime, when people will begin to queue about half an hour before time. Food is the focus of the day and always a topic of conversation. Lunch and dinner are basically the same: rice, noodles or spaghetti, beans and some form of meat – chicken, beef stew and canned or fresh fish. The flavour never changes from one meal to the next, but there's always plenty to eat. Your fellow passengers will always tell you when it's time to eat and will even wake you up if you are asleep. I was amazed that many of my fellow travellers showed genuine concern that I might miss out on a meal although I always preferred to go last. That way I could take more time and not be in a hurry to let in the next shift. Brazilians sprinkle *farinha* (dried manioc flour) on everything. I found it tasteless and that it made me thirsty, but the Brazilians don't seem to be able to eat food without it.

I would make a point of trying to compliment or at least thank the cook after each meal, as no-one else seemed to. On some boats it produced little treats and, particularly something I really enjoy, strong black coffee for breakfast; on others I received just a smile. On the little family boats it was always appreciated and went down very well, although it seemed to me that the woman of the boat thought it a somewhat unusual thing to do, with embarrassed smiles everywhere. Without having any spoken Portuguese, I found it endeared me to everyone, especially on the small boats.

The showers and toilets are a simple and mixed affair. The shower is river water pumped up to the top deck, stored in big tanks and then gravity fed to the showers; the water also flushes the toilets. All the run-off returns to the river. It is fairly basic and the smell isn't too salubrious. On most boats, I found that the toilets were cleaned on a regular basis but most Brazilians' basic hygiene leaves a lot to be desired. I never discovered a boat with private toilet facilities but I believe that they do exist. I also found that everyone on board showers often to cool off and to relieve the boredom.

On the smaller boats, the shower was either a hose from the roof, a bucket over the side, or you in the river. Toilets were the very basic backside-over-the-side affair.

WHITEWATER, BLACKWATER AND CLEARWATER RIVERS

One of the great phenomena of the Amazon region is an occurrence called the 'meeting of the waters'. This is where rivers of different water colours meet and either blend or, as in the case of the Rio Negro and the Rio Solimões joining near Manaus, flow side by side for several kilometres before actually blending and becoming a major tourist attraction.

There are three types, or rather water colours in the Amazon region: whitewater, blackwater and clearwater.

Whitewater rivers, such as the Rio Solimões, Rio Madeira and the Amazon itself originate in areas where the soil is extremely rich in nutrients, an area much younger geologically than the rest of the continent, perhaps barely 60 million years old. The sediment from the nutrient-rich soils is washed into the rivers by rain and held in suspension as the river makes its way to the sea. The Amazon originates in the high Andes Mountains in Peru, and the Rio Madeira begins its journey in the Bolivian Andes – geologically young mountains. These rivers are rich in aquatic life, but this includes mosquitoes and other biting insects.

Blackwater comes from white, sandy soils of the type that occur in the area of the Guianan Shield – a geologically old area once connected to the African continent (see the section on *Amazon Geology*). These soils are very poor in nutrients and the dark colour comes from tannins and phenolics, the poisonous protective compounds found in leaves and plants to discourage herbivory, extracted from fallen vegetable matter. In poor soil areas, leaves are at a premium as a source of nutrients. When an old leaf falls the rainfall leaches out the tannins and phenols, called blackwater, and drains into the rivers. The main blackwater rivers are the Rio Negro, Trombetas, the Rio Guaporé and Juruá. Although still rich in aquatic life, insects that metamorphose in water find the blackwater rivers too acidic to breed.

Clearwater rivers flow across the crystalline shield regions of resilient rocks and lixiviated surface formations that are high in silicates. These rivers are low in suspended materials and have high stable banks which further reduce the bleaching of organic matter. They flow clear and clean to the eastern end of the Amazon basin. The Riós Xingu, Tapajós and Jari are the main clearwater rivers.

The most amazing thing is that all these regions, regardless of soil type, still produce and support equally impressive rainforests.

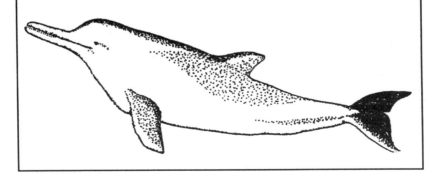

Drinking water is usually to be found in a drinking fountain, like the type you find in big offices. On some boats, the bottles that supply the water are sealed and fresh; others are filled from the ship's own water supply. I never saw any being filled from the river. Some travellers will only want to drink bottled (and expensive) water, so they must bring their own. Whenever I was dubious about the water's origins I used purification tablets in my water bottle. I always carry a two litre soft plastic US Army water bottle. It allows me the privilege of not having to queue for water several times a day and, if necessary, to purify several litres at once. It also doubles up as a pillow!

The whole world changes at night. Brazilians have discovered satellite TV (but not *The Simpsons*) and it's opened up a whole world to them. Not only can they get all the football they can digest, but that all-important social necessity, the soap opera (*novela*), has arrived at the most upper reaches of the jungle. Even the most basic of *caboclo* houses has a satellite dish outside and so does almost every boat that sails up and down the Amazon and its tributaries. Everyone huddles around the TV to watch a seemingly endless stream of half hour soaps followed by the match of the day. When it's all over they go to bed if a party hasn't started. There are bars on board the bigger boats and they are open all day, selling everything from biscuits and chocolate to beer and *cachaça*, a local spirit that poisons the brain (fire-water would be an understatement for this stuff).

Well after dark, the crew roll down the tarpaulin along the sides of the boat to keep the chilly winds out. Sadly, rolling down the sides not only keeps the wind out, it causes the stars to disappear, turns stunning tropical thunder storms into a dull rumble, and changes dawn into a dismal blue hue draped over everything.

Arrival at a port is quite exciting. There is cargo to be unloaded and more cargo to take its place. The ship is a hive of activity. Travelling upstream, the cargo usually consists of consumer goods such as wire, steel, food stuffs, canned goods, electrical appliances, cars, cement and booze. Downstream, it is the natural forest produce: coffee beans, brazil nuts, piassava fibre (used for brooms), fish, palm oil and palm hearts, fruit and animals (including endangered species here, particularly turtles). In the larger ports where loading and unloading takes a considerable amount of time, there is often opportunity to go ashore and stretch your legs exploring the riverside towns. People are coming and going, and it seems that the entire town comes to a standstill when the boat comes in. Some of the bigger towns along the river appear to be stuck in a time warp, having never changed their outward appearance in 50 or so years. If there is only a small amount of cargo to unload, or maybe a passenger or two to be put ashore, the boat's outboard skiff is quite adequate for the job and saves the boat losing time by docking.

NIGHT WALKS IN THE RAINFOREST

Spend the whole day in your hammock if you must, but make sure you see the forest at night. Much of the wildlife activity takes place high in the forest canopy during the daylight hours, frustrating all but the most patient observers and straining even the toughest necks. After dark, on the other hand, the canopy slumbers while the forest floor surges to life. What's more, nocturnal animals are by and large a more sluggish, easily observed lot than their diurnal brethren. And besides the opportunity it provides for watching animals, night transforms the forest into a magical and eerie place.

It's entirely normal to feel nervous traipsing around after dark in a jungle setting. But the rewards are so great, the experience so unlike that of the daytime forest, that you'll find yourself counting the hours till darkness, bounding out of your hammock, and grabbing your headlamp. Remember, you are undoubtedly far safer here than on the streets of your own city at night. The only fear with any rational basis, in fact, is the fear of getting lost; and that much you can easily prevent by always carrying a spare light and batteries and marking your path as you go.

Don't start your walk right after dusk. Waiting until about 20.00 will give nocturnal animals a chance to ease from their hiding places and take over the forest. Take along a standard flashlight as a backup, but for your primary light you'll want a headlamp. Bring your camera if you've got a flash; you'll be able to get amazingly close to many nocturnal animals without disturbing them.

Choose a path you've taken during the day, or follow the path of a small creek. Walk as slowly as you possibly can, sweeping the area around you with your headlamp. Don't forget the creek itself; a number of fish are nocturnal, and you stand a good chance of spotting a *traíra* or a huge cichlid cruising the shallows. Familiar creek banks that you've walked before suddenly glow with luminescent fungi. It's normal to search the ground for animals, but budding herpetologists shouldn't overlook small trees and branches just above eye level. Here you may find numerous tree-dwelling frogs, as well as arboreal snakes such as boa constrictors. Much of the best night-viewing, in fact, centres on twigs and branches at or just below eye level. Lots of the larger insects – mantids, moths with bright red eyes, and stick insects – can be seen here.

Watch for eyeshine. Reflective eyes of every colour and size really do peer from the forest at night – it's one of the few cinematic jungle cliches that actually holds water. Nocturnal animal eyes have been outfitted with a reflective lens called the tapetum which bounces dim night-time images off the retina. It is this tiny mirror which allows nocturnal animals to forage so effectively in what appears to be 'total' darkness; it also creates the eerie glow of jungle eyes reflected by your headlamp. A headlamp, in fact, allows you to see animal eyeshine much better than a hand-held light (which, since it isn't aligned with your line of sight, often fails to reflect directly off the tiny tapetum).

After about 23.00, nocturnal animal activity tapers off for reasons not well understood, and there is a marked period of inactivity from midnight until an hour or two before dawn. This pre-dawn period provides another excellent opportunity to view nocturnal animals. As dawn approaches, these animals retreat once again to their burrows under rocks, logs or vegetation.

Night walks work best when the moon is waning or the sky is overcast. Moonlight filtering down into the forest keeps many animals 'indoors'. Rainy nights provide excellent, if inconvenient, opportunities for wildlife viewing.

Finally, don't forget occasionally to turn off your headlamp and savour the forest in near-total darkness for a few minutes.

Getting lost

Hollywood myths aside, the Amazonian jungle is not a risky place to wander about for short periods. There are plenty of troublesome animals, but almost none that are actually dangerous. Hostile tribes – as well as non-hostile tribes – have been pushed to the brink of extinction. There are no extremes of weather, and lots of shade and water. So even if the worst happens and you find yourself lost, take heart; the Amazon rainforest is a rather benign place, particularly when compared to the mountains and forests lots of us like to hike through at home.

To avoid getting lost in the first place, mark your path. You can do this simply by cutting underbrush every few metres or putting small notches in tree trunks. A more elaborate system requires a roll or two of plastic flagging tape, preferably international orange or red. Simply pull off a 20cm strip and tie it to some nearby vegetation at eye level; do this every ten metres or so. These gaudy trail markers will eventually weather and degrade – some animals will even eat them – but try to remove as many as possible on your return. Always carry a compass and know how to use it. Streams often provide a sure route to follow through the forest, but beware when they fork.

BELÉM

As one would expect from being so close to the Atlantic Ocean, Belém is one of the oldest cities in the Amazon. It been there since 1621, when the town was placed strategically at the junction of the Rio Tocantins and the Amazon estuary. Originally called Nossa Senhora do Belém do Grão-Pará, the name is now shortened to Belém do Pará, or just Belém.

Pará is the richest state in Brazil, sitting on huge deposits of gold ore, and it is larger than most European countries. Belém is very much like the rest of the Amazonian region, coming into being during the rubber boom. Art-nouveau structures and neo-classical buildings embellish the pavements of the tree-lined avenues and plazas. Victorian arches and Italianate palazzos have turned a small and bustling little port into a graceful city with an elegance and style that's lost on other Amazonian towns of the same period. The entire centre of town all lies well within easy walking distance. Hotels, restaurants, the Ver-o-Peso market, moneychangers and banks are all within that central square kilometre fronting the river.

Traditionally, most people have headed for Manaus for that once-in-a-lifetime jaunt into the 'Green Hell' but expeditions from Belém are equally as good, less commercial, and there seems to be less pressure from the tour companies. There is also more chance to experience a wider variety of vegetational zones with the nearby Ilha de Marajó. You are more likely to see birds, monkeys and caimans here than in the jungle further upstream. The island is the size of Switzerland and there are huge buffalo ranches in the savanna, palm tree-lined beaches and mangrove forests along the coast, and jungle on the western half of the island.

Getting there

Belém can be reached on daily flights from all major Brazilian cities via the national airlines, including those offering airpasses: Varig, Vasp and Transbrasil. Within Brazilian Amazônia, there are daily flights to Santarém, Manaus, and Macapá. There are a number of international flights: Varig service to and from Miami; Air France, Suriname Airways, and Taba flights to Cayenne (French Guiana); Taba flights to Oiapoque (French Guiana); and Suriname Airways flights to Paramaribo (Suriname). All these national and international flights operate from Belém's Val de Cans airport, about 13km or 30 minutes by bus from the centre of town. The cheapest way to reach the city centre from the airport is to catch the local bus marked 'Perpétuo Socorro', which runs roughly every 20 minutes throughout the day. At night, or if carrying lots of baggage, you're better off with a taxi; buy tickets (roughly US$15–20 for up to three passengers) from the booth inside the airport terminal. There is also a Banco do Brasil branch inside the airport which changes cash and cheques, and an information booth run by Paratur, the state tourism authority.

Several companies fly air taxis and small aircraft throughout Amazônia and operate from Belém's municipal airport, Júlio César, at Avenida Senador Lemos 4700, about 8km from the centre.

All interstate buses run from the rodoviária at the corner of Avenida Almirante Barroso and Avenida Ceará, about 5km from the city centre. There are daily buses to all the major Brazilian cities, including Rio (52 hours, US$150), Fortaleza (24 hours, US$59), São Luís (13 hours, US$30) and Recife (35 hours, US$80). The once-weekly bus to Santarém was not operating when we went to press. The local buses marked 'Aeroclube' or 'Cidade Nova' run between the city centre and the bus station.

Boats leave from along the riverfront near the Ver-o-Peso market. The trip to Manaus takes about six days; Santarém takes roughly three days. There are usually departures every day.

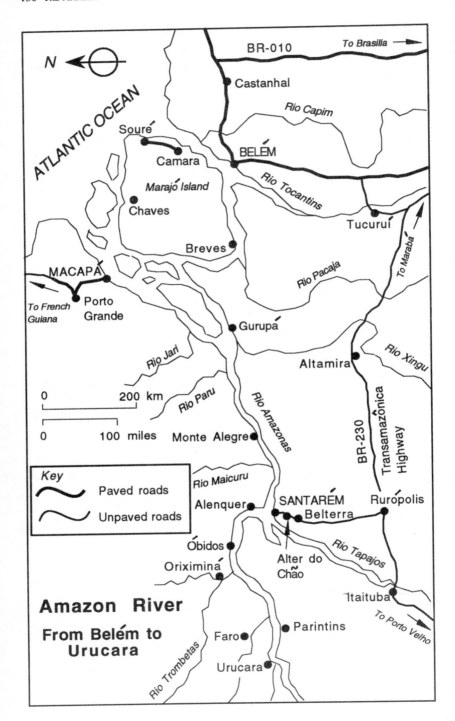

N

ATLANTIC OCEAN

BR-010

To Brasilia →

Castanhal

Rio Capim

Souré

Camara

BELÉM

Marajó Island

Rio Tocantins

Chaves

Tucuruí

To Marabá

Breves

MACAPÁ

Rio Pacaja

To French
Guiana

Porto
Grande

Gurupá

Rio Jari

Altamira

Rio Xingu

0   200 km

Rio Paru

Rio Amazonas

BR-230

Transamazônica
Highway

0   100 miles

Monte Alegre

Key

Rio Maicuru

Paved roads

Alenquer

SANTARÉM

Ruropólis

Unpaved roads

Belterra

Óbidos

Alter do
Chão

Rio Tapajos

Oriximiná

Itaituba

Amazon River

To Porto Velho

**From Belém to
Urucara**

Faro

Parintins

Rio Trombetas

Urucara

Where to stay and eat

The city's top hotel is the Hilton Belém at Avenida Presidente Vargas 882 near the Praça da República. There are several cheap hotels along the waterfront, but I didn't feel safe in them with all my photographic kit, so I went for the newish Hotel Vitória Régia at Travessa Frutuoso Guimarães 260 – it's closer to the centre of town, but easily within walking distance of the river. It is clean, neat and has a bit of style. Others like the venerable Hotel Central at Avenida Presidente Vargas 290 (US$20–35). Another recommended hotel is the Sete Sete, at Travessa Primeiro de Março 673 (US$15–20).

Of all the places in the Brazilian Amazon, Belém has the best range of cuisines, especially the local dishes. Try the Inter Restaurant at Avenida 28 de Setembro 304. It serves large helpings of local specialities and is popular with locals. The most famous dish in this part of the Amazon is *pato no tucupi*, duck which is roasted in the oven, cut in pieces, and then cooked in *tucupi* (a sauce extracted from grated manioc cooked with garlic), and *jambú*, a leafy green. Although not to everyone's taste, it's typically Amazonian, and can be found in many of Belém's restaurants. Probably the best and cheapest way to savour Amazonian specialities is to frequent the many outdoor food stalls and carts near the waterfront and in the city centre. The most popular dish is *maniçoba*, a stew made from manioc leaves, sun-dried beef, and bits of sausage, oxtail, bacon, and pork head, chopped mint, cumin, garlic and hot peppers. Another street stall favourite is *tacacá*, a soupy dish made with dried shrimp, *jambu* leaves, manioc, hot peppers, all swimming in *tucupi* sauce.

Other local specialities include Amazonian fish like *filhote* and the delicious *tucunaré*. Finally, visit the Ver-O-Peso market and sample the scores of exotic Amazonian fruits – even most Brazilians from other parts of the country have never heard of them. If you balk at digging into these strange fruits – or can't figure out how to eat them – try the local ice creams made with Amazonian fruits like *cupuaçu*, *açerola* and *bacuri*.

Information and useful addresses

The Banco do Brasil, which changes cash and cheques, is at Avenida Presidente Vargas 248. Beware – they charge US$20 for all transactions, no matter what the amount. There is also a Banco do Brasil branch at the airport. There are a couple of câmbios along Avenida Presidente Vargas, including Turvicam at number 640 and Loja Morpho at number 362. Another *câmbio* is the Casa Francesa at Travessa Padre Prudêncio 40.

Paratur, the state-run tourist agency is on Praça Kennedy near the waterfront (tel: 091 224 9633). They're open Mon-Fri 08.00–18.00. Attached to the office is a small zoo full of native animals including the elusive *saguis*, and handicrafts from the area are sold in the adjacent gallery. Paratur also staffs an office at the airport.

There are literally dozens of shops selling hammocks (*redes*). Many are along the waterfront and you can't miss them – their wares are hanging up outside the shops. Hammocks can also be found inside the Ver-o-Peso market. Prices vary according to style, size and material. Don't forget you'll need a couple of metres of rope to hang it with. If you are only sailing up the mainstream Amazon you won't need a mosquito net, but if you intend to take in that jungle experience, then many of the shops sell nets that are designed for use with hammocks. Prices again vary depending on type, netting and material.

SANTARÉM

Santarém is often left out of any journey up the Amazon. It's about halfway between Belém and Manaus and, although the third biggest city on the Amazon, it's a sleepy backwater compared to the other two. Situated at the junction of the Amazon and the Tapajós rivers, a village was founded around the site of a Jesuit mission in 1758 and named after a town in Portugal. In 1867 a group of Confederates from the southern states of America came here to establish a new life for themselves. Only a few of these settlers survived the jungle. The rest either died or went back to the US. Rubber and gold has brought prosperity and doom at varying times throughout the town's brief history. Forest products as well as gold and bauxite have kept the town going in recent years, as did the construction of the Santarém-Cuiabá highway and the Curuá-Una hydro-electric dam. Tourism is now very slowly coming into its own. The town is easy to walk around, and after a couple of days on a boat, a bit of exercise will do you the world of good.

Getting there

The airport is about 13km outside the town. There are almost daily flights to Alta Floresta, Belém, Fortaleza, Manaus, Recife and São Luís. There are taxis to and from the airport (US$15), and a courtesy shuttle bus to the Tropical Hotel – the best in town. Buses leave from the rodoviária 5km outside town on the Santarém-Cuiabá highway, with regular departures for Cuiabá, Belém, Itaituba and Marabá. Bus travel to any of these destinations is unreliable, however, and totally dependent on road conditions. The local bus marked *Rodagem* plies between the bus station and the town centre.

Then, of course, there are the boats. Manaus is three days upriver; Belém is three days downriver; Itaituba is about 12 hours upstream on the Rio Tapajós. All boats leave from the riverfront docks near the town centre. Boats leave daily both upstream and downstream.

Where to stay and eat

The best hotel in town is the Tropical Hotel Santarém at Avenida Mendonça Furtado 4120. For a mid-range hotel, I recommend the Santarém Palace Hotel (Avenida Rui Barbosa 726). It is more of an upmarket budget hotel, but it is clean, pleasant and air-conditioned. At the bottom, try the New City Hotel (Travessa Francisco Corrêa 200, US$33). Another recommended place is the Hotel Brasil Grande (Travessa 15 de Agosto 213, US$32). The best fish place in town is the Peixaria Canta Galo (Travessa Silva Jardim 820), which is a short taxi ride from the centre; they also offer the traditional Amazonian duck dish *pato no tucupi*. The Mascote Restaurant (Praça do Pescador 10), near the waterfront, is another good place for fish, particularly local dishes; it also does pizzas. A mini version of this restaurant is the Mascotinho, perched on the river bank, and a great place to enjoy the sun going down.

Information and useful addresses

Banco do Brazil is at Avenida Rui Barbosa 794, and you can get cash advances on VISA cards. But don't count on them changing dollars; bring enough *reais* with you to Santarém. Try the Divisão Municipal de Turismo for information and maps; they are at the Centro Cultural João Fona, Rua da Imperador on the waterfront.

MANAUS

Originally called Barra, Manaus was founded by the Portuguese in1669 as a small garrisoned village and fort to monitor the land-grabbing aspirations of Brazil's neighbouring Spaniards. By the mid 19th century, it was noted by the botanist d'Orbigny that Barra had a ragtag and impassioned trader population selling everything the region had to offer: Brazil nuts, turtles, dried fish, sarsaparilla and, by then, rubber. Barra rose to great prominence during the great rubber boom of the late 1800s and early 1900s, becoming the provincial capital of Manaus and exporting over 20,000 tons of rubber annually. The city's population swelled to 50,000, and the rubber barons, attired in the latest European fashions, did all their business in gold. In 1897, electric trolleybuses arrived and there were 300 telephone subscribers. A chicken cost 27 dollars and a bunch of carrots went for nine dollars. At its peak, from 1908 to 1910, 1.2 million square miles of forest with some 80 million rubber trees were producing 80,000 tons of rubber a year; the export duties alone paid for 40% of Brazil's national debt.

But all good things must come to an end. In 1870, a young Englishman called Henry Wickham smuggled some seeds of the *Hevea* tree to England with some help from a group of disgruntled Indians of the Tapiu tribe and a bent customs official. The scam, in conjunction with Kew Gardens, led to seedlings being planted in Ceylon, subsequently forming the basis of the great rubber plantations of Malaysia. Within 24 years, the trees matured and Southeast Asian production readily outstripped the Amazonian market, which went bust in 1923. Everybody left town – rubber barons, prostitutes, tycoons, traders and speculators. They left behind a decaying city with a boarded-up opera house and cobblestone streets full of weeds.

I like Manaus! I can't quite explain why, because it's a dump. It has no style or class, and it's dirty, smelly, noisy, polluted and overpopulated, as

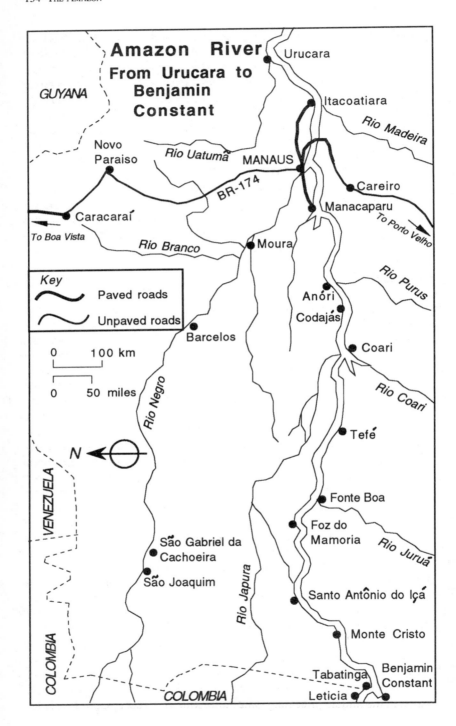

Amazon River
From Urucara to
Benjamin
Constant

you would expect from any city with a population of almost two million.

If you're only after a quick taste of the Amazonian rainforest and don't want to be too far away from some or any form of true civilisation, complete with slums and highrises, then Manaus is the place. Tourism here is rather overrated, and the places have been done to death – the trails and waterways have ruts in them from so many people gaining that jungle experience. If you've never been into the true forest before, and are a little wary about whether you can handle it or not, then Manaus is the place to go. Escape is not that far away. But as a stepping off point for that journey into the interior, Manaus can't be bettered.

Anything worth seeing is located within easy walking distance of most of the hotels, particularly the cheap ones. The Mercado Municipal, the Teatro Amazonas and other sites of interest are all within twenty minutes of each other. The Escadaria dos Remédios Port, where most of the boats leave from, is just outside the Mercado Municipal and is a hive of activity. There are taxis, but ensure that the meters work. There is also a good local bus network that's cheap – about US$0.20 a ride – and the central bus station near the docks has a list of destinations and bus numbers.

Getting there

Manaus' Eduardo Gomes International airport is 16km out of town and costs US$24 in a taxi to the city centre. There is a booth at the airport for the taxi cooperative, the fare is fixed, and they'll drop you off at the hotel of your choice. There are daily flights to the major Brazilian cities on Varig, Vasp and Transbrasil, all of which offer airpasses. In addition, there are international flights to and from Miami and Orlando (on Varig most days of the week), Buenos Aires (on Transbrasil), La Paz (Bolivia, on LAB), Caracas (also on LAB), and Aruba (Netherlands Antilles, on Vasp). There are also weekly flights to several destinations in Europe such as Amsterdam, Madrid, Paris, Rome, Brussels and London.

The bus station is 5km outside the city, with regular buses to Boa Vista (18 hours if the weather is good, US$55), Caracarai and Humaita.

Boats go to everywhere in Amazônia with literally hundreds of destinations to towns along the Amazon Basin's river system. The Escadaria dos Remédios Port has boats for all destinations up and down the mainstream Amazon and destinations on most of the tributaries. The port of São Raimundo northwest of the city centre is for boats up the Rio Negro to Barcelos and São Gabriel da Cachoeira, and for boats up the Rio Branco via the Rio Negro to Boa Vista. There are daily departures as well to Santarém and Belém. For other destinations, departures are usually weekly or bi-weekly.

Where to stay and eat

In Manaus the top hotel is the Tropical Manaus. This is a really flashy joint complete with its own zoo and a price to match. It takes all the usual credit cards. In the middle price range, the Hotel Monaco is acceptable at US$45, has a reasonable restaurant and takes all credit cards. At the bottom end of the price range is the Hospedaria de Turismo 10 de Julho (Rua 10 de Julho 679, US$20 pp). I found this popular hotel a bit run down and noisy, but the breakfast is OK. My favourite hotel in Manaus is the Rio Branco (Rua das Andradas 484, US$8–20). It's full of gringos and overlanders and one of the best places to organise that all-important jungle tour. It has a great breakfast included in the price. It's run by nice friendly people, but doesn't take credit cards. Hotel Dona Joana across the road looks like a front for a brothel and probably is, but it's cheap (US$8–20) and convenient; no cards.

The best fish restaurant in Manaus is the Bar Galo Carijó near the Rio Branco Hotel and Dona Joana's. A big plate for US$5. Some restaurants do food by the kilo, best value as you only pay for what you take. Churrascaria Búfalo does an all you can eat multi-meat special for US$15. Popular, but over the top in price. There are several pizza places in town, just look around.

Information and useful addresses

The Banco do Brasil at Rua Guilherme Moreira 315 changes cash and cheques; it also gives VISA card cash advances, but charges US$20 per transaction. A better place is the Casa Cortez on Avenida 7 de Setembro 199, which buys and sells cash and cheques. Emamtur, the state tourist office, is now located on Avenida 7 de Setembro just past the Palácio Rio Negro. They haven't very much to offer and can be hard to find.

Swallows and Amazons (tel/fax: 55 92 622 1246), a river and jungle tour company based in Manaus, can be found at Rua Quintino Bocaiuva, a couple of blocks down from the Banco do Brasil. Ariaú Jungle Tower, Rio Amazonas Turismo, Rua Silva Ramos, 41 (Centro) Manaus; tel: 92 234 7308; fax: 92 233 5615, is an expensive, but all-inclusive superb jungle lodge on the Ariaú River about 85km north of Manaus.

SÃO GABRIEL DA CACHOEIRA

Situated 1,600km up stream from Manaus along the Río Negro, São Gabriel da Cachoeira is probably the best place to see indigenous peoples. There are 13 large groups in the upper Río Negro region, including the well-known Yanomami. It is from here that the 19th century German naturalist Alexander von Humboldt discovered the Casiquiare Canal. At certain times of the year it is believed that this canal links the Orinoco Basin to that of the Amazon. The region is extremely rich in flora and fauna, with many species unfamiliar to science. There are also high concentrations of gold, and the world's largest reserve of the metal niobium (used in making stainless steel and other alloys for jet engines and rockets, and for making superconductor magnets). There are several national parks in the area, and a distinct mountain range called Bela Adormecida (Sleeping Beauty) – so called because it resembles a reclining woman – and the river has several sets of rapids and islands during the low water period.

Getting there

You have only two options: air taxi or boat. Boats (US$60 in hammock space) take about seven days upstream and five days down, stopping at Novo Airão, Moura, Carvoeira, Barcelos and Santa Isabel do Rio Negro, among other ports. Boats leave Wednesdays and Thursdays from the São Raimundo Port in Manaus.

TABATINGA AND BENJAMIN CONSTANT

At the far western end of Brazil and a thousand miles from Manaus is the tri-frontier between Brazil, Peru and Colombia. Here the Peruvian Rio Amazonas becomes the Brazilian Rio Solimões as it continues on its way from its source high in the Peruvian Andes to the Atlantic Ocean. The towns along the river here look like they have stepped right out of the 1950s. You can't possibly be any further from anywhere else in the world than here. This is real jungle frontier country. It's brilliant! Benjamin Constant is an hour and a half away from Tabatinga and next to the Peruvian town of Islandia. Boats always stop here to load and unload cargo before going to Tabatinga, and on their way back downstream to Manaus. Tabatinga is next door to Leticia (Colombia) and across the river from Santa Rosa (Peru).

Getting there

There are two flights weekly with Varig to Tabatinga (US$230) and air-taxis run an irregular service (US$90–190). From Leticia there are daily flights Bogotá with Aero República and twice-weekly flights with Avianca to Bogotá. Fawcett flies weekly to Iquitos in Peru. There are also numerous cargo planes that take passengers to Bogotá. Boats leave Manaus heading upstream on Wednesdays and Saturdays; the journey takes from eight to ten days, depending on the river and the number of stops (US$80 in hammock space). The return journey takes five days. There is a twice weekly Expresso Rapido speedboat service to Iquitos from Leticia (12 hours, US$50) and an irregular boat service from Santa Rosa to Iquitos (3 days, US$25).

Where to stay and eat

Tabatinga is a dump, and a well spread out one and I wouldn't stay there. Five minutes away by combi collectivo (mini-bus) or a 20 minute walk is Leticia, Colombia – a far more salubrious place to stay, with good restaurants and plenty of respectable yet inexpensive hotels.

PORTO VELHO

When I first began poring over maps of the Amazon Basin to gain some inspiration and decide where I wanted to go, my mind was constantly pulled to Porto Velho. It seemed to me that all roads in the Amazon went either to or from it. My map showed a road northwest from Cuiabá (BR-364) in

Mato Grosso joining the Pantanal with the Amazon; southwest (BR-230, the Trans-Amazon Highway) linking Santarém and Belém to the frontier with Bolivia and southern Peru; roads west and north from Peru and Bolivia; south from Manaus (BR-319), where another road linked Manaus with Venezuela. It appeared that the entire Amazon where I wanted to explore by boat was a network of roads that all seemed to originate in Porto Velho.

Porto Velho is the capital of Brazil's Rondônia state and is situated on the right bank of the Amazon's longest tributary, the Rio Madeira. My first impression is that this town is right out of a ten-cent cowboy novel with a modern twist. Gold shops were everywhere and the buildings had a distinctly 50s facade. I had read in one guidebook that there was a hotel with a very distinct sign that was appropriate to the persona of the place: 'Spit neither on the floor, nor on the walls, nor beside the bed'. I never found the sign, but it did fit the place. The 'wild west' atmosphere came from the opening of the east-west counterpart of the Belém-Brasília Highway linking Cuiabá to Peru and Bolivia, and the discovery of cassiterite (tin ore) and gold in 1952, but the town's fame came from the railway built during the rubber boom to link Bolivia and Peru to the Atlantic coast. This 200 mile Madeira-Mamoré railway, nicknamed Mad Maria, finished in 1912 and inaugurated in 1923 (the year of the rubber bust), was an awesome accomplishment with all the raw materials imported: coal from Wales, steel from Pittsburg, and termite-resistant wood from Australia. The construction cost over 6,000 lives due to Indian attacks and disease, mainly malaria; it took fifty years from conception to completion, and was hardly used. The line closed fully in 1960 and the tracks were pulled up to make room for a road.

Most of the hotels and restaurants are around the town's centre and are within walking distance from the docks (one kilometre). There are plenty of taxis and a local bus service.

Getting there

Ter Guaporé airport is just seven kilometres outside town. There are daily flights to the major Brazilian cities plus several smaller towns and cities. Buses leave from the rodoviária on Avenida Jorge Teixeira about two kilometres from the centre. They go to Brasília, Cuiabá, Rio Branco, Manaus, Humaita, Abúna and, via connections, to several other destinations.

And then there are the boats. There are several sailing each week to Manaus plus some smaller destinations and towns or villages. Manaus is three to four days downstream, and about five to seven days upstream, depending on stops and cargo.

Where to stay and eat

The best in town is the Hotel Vila Rica at Avenida Carlos Gomes 1616. You can't miss it, it's the tallest building in town. The Hotel Nunes at Avenida 7 de Setembro and the Cuiabano on the opposite side of the road are good budget hotels that are both clean and comfortable.

Like most other towns on the rivers, Porto Velho is not famous for its food, but there are many good restaurants serving local fish dishes. The best is the Remanso do Tucunaré at Avenida Brasília 1506 in the Nossa Senhora das Graças neighbourhood. The town even has a proper Chinese restaurant, the Oriente at Avenida Amazonas 1280.

Information and useful addresses

The Banco do Brasil is on the corner of Avenida José de Alencar and Rua Dom Pedro II. The DETUR office (Departamento de Turismo de Rondônia) is at Avenida Padre Chiquinho 670, Esplanada das Secretárias.

THE DISAPPEARING RAINFOREST

By now everyone realizes that the Brazilian rainforest is being methodically chopped and burned down for cattle, farm land and mineral exploration. Unlike our own temperate forest soils, which have been subjected to the mineral-enriching activities of glaciers and mountain-building fairly recently on the geological timescale, rainforest soils are ancient. Pounded by tropical downpours for over 200 million years, jungle soils have become thin and nutrient-poor. Clearing and burning destroys the mycorrhizal fungi-and-root network which normally recycles nutrients so effectively (see *Plant Life of the Rainforest*). After a few seasons, the nutrients released by slash-and-burn have been washed away, the earth turned hard as concrete. Farmers must move on and clear another plot after just two years; ranchers get about eight to ten years out of their pastureland before abandoning it.

Amerindian tribes have successfully practised this slash-and-burn agriculture for centuries, so why the outcry from environmental groups? The important difference, of course, is scale. A tribe cannot possibly clear more than a hectare or two of land every couple of years. Such tiny tracts of land regenerate naturally over about 20 years when left fallow; seeds from neighbouring trees easily reach the cleared area, and the mycorrhizal network again infiltrates the tract. Fallow time is perhaps irrelevant, since the tribe isn't likely to return and clear this land again anyway.

Modern agribusiness plays the game on a far larger (and far more destructive) scale. Most fazendas span hundreds of thousands of hectares. Reseeding and re-establishment of the mycorrhizal network cannot possibly

CITES

The Black Caiman (*Melanosuchus niger*), the Giant or Brazilian Otter (*Pteronura brasiliensis*) and the Amazonian or South American Manatee (*Trichechus inunguis*) are all on the CITES Appendix 1 Endangered Species list.

CITES Appendix 1 species are totally protected under international agreement allowing no trade whatsoever in any of the species on the list. CITES Appendix 2 species list allows some limited but fully monitored trade in each individual species. Trade includes use as a food source.

occur except at the margins of such an expanse. Besides, the flood of Brazilians into Amazônia limits the amount of time a farm or pasture can lie fallow. Despite this poor outlook, investors continue clearing, in large part due to government incentives which reward even money-losing operations.

Mining, logging, and hydro-electric dams also take their toll. The scale of the Grande Carajás Project, which includes all three enterprises along with cattle ranching and agribusiness, is almost beyond comprehension; 895,000 square kilometres, or 10% of the entire country, developed for US$70 billion. The Project began in the mid-1970s with a surprisingly enlightened plan that included deforestation of only a tiny percentage of the total concession. Mismanagement, corruption and chaotic development by hordes of immigrants has undermined the Project, however.

The rainforest remained largely untouched until 1969, when Brazil inaugurated its National Integration Program, aimed at settling the area and turning a profit with cattle ranching. Following the completion of the Transamazon Highway, wealthy ranchers and thousands of *nordestinos* from the Drought Polygon began pouring into the area. The Smithsonian Institution estimated in 1988 that about 0.33% of the Amazonian rainforest is being destroyed each year. Obviously, some areas have been harder hit than others, notably the state of Rondônia, where experts believe 20% of the forest has already been cleared. Just how much of the entire forest is gone and how much is left remains open to debate: in April 1989, ex-President Sarney claimed that a mere 5% of the nation's rainforest had been destroyed, based on satellite photos. The *New York Times*, however, estimated that 3% had been taken down as far back as 1977, and more recent estimates based on satellite photos estimate that 10% of the forest was lost from 1970 to 1989.

Why should we worry if Brazil decides to level its forests? There are plenty of practical considerations, but the one we used to hear a decade ago – that our oxygen would disappear along with the forests – has been largely debunked: a mature rainforest consumes almost as much oxygen as it produces, and most scientists now agree that phytoplankton in the oceans is responsible for our oxygen supply. Concern today centres instead on potential climatic changes caused by the destruction of the forest. Carbon dioxide released into the atmosphere by burning fossil fuels is already credited with global warming and rising sea levels; rainforest slash-and-burn on the current scale may magnify the problem. And since the forest creates about half its own rainfall, the potential exists for massive droughts when the trees have been taken down.

A huge bank of genetic diversity will also disappear with the rainforest. If the modern-day agricultural strains of corn, tomatoes, potatoes, sweet potatoes and manioc are to thrive in the face of diseases and pests, they will need an occasional genetic shot in the arm from their wild ancestors, which originated in the Latin American rainforests. The WWF estimates that fully one-quarter of the drugs prescribed in the United States contain plant ingredients from tropical rainforests, and Amazônia accounts for the lion's share. Those of us who love wild places have other, less tangible reasons for wanting the great forest saved. But only economic incentives are likely to sway a government staggering under the burden of a US$109 billion debt. If Brazil can be convinced that the living forest is worth more in cash dollars than pastureland, there may be hope for Amazônia.

Such hope glimmered briefly in Acre, where a poor rubber tapper named Francisco Mendes Filho had organized his fellow *seringueiros* to protect the forest where they traditionally made their living. 'Chico' Mendes proposed the idea of '*extractive reserves*', large tracts of jungle set aside in their virgin state, where the forest's bounty of rubber, brazil nuts, fruits and valuable plants could be harvested without destroying the source. Mendes organized blockades to prevent illegal razing of the forest, and successfully persuaded the Inter-American Development Bank to suspend funding for the paving of BR-364 between Rondônia and Acre. Mendes was not only a Brazilian but a native Amazonian; the Brazilian government could no longer complain that it was being unfairly badgered by smug

TURTLES

Brazilians love turtles – to eat. The eggs, the flesh, the lot. Turtles are considered a delicacy but they are becoming quite expensive, leaving their consumption to the more wealthy Brazilians. They are eaten at all celebrations such as festivals, birthdays, weddings – but any excuse will do. Sometimes I think that Brazilians don't need an excuse. It's very sad. Only breeding adults are eaten and this is having a devastating effect on the Amazon turtle population.

Besides hunting and egg collecting, deforestation of the flood plain is also contributing to their extinction. Turtles migrate into these areas during flooding to feed on the fallen fruits and seeds. Although on the endangered list and supposedly protected from such attention, no-one takes much notice. One boat I was on was searched by the authorities for contraband (drugs, etc.) but the twenty or so turtles in the hold were conveniently overlooked although the boat captain had made a point of showing me the turtles (all alive) along with the boat's boa constrictor – their ratter. The only other times I saw turtles were either on a barbecue, surreptitiously displayed in the market place or in someone's house awaiting its unpleasant demise. The most popular species eaten are the four species of side-necked turtles and the Amazon River turtle, the largest freshwater species in the world. The remaining 15 species are normally too small or too rare, and appear to me to hardly be worth the effort, but nothing would surprise me about the Brazilians when it comes to turtles. The turtles can't win.

There have been some efforts at small-scale farming of turtles but with little success. Breeding them in captivity has proved difficult to say the least. Even experimenting with artificial water levels to induce breeding has failed. There have also been some attempts made to protect nesting sites but caiman, catfish, piranhas and dolphins still prey on the young turtles and the birds feed on the eggs. With man also not obeying the rules, the turtle has little chance in the greater scheme of things. The big headed Amazon River turtle (*Peltocephalus dumeriliana*) and all river and side-necked turtles of the genus *Podocnemis* are on the CITES Appendix 2 Endangered Species list.

THE HAMBURGER-RAINFOREST EQUATION

Since beef production is the rationale behind much 'development' in Amazônia, it makes sense to ask two simple questions: just how much beef does the world stand to gain from the deal; and what will it cost? Christopher Uhl, a visiting biologist from Pennsylvania State University, did some basic cost-benefit calculations in Belém's daily newspaper *O Liberal*. Uhl estimates that a single hectare of virgin Amazonian jungle contains close to 800,000kg of plant and animal matter. Once cleared, how much food can we expect this chunk of land to produce? A steer grazing this single hectare is expected to put on about 50kg of weight per year, or some 400kg in an average eight-year life span. Subtracting hide, bones, and other non-edible parts of the steer, we end up with approximately 200kg of beef, enough to produce 1,600 hamburgers.

I happen to enjoy a good burger, and this would strike me as a reasonable trade-off if we could continue fattening steers on this hectare of former jungle land. But it doesn't work that way in Amazônia. By the end of eight years, this hectare of thin, nutrient-poor soil will be as dead as the steer that grazed it; our stack of burgers is a one-time transaction. Thus, 800,000kg of living jungle have been effectively converted into just 1,600 hamburgers – or about half a ton of jungle per burger. Considering the loss in terms of area – 10,000m² per hectare divided by 1,600 hamburgers – we discover that each burger represents 6.25m² of rainforest. As Uhl puts it, 'that's almost the size of a small kitchen!'

First World environmentalists. As Mendes put it, 'We became ecologists without even knowing the word'. But his efforts had angered powerful ranching interests. On December 22, 1988, Chico Mendes was gunned down outside his home in Acre. Already, Japanese investors are renewing efforts to pave BR-364 all the way to Peru.

Prodded by international outrage at Mendes' murder and the wholesale destruction of the rainforest, ex-President Sarney outlined in April 1989 a plan to protect Amazônia. '*Nossa Natureza*' ('Our Nature') includes 17 presidential decrees and seven bills to be sent to Congress. These include ending incentives for cattle ranching, controlling the sale of toxic mercury (used by miners to extract gold), and creation of a special forest police. How effective these measures will be remains to be seen. Brazil already has environmental laws on the books which are quite strict by international standards; enforcement of those laws, on the other hand, is lax to nonexistent, and funding for everything from game wardens to pollution monitoring is scanty at best.

What you can do to help

Those of us who live in developed countries can't get overly smug on the topic of rainforest destruction. The United States, for example, is responsible for the bulk of the carbon dioxide being added to the earth's atmosphere, while nations like Switzerland continue to log off their remaining forests at an astonishing rate. If we hope to convince Brazil of our sincerity, we must take an active role in cleaning up our own back yards as we lecture other nations. If you're not already a member of a local environmental group in your own country, join now and press for stiffer controls on vehicle emissions, air standards, water pollution, and logging.

One of the most promising tactics in protecting the forests is the so-called debt-for-nature swaps. Forgiving a portion of Brazil's foreign debt in return for either total protection or rational development of certain forest tracts is now being discussed by creditor nations; such schemes have already worked in Bolivia and Costa Rica. Urge your local politicians to support these measures.

Consider joining at least one of the following organisations, all of which work to save rainforests in Brazil and throughout the world:

World Wide Fund for Nature (WWF), 1250 24th St NW, Washington, DC 20037

Rainforest Action Network, 301 Broadway, Suite A, San Francisco, CA 94133

Rainforest Alliance, 270 Lafayette Street, Suite 512, New York, NY 10012

Fundacão Pro Natureza (FUNATURA), Latin American Program, 1785 Massachusetts Avenue NW, Washington, DC 20036

Environmental Defense Fund, The Chico Mendes Fund, 257 Park Avenue S, New York, NY 10010

Conservation International, 1015 18th Street NW, Suite 1002, Washington, DC 20036

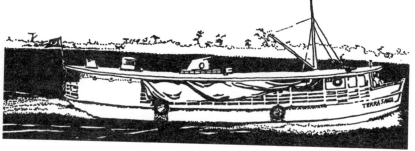

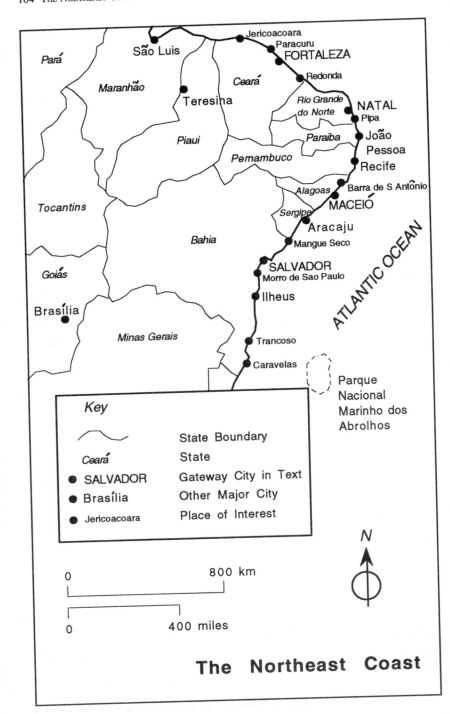

Key

State Boundary

Ceará   State

● SALVADOR   Gateway City in Text

● Brasília   Other Major City

● Jericoacoara   Place of Interest

0   800 km

0   400 miles

N

The Northeast Coast

Chapter Seven

The Northeast Coast

As far as most of the world is concerned, there are exactly two Brazilian beaches: Copacabana and Ipanema. I wouldn't suggest that Rio's famed twin beaches don't have their charms: miles of sugar-white sand jam-packed with Brazilians at play – eating, drinking, making music, playing soccer, flirting, gossiping and even, occasionally, swimming.

Yet there is another kind of Brazilian beach – which is not too surprising in a country that boasts over 7,000km of Atlantic waterfront. This beach is fringed not with skyscrapers but with slender coconut palms. Here, the big entertainment involves the afternoon arrival of the *jangadas*, primitive fishing boats powered by the wind. And the only traffic you'll have to avoid on this beach will be the occasional donkey-drawn cart.

Welcome to the northeast coast, a stretch of shoreline with beaches so spectacular that even *cariocas* sometimes search them out. Northeastern Brazil encompasses nearly 20% of the entire country, including the states of Bahia, Sergipe, Alagoas, Pernambuco, Paraíba, Rio Grande do Norte, Ceará, Piauí and Maranhão. Much of the interior is dry scrub desert, sparsely-populated badlands known as the *sertão*. While the narrow coastal strip has attracted all the northeast's major cities – among them Salvador da Bahia, once the nation's capital – it also includes hundreds of kilometres of pristine beaches punctuated with rustic fishing villages.

Northeastern Brazil can boast a richer human and historical fabric than any other portion of the country. It was here that Portuguese navigator Pedro Cabral first landed in April 1500, near present-day Porto Seguro, Bahia. And it was here that colonists from the Azores introduced the colony's first boom crop, sugar cane. Over the following three centuries,

Portuguese slavers delivered between 3 and 15 million Africans to work the plantations. (No one today can be sure of the number, because Brazil destroyed all records of the slave trade in 1891.) Regardless of the correct number, the vast majority of slaves landed in the northeast, which remains to this day the most distinctly African region of Brazil. Catholicism and African deities mingled here to form *candomblé*, the equivalent of Haiti's *vodoun* (voodoo) and Cuba's *santería*. Music, dance, even the rich and spicy food of coastal Bahia reflects the region's African heritage. That influence fades as you move north, toward Rio Grande do Norte and Ceará, being replaced by a mixture of Amerindian and European elements. Here you'll often come across beige-skinned Brazilians with frizzy hair and green eyes, living reminders also of the short-lived French and Dutch occupations of the 17th century.

Northeastern Brazil remains the country's most impoverished region. Even in the best of years, inhabitants of the *sertão* find it hard to scrape a meagre existence from its parched soil; when periodic droughts strike, the hardy *sertanejos* migrate by the thousands to crowded shantytowns in the coastal cities or industrial centres in the south. Such migrations are the stuff of legend in Brazil, inspiring songs, films and novels, but they are by no means a thing of the past; in Alagoas, we've seen buses stop along the highway to accommodate whole families of drought-stricken *sertanejos* dragging aboard everything they own. Despite these hardships, or perhaps because of them, *sertanejos* are Brazil's friendliest people.

Sugarcane remains a major crop along the coast, and until recent years an important portion of the harvest went to make fuel alcohol for cars. But the government fuel alcohol programme, which subsidized the relatively high cost of cane alcohol production, is being slowly phased out. Of course, cane sugar remains in demand for other, more traditional uses; Brazil's most popular brands of *cachaça* (sugarcane rum) comes from the northeast. Cacao, corn and cotton exports also fuel the regional economy. The *sertão* is primarily cattle and goat country. The northeast also produces Brazil's finest crafts, including gorgeous lacework, clay figures, woodcarvings, hammocks and embroidery.

LEGUAS

When you're asking directions, be aware that backcountry residents in this part of Brazil sometimes use *leguas* (leagues) rather than kilometres as a measure of distance. One *legua* equals 6km. Another cautionary note: the locals here customarily travel enormous distances daily just to sell fish, buy coconuts, or wash laundry. Consequently, when you ask for directions, try to get as specific a distance estimate as you can squeeze from your source. *Pertinho* (extremely close by) often translates into an eight-hour trek!

GETTING THERE

Gateway cities for the northeast coast include eight of the state capitals: Salvador, Aracaju, Maceió, Recife, João Pessoa, Natal, Fortaleza, and São Luis. (Teresina in Piauí lies far inland). Varig, Cruzeiro do Sul and Vasp all run daily flights from Rio and São Paulo. From Belém, there are direct flights to Recife, Fortaleza and São Luís. Buses run daily to all the gateway cities from Rio and São Paulo; from Belém, you'll find direct buses to all the gateway cities except Aracaju.

GETTING AROUND

Buses will get you within striking distance of most of the beaches; in some cases, you can simply step off the bus in a tiny fishing town within minutes of the water. Most of the time, however, you'll either have to walk or rely on more sporadic local transport to reach the truly pristine beaches.

Even when the road runs out and formal transportation ends, you can be sure there's some way to get to the beach. Local fishing villages, after all, need to get their fish to market and to receive supplies. So in many cases you can hop a ride with the supply truck or jeep as it passes through town. Popular forms of transport include *kombis* (Volkswagen vans) and *bugues* or *bugres* (dune buggies, four-wheel drive vehicles with balloon tyres, especially suited for dune- and beach- driving). *Pau de araras* – large supply trucks that also hold up to 60 paying passengers – still ply many kilometres of coastline on a daily basis. The *pau de arara* (literally, the parrot's perch) enjoys the same legendary status in Brazil that the *Conestoga* wagon does in North America – ride one if you get the chance. Finally, in the really remote spots (or those where shifting sand renders roads useless), you may have to hire a local to walk you from some inland point to the beach.

Walking the coast is supremely easy except when you run up against rivers and high tides. The former rarely present major problems, since fishing villages tend to spring up around a river mouth and boats are easily hired for the crossing. In some cases, there are small ferries that run on what passes for a schedule in the *nordeste*. Tides are a different matter. Be very alert to the tide level, since many of the beaches in the northeast are fringed with steep sandstone cliffs that can't be scaled. In this situation, take careful note as you hike of escape routes that will take you up to the ridge tops. You'll sometimes find beaches that are blocked by headlands jutting out into the water; some, but not all, are passable at low tide. Never attempt to pass such headlands during a flooding tide. When in doubt, look for a way to climb the headland rather than risk being trapped.

Drinking water can be scarce along the beach. Coastline fringed with steep sandstone cliffs often contains small springs issuing from the bank, but be sure to ask locals if it's potable; such springs are in many cases used strictly for washing clothes. The only fresh water you're likely to find along coastline backed by sand-dunes is river water, and this is likely to be polluted. Freshwater lagoons sometimes occur between the dunes; once again, check with the locals before drinking. Fishing villages almost always rely on wells for their drinking water and you can often fill a canteen from the local hand pump. Frequently, well water will contain small amounts of salt water, and we've even run into faecally polluted well water. In short, you should bring as much water as you possibly can when hiking deserted and semi-deserted coastline. Coconut milk is an excellent substitute; coconuts are available almost anywhere you find a fisherman's hut along the beach, and they are much safer than well water. Coconut milk is an almost perfect electrolyte, so it's excellent if you have diarrhoea. Ask for the coconuts to be opened, and insist on paying for them.

When to go

In terms of weather, virtually any month is splendid in the northeast. Heaviest rainfall occurs from March through to July, but rarely will you be rained out for more than a day or two in a row; more often than not, all the day's rain will be dropped in a single downpour of short duration. Temperatures vary little year-round, averaging 28°C and virtually never dropping below 20°.

If at all possible, let the Brazilian vacation schedule determine when you go rather than weather. Avoid January and February, the first week of March in those years when Carnaval spills over, and July, when vacationing Brazilians from the south invade the northeast in droves.

A caution

Unlike the Pantanal and Amazônia, which are seldom visited by Brazilian tourists, the northeast coast draws more and more people every year. Many a peaceful fishing village or deserted stretch of beach has been 'discovered' and completely transformed within the space of a few years; witness Trancoso in Bahia, and Canoa Quebrada and Jericoacoara in Ceará. These places are still pleasant enough, but the towns themselves no longer meet my admittedly vague definition of 'backcountry'. Therefore, be forewarned that the information contained in this chapter concerning specific beaches may well be outdated six months from publication. Remember that the northeast boasts 3,000km of shoreline and literally thousands of named beaches and fishing villages; what Canoa Quebrada was fifteen years ago exists today elsewhere. You'll find here a starter course featuring the states of Ceará, Rio Grande do Norte, Alagoas and Bahia. And keep in mind that you can frequently escape a touristy resort town by simply walking a couple of kilometres or grabbing local transport to a neighbouring village. Finally, some villages go through seasonal transformations during Brazilian holidays and vacation periods; visit these places in the off-season and you'll often find them as tranquil as they were decades ago.

What then qualifies a fishing hamlet as 'backcountry?' I suggest the simple litmus test developed by our Brazilian friend Wellington Franklin, a native of Ceará: ask the locals if someone can fix you a cheeseburger (*X-burger*, pronounced shees-BUR-gee). If no one can produce a cheeseburger, you've landed in bona fide backcountry; if they don't know what a cheeseburger *is*, stay put, because you've stumbled into Eden.

AFRO-BRAZILIAN RELIGIONS

Uprooted from their homes in Angola, the Congo, Guinea, Mozambique, Dahomey, the Sudan and all over West Africa, black slaves were landed by the millions in northeastern Brazil. Many of them had been wealthy tribal leaders before being sold into slavery; some even had slaves of their own. But when the Portuguese loaded them aboard the ships, they left everything behind. Everything, that is, except their *orixás*. Ethnologists have identified at least sixty separate *orixás*, or deities, which made the trip from West Africa to Brazil. Heading the list are Oxalá, the chief spirit; Iemanjá, the goddess of the sea; Xangô, the thunder god; and Oxóssi, god of the hunt.

Once in Brazil, the slaves mingled with Tupi Indians and ended up borrowing a number of their local forest gods, making them *orixás* as well. Always ready to accept new spiritual allies wherever they found them, blacks enlisted the Tupi spirit Japetequara (the Alligator) and Tapinaré (the Jaguar). Some of the tribes sold into slavery had been Muslims, and an element of Islam crept in as well. Before long, the slaves were celebrating a distinctively new kind of religion.

To appease their Portuguese masters – who had summarily banned the worship of African deities – slaves simply merged their traditional *orixás* and the new Catholic saints. Iemanjá, with her white gowns of sea-foam, became the Blessed Virgin. Xangô, the spirit of wilderness, was now St John the Baptist. Omulu, the spirit of disease, merged easily with St Lazarus. And Ogun the warrior god became St George the Dragonslayer.

This spiritual gumbo of African, Catholic, Amerindian and Muslim elements simmered for a few decades before spilling throughout Brazil. In Bahia (where the purest, most African form is practised), this hybrid religion is known as Candomblé; in Recife you'll hear it referred to as Xangô; and in Rio, the original term, now much abused, was Macumba. Umbanda is a less orthodox form, nowadays extremely widespread throughout the northeast and Brazil as a whole. Crossing all racial and economic barriers, Umbanda is practised not only by manioc farmers in Pitombeiras but also by Fortaleza office clerks. This new yet ancient form of worship has augmented rather than replaced Catholicism; many Brazilians attend the spirit tents on Saturday night and go to Mass on Sunday.

Long before we attended our first full-blown Umbanda ceremony in the northeast, Jayne and I – quite literally – stumbled upon an offering to the *orixás*. There it was, at the intersection of two dirt paths in the backcountry: a paper plate filled with dried corn kernels, cooked beans and manioc flour.

Umbandistas (practitioners of Umbanda) gather on a beach in Ceará beneath an effigy of Iemaná, Goddess of the Sea

A candle sat upright in the centre of the plate, its base supported by the beans, and an empty bottle of cane rum lay alongside. We later learned that such offerings are typically placed at crossroads, being meant in this case for the messenger spirit Exu. Actually, there is not one Exu, but rather a series of Exus, each with different traits, powers, and appetites. Most Exus appreciate offerings of rum, tobacco, or meat; we've seen cigars and *cachaça* placed alongside a pair of sacrificed chickens. Since some of the Exus tend towards mischief (there is one which is said to destroy happy marriages, another which promotes venereal disease), it was easy for Christian observers to confuse Exu with the Devil. The many Exus, however, all serve as messengers between worshippers and the gods; as such, they are invoked at the beginning of virtually all rituals, even the most benign.

And, sensationalism notwithstanding, the Afro-Brazilian religions concern themselves almost exclusively with good works. Quimbanda, officially outlawed in Brazil, is the single splinter sect which deals in black magic. Animal sacrifice plays a part in all the Afro-Brazilian religions, but the killing itself is done in private by the priest and a few assistants, well before the public ceremonies held in the evening.

One of the most impressive and easily-witnessed Umbanda rites along the northeast coast is the Festival of Iemanjá, goddess of the sea. Ceará honours Iemanjá on August 15th, with the largest celebration in Fortaleza. The faithful from some 200 local *terreiros* (churches) arrive by bus at noon, each *terreiro* claiming its own particular piece of beach at the Praia do Futuro (take a bus of the same name from the centre).

Terreiro members beat drums, chant and parade likenesses of Iemanjá about the beach. Iemanjá favours long, flowing, white-and-blue robes, and worshippers usually follow suit. Priests (*pai-de-santos*) and their female counterparts (*mãe-de-santos*) enter into inspired religious trances, dancing spasmodically, spittle dribbling from their mouths, eyes rolled up so that only the whites show. We once watched a transfixed *mãe-de-santo* repeatedly cut herself with a fish knife, but self-mutilation is rare. Usually, *terreiro* members are on hand to steady and protect those who enter into trances.

Visitors (foreigners included) may enter the circle of worshippers to *pegar um passo* (enter into a brief trance) at the hand of the *pai-de-santo*. As drummers beat a frantic rhythm, the priest takes the initiate's hand and twirls her or him in circles, puffing clouds of cigar smoke and chanting all the while. Church members stand ready to catch the initiates if they stumble during trance. The entire *passo* lasts only a few minutes.

Though deeply spiritual, Umbanda has an openly earthly element as well, and a great deal of drinking (usually cane rum) and smoking (cigars and long-stemmed pipes) goes on. Many of the *pai-de-santos* and their assistants (*filho-de-santos*) are homosexuals or bisexuals; indeed, many of the *orixás* themselves are sexually ambiguous. Iemanjá, a fancier of carnal pleasures herself, adores jewellery, perfume, roses, champagne and *cachaça*; these are loaded upon tiny wooden rafts and pushed to sea at dusk, then overturned.

In smaller celebrations, worshippers simply throw these offerings into the surf.

Authentic Candomblé rites can best be seen in Salvador. The state tourist bureau in Salvador, Bahiatursa (tel: 071 241 4333), offers lists of the many local *terreiros* which allow visitors. These operate daily on a year-round basis, except during Lent (the forty days following Ash Wednesday and Carnaval), when no public rites are performed. Bahiatursa's monthly calendar of events includes those candomblé ceremonies which may be visited. Some of the *terreiros* which allow visitors include: Casa Branca, Avenida Vasco da Gama 463 (Salvador's oldest and most frequently-visited by travellers); Olga da Alaketu, Rua Luíz Anselmo 67 (tel: 071 224 2285); Terreiro do Gantois, Alto do Gantois 23 (tel: 071 247 3302); Pilão de Prata, Rua Tomaz Gonzaga 298 (tel: 071 231 9055); Terreiro de Oxóssi, Rua Queira Deus 78 (tel: 071 891 2881); and Axé Opô Afonjá, Rua Direita de São Gonçalo do Retiro 245 (tel: 071 384 9801). Virtually all of the *terreiros* are located outside the city centre, and you'll want to either join an organised tour or take a taxi. Ceremonies start around 21.00. Dress conservatively (no shorts of any kind). Men and women will be expected to sit on opposite sides of the *terreiro*. These are not shows, and no real *terreiro* allows cameras or tape recorders. In the suburban and rural areas of the northeast, visitors may be grudgingly accepted to private rites. These generally occur just once or twice a week, and your only chance of seeing one is through a Brazilian friend with contacts.

FORTALEZA

A sprawling city of 1.8 million people and capital of Ceará state, Fortaleza provides access to what are some of the finest beaches in all of Brazil. Not too long ago, the national edition of *Playboy* magazine featured no less than six nearby beaches on its list of the 'Twenty Most Afrodisiacal Beaches of Brazil'. Ceará's coast, spanning some 540km, is noted for its towering sand-dunes – one story has it that the state's name itself is a bastardisation of 'Sahara'.

In recent years, the city of Fortaleza has undertaken many civic improvement projects, and some downtown areas that were formerly dilapidated or even dangerous have been transformed into attractive waterfront promenades, café districts and artist hangouts. The city centre itself isn't of much interest to travellers, unless you've got business with airline offices or banks, and it becomes fairly deserted at night. The beachfront and neighbouring streets, however, are alive year-round and far into the night with outdoor cafés, handicraft stalls, dance clubs, bars and street vendors.

Most travellers spend most of their time in the Iracema and Meireles districts. Iracema is east of the city centre along the beach, where the Ponte Metállica (Metal Pier) juts out over the sea. The area surrounding the Ponte – especially Rua dos Tabajaras – is loaded with cafés, bars, bohemian art stalls, shops, vendors and pousadas, and it's a great place for an evening stroll. Further east along Avenida Presidente Kennedy (*Aka* Avenida Beira Mar) is the Praia do Meireles, another busy area of restaurants, clubs, pousadas, open-air craft markets and shops. Further east is Praia do Futuro, a high-rise hotel area considered to be the best beach within the city itself. It's the scene of a great annual Afro-Brazilian religious festival for Iemanjá, the goddess of the sea.

Getting there

Pinto Martins airport lies 6km south of the city centre. Daily flights go to and from Rio, São Paulo, Belém, Salvador, Recife, Manaus, João Pessoa, and Natal. There are weekly international flights from Miami, Rome, and Milan on Varig, as well as from Washington DC, New York, Miami, Buenos Aires, Vienna and Amsterdam on Transbrasil. Cheap city buses run from just outside the terminal to Praça José de Alencar, located in the city centre, from where you can catch buses to the hotel districts near the beach. A taxi from the airport to these hotel districts will cost around US$8–$15. There are several information booths at the airport, as well as self-service computer terminals with tourist information.

The spacious bus station is about 4km south of town, within 2km of the airport. Buses run daily to hundreds of small towns in the state, as well as Belém (US$60, 23 hours), Rio (US$110, 48 hours), São Paulo (US$120, 48 hours), Salvador (US$52, 22 hours), Natal (US$20, eight hours), Recife (US$32, 12 hours), São Luís (US$44, 16 hours) and many other state capitals. To get to the city centre from the bus station, catch any city bus headed for Praça José de Alencar, or those marked 'Aguanambi' or '13 de Maio'. A number of buses make the return trip from the Praça, and are marked 'Rodoviária'. Taxis from the bus station to the centre or hotel districts generally cost around US$5.

FOOD AND DRINK IN THE NORTHEAST BACKCOUNTRY

The food and drink served in remote fishing villages isn't one of those travel experiences you'll get nostalgic about back home. In one village, we always dreaded Sundays, when the fisherman didn't fish. This meant that we would be eating chicken, and the only reason we could see for slaughtering these pathetically scrawny and diseased birds might have been to put them out of their misery.

Nevertheless, much of the food you'll eat is particular to this region of Brazil, and there are pleasant as well as unpleasant surprises. You'll often start the day off with *tapioca* cakes instead of bread; this is a granular form of manioc starch baked into rounds with coconut milk. Fish dishes include mackerel (*cavala*), hammerhead shark (*tubarão martelo*) and skate (*arraia*). Stingray stew (*ensopada de arraia*) can be particularly tasty. *Nordestinos*, like all Brazilians, love sweets; in the backcountry you'll get *cocada*, a chewy macaroon-like concoction of shredded coconut and sugar. For real sugar-holics there's always *rapadura*, a hardened cake of raw cane broth that's been boiled down to its sugary essence. *Cachaça* is, of course, the national drink, but here you'll often take it with cashew fruit syrup (*mel de cajú*).

Where to stay and eat

There are literally hundreds of hotels in Fortaleza, ranging from bare-light-bulb dives to chic penthouses with a view of the beach. Because Fortaleza is a major centre of tourism for both Brazilians and foreigners, it's never been a cheap city for lodging, but there are good deals to be had, especially if you look around a bit. Remember that outside the high season, you can often receive far cheaper rates than those posted if you're willing to do a little bargaining. The most pleasant hotels and pousadas tend to concentrate in the Iracema and Meireles neighbourhoods near the beach. Staying in these two areas, you'll be close to most of the good restaurants, bars, dance clubs and handicraft markets of the city, most of them within easy walking distance day or night. There are so many hotels and pousadas in these areas that your best bet is to simply walk within a few blocks of the beach and check them out personally. There are two youth hostels in the Iracema/ Meireles area: Albergue da Juventude Praia de Iracema at Avenida Almirante Barroso 998 (they charge US$14 pp, and will pick you up from the bus station for about US$5 for four people); and Albergue da Juventude Coqueiro Verde at Rua Frei Monsueto 531, charging US$15 pp. There's also a third hostel in the Aldeota district, Albergue de Fortaleza, at Rua Rocha Lima 1186, also charging US$15 pp.

Fortaleza is a good restaurant town, where you'll be able to eat anything from lobster to sushi to traditional dishes of the *sertão*. See the box on *Food and Drink of the Northeast Backcountry*; you'll be able to sample many of these dishes in Fortaleza (and, quite frankly, they'll often be better prepared in the city.) Typical northeastern dishes to watch for include *paçoca* (sun-dried beef which is first fried and then mashed together with toasted manioc flour), *carne de sol* (sun-dried, salted beef), *baião-de-dois* (a mixture of beans, butter, rice and cheese), and *macaxeira* (deep-fried manioc). As with hotels, Fortaleza's restaurants are so numerous and constantly-changing that the best advice is to simply explore the streets of Iracema and Meireles. Rua dos Tabajaras and the entire area around the Ponte Metállica in Iracema is jam-packed with good restaurants and cafés. There's also good cheap food to be had at the makeshift stalls at the nightly crafts market on Avenida Presidente Kennedy in Meireles. The most famously eccentric restaurant in Fortaleza is Osmar, in the Mucuripe district (take a cab; everyone knows the place, it's a bit out of town, and you'll never find it on your own!). This unlikely place is in Osmar's tree-shaded back yard, accessed through a narrow space between two houses.

Information and useful addresses

There are now many *casas de câmbio* springing up throughout Fortaleza. Ask at one of the tourist information offices listed below for a *câmbio* nearby. There are a number of câmbios in the Iracema hotel area on Avenida Monsenhor Tabosa. Banco do Brasil changes cash, cheques, and gives VISA cash advances at their branches in the centre (Rua Barão do Rio Branco

1500) and in the Meireles district. The Centro de Turismo at Rua Senador Pompeu 350 also changes cash and cheques.

Fortaleza and the state of Ceará have made a big push to provide travellers with easy access to information. Travellers arriving at the Fortaleza airport are frequently met by representatives of the state travel authority (Coditur), who hand out informational brochures, a list of cultural events and sometimes even free straw hats. At the baggage claim area, there are computer terminals with information for travellers, and if you still need help, they staff an airport booth 24 hours a day (tel: 085 272 1335). A similar booth at the bus station is open 06.00–18.00 daily (tel: 085 227 4080). Once in the city centre, you can visit the pleasant Centro de Turismo, a prison during the 1850s and 1860s which has been converted into a series of handicraft stores, with a shaded outdoor cafe and an information centre. The Centro, taking up a whole city block at Rua Senador Pompeu 350, is open Mon-Fri 07.00–18.00, Sat 08.00–14.00, and Sun 08.00–12.00. Maps, brochures, and general information on travel throughout Ceará are available. Cultural events, including musical performances, are presented outdoors at the Centro. There are also smaller information booths open along the beach in Miereles. And making things easier yet is the phone service *Disque Turismo*, available by dialling 1516 from any city phone.

There are plenty of tour operators in Fortaleza offering trips to the Ceará beaches and interior hinterlands. The most informal of these are guides operating out of vans parked along the busy Avenida Presidente Kennedy in Meireles, each with photos of their destinations, descriptions of the tours, and prices posted on the van exteriors. One of the best guides to Ceará, be it coast or inland, is Wellington Franklin, who operates Faciltur (Avenida Santos Dumont 905, room 7, in Aldeota; tel: 085 289 2013 or 085 984 3247). Despite the name, Wellington is pure Brazilian and pure Cearense, always ready to lead foreigners well off the beaten path and into the 'real Brazil'. Young as he is, Wellington is already something of a local treasure, brimming with the lore and fact of Ceará. He speaks excellent French, Italian and German, good English, he's learning Russian, and his sense of humour manages to transcend all linguistic barriers. He was one of the first guides to bring travellers to places like Jericoacoara (via local transport and on foot), and continues to promote low-impact travel to unspoiled villages of Ceará.

Fortaleza inspires even non-shoppers like us to shop. Typical Cearense crafts include fine lacework, leather goods, clay figurines, and coloured-sand artwork. Everywhere you'll see ceramic likenesses of Padre Cícero, a backcountry cleric and religious fanatic disavowed by the Vatican but revered by *nordestinos*. But first stop for backcountry travellers should be a hammock (*rede*) shop. Fortaleza vies with Manaus as the best place in Brazil to buy hammocks, and Fortaleza's hammocks tend to be far more handsome. Many hammock factories sell their own products out front; ask for a tour of the factory as long as you're browsing. Some good ones include:

MUSIC AND DANCE OF THE NORTHEAST BACKCOUNTRY

Nowadays you'll find chic urbanites dancing the *forroá* in clubs throughout Brazil. But it's originally a creation of the northeast backcountry, a dance you're sure to experience in its purest form if you spend a weekend in one of the fishing towns mentioned in this chapter. We saw our first *forroá* in 1984 at Jericoacoara; under a tin-covered shed, villagers had rigged a phonograph to a 12-volt truck battery, and there they danced to the infectious beat of Luiz Gonzaga's accordion. The *forroá* demands a series of quick shuffling steps, and the sounds of perhaps 40 plastic sandals scraping in time over that concrete floor added considerably to the recorded music. The smallest villages generally rely on record players or even radios for their *forroá* music. To really appreciate this local tradition, though, try to catch a live band in the hinterlands. In addition to the ever-present accordion player (*sanfoneira*), you can expect a drummer and a steel-triangle player, often augmented by a tambourine. One or more of the players will sing. We attended one *forroá* where a small child spent the entire evening holding a microphone up for the singer, resting his arm between verses. The tunes themselves are fast and rambunctious, sounding a great deal like Mexican music (though I assume that's purely coincidental). Partners cling to each other tightly in this deceptively simple dance. The setting for a good *forrozinho* can often be as intriguing as the music and dancing. We attended one in Peixe Gordo ('Fat Fish'), Ceará, which the band had enclosed within a makeshift barrier of palm fronds to prevent non-paying customers from interloping. On another occasion, the hut where we rented hammock space became the dance hall on Sundays. The name *forroá* reportedly originated when English bosses held dances 'for all' their Brazilian and English employees. Most backcountry *forroá* occur on weekends, especially during religious and other holidays. Those with live music will charge you an admission if you're a man (ridiculously cheap); women dance for free.

The backcountry of the northeast also spawned the unique singers known as *repentistas*. Accompanied simply by guitar, tambourine or triangle, the *repentista* actually makes up lyrics as he goes, singing in a fast, typically harsh monotone. Poverty, politics, drought and the suffering of the *nordestinos* are common themes, but sly humour plays a big role as well; *repentistas* frequently poke good-natured fun at members of the audience, and a foreigner is always fair game. This isn't dancing music.

If you happen to be visiting around June 23rd, particularly in the state of Maranhão, you may well see the *bumba-meu-boi* festival. The spectacle revolves around an ox, usually portrayed by two local men beneath a fabulously decorated sheet. Dancing, singing and poetry all play a part in this festival, which may or may not have religious overtones, depending on which Brazilian you happen to ask.

Feirão das Redes de Elilton Pinheiro (tel: 085 231 9339); Fábrica de Redes Santa Lourdes (tel: 085 260 4926); and Fábrica de Redes Rafael (tel: 085 295 2906). See the section on camping *Chapter Two* for more on hammocks. Mosquito nets (*mosquiteiros*) aren't as easily purchased here as in the Amazon.

For hammocks and all other sorts of Cearense craftwork, try the Centro de Turismo in the centre, the Centro de Artesanato Luiza Távora (Avenida Santos Dumont 1589) in Aldeota district, and the Mercado Central, Rua

General Bezerril 14 . One of the liveliest places to shop for Cearense crafts is at the huge nightly outdoor market at the Praia do Meireles. Here, hundreds of makeshift stalls along the beach on Avenida Presidente Kennedy sell everything from cheap junk to stunning lacework to cashew nuts roasted on the spot. There are also lots of stands selling barbecued fish, beer, *caipirinhas*, and sweets. Ask about the schedule of outdoor crafts markets at any of the Coditur information booths (see above).

Fortaleza is a popular place for music and dancing, especially the traditional northeastern dance called the *forró*. Once again, there are scores of music and dance clubs in the Iracema and Meireles districts; probably the most famous dance hall is Piratas, at Rua dos Tabajaras 325 in Iracema. For a quiet evening, take a cab up to O Mirador, a hilltop community of small cafés and restaurants with spectacular views of the city.

Excursions
South of Fortaleza

Unpolluted white-sand beaches begin just 32km south of Fortaleza, near Aquiráz. Prainha, Iguapé, Caponga, Barra Nova, Morro Branco and Uruaú are all relatively small coastal villages accessible by public bus from the Fortaleza terminal. *Jangadas* return daily with their catch, and you can join the locals as they barter for fresh hammerhead shark, skates and mackerel. Tiny beachfront shacks (*barracas*) roofed with palm leaves serve beer, fried fish, manioc meal, rice and beans. Gorgeous as these beaches can be, they lie so close to Fortaleza that residents of the big city flock to them in droves, especially on weekends. Prainha and Morro Branco get most of the crowds. None of these beaches therefore qualify as particularly remote, although backpackers will find deserted stretches just beyond the villages. Unfortunately, a series of rivers makes a complete traverse of this coastal stretch impossible.

The more isolated shoreline begins south of Aracati. An inland town of 60,000 people with some nice colonial architecture and Portuguese tile work, Aracati is accessible via seven daily buses from the main terminal in Fortaleza. The trip takes about 3½ hours and costs US$7. Getting off the bus, you'll be besieged by *kombi* and *bugue* drivers offering rides to Canoa Quebrada, 11km to the east (regular and much cheaper buses leave Aracati for Canoa at 12.00 and 18.40 daily). Canoa inherited Arembepe's reputation as Brazil's 'in' beach town, and the once-idyllic fishing hamlet hasn't really qualified as 'remote' since about 1982. Drugs, venereal diseases, crime – including at least one rape – and terminal hipness long ago scratched Canoa from our list. I mention it here mainly because you will be steered there frequently by well-meaning Brazilians who still regard it as primitive.

Canoa's beach itself, however, flanked by massive white sand-dunes, is still fabulous, and provides a starting point for backpacking trips to the south. From Canoa, you can hike south along the coastline all the way to the state border, crossing into Rio Grande do Norte and arriving at the

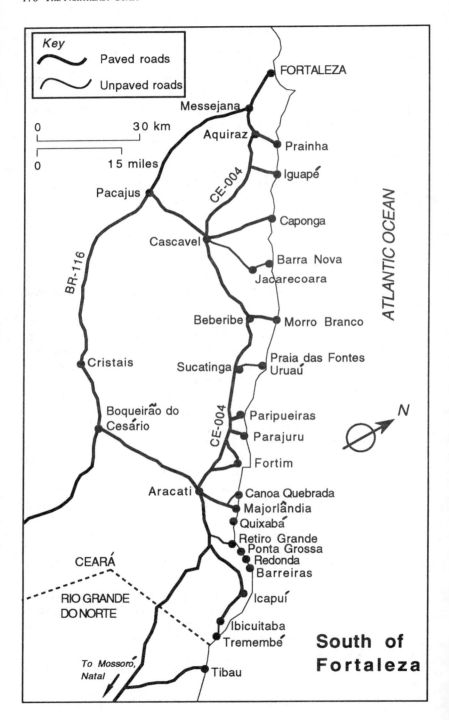

town of Tibau. Only just before Tibau will you run into an unfordable river, but it's served by a makeshift ferry.

About 70km separates Canoa Quebrada from Tibau. Only three spots along this stretch are accessed by decent roads, so the coast is largely deserted, punctuated here and there by truly primitive fishing settlements and some breathtaking scenery. Sadly, the unobstructed shoreline also tempts jeep and *bugue* drivers to make the trip, occasionally spoiling a quiet day of hiking. This is most likely to happen on weekends and Brazilian holidays, and even then only at low tide. Most of the time, you'll encounter only donkey-drawn carts hauling firewood and fish.

Hiking down the coast, you'll first hit Majorlândia, just 7km southeast of Canoa. Majorlândia is a fishing town and popular beach resort, quite crowded on weekends. From here, travellers often hire *bugue* drivers to take them along the beach as far as Ponta Grossa; this trip takes about an hour and costs US$50 for 3–4 people. It's also a popular place to hire rides in *jangadas* (US$5–$7 pp for about an hour trip, but bargain). If you want to skip this 7km stretch, take the bus to Aracati from Fortaleza (see above), then hire a jeep to take you directly to Majorlândia, 12km east, continuing on foot from there. About 3km south of Majorlândia lies Quixabá, much smaller than its neighbour to the north, but still with electricity and simple overnight accommodation. Sandstone cliffs and deserted beaches occupy the next 15km to Retiro Grande, 6km from the highway and served by a dirt road. The cliffs are a vivid orange-red, spattered as if by paint with white, purple and brown splotches. Now and then you'll meet women, clothing piled high in pans balanced on their heads, going to wash in freshwater springs. Goats bleat from the cliffside. Here the coast turns slightly northeast, towards the tiny fishing village of Ponta Grossa, which lies another 6km from Retiro Grande.

We stopped here late one afternoon and bought yellow coconuts from the villagers. Sipping the cool, watery milk, Jayne felt a curious kinship with the local fisherfolk; like her, at least half the villagers sported blonde hair, a legacy of 17th century Dutch invaders. They seemed unaccountably shy by Brazilian standards, but we lingered anyway, taking in the bucolic setting. Draped on crude wooden frames lay a handful of nylon fishing nets, the village's single concession to the 20th century. Even the anchors for the half-dozen or so *jangadas* were rustic, hand-made affairs: stones encircled by saplings, then lashed with reeds.

Just beyond Ponta Grossa lies Redonda, a much larger fishing village with electricity and served by a dirt road from Icapuí. (Icapuí, incidentally, is widely reputed to have Ceará's most beautiful women). A bus runs daily to Redonda from Icapuí, which in turn is served by three daily buses from Fortaleza (US$10). A third way to reach Redonda involves catching the so-called 'Misto', an hilariously claptrap cross between bus and *pau-de-arara*. On a daily basis, the 'Misto' leaves the inland city of Mossoró in Rio Grande do Norte, heads to Tibau on the coast, then plies the beach

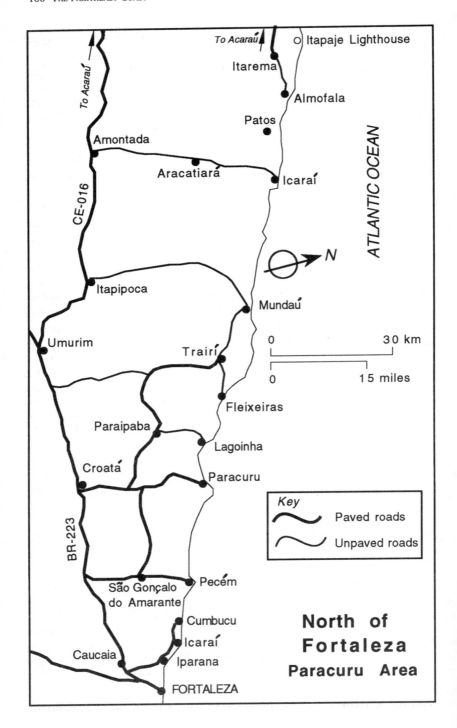

To Acaraú
To Acaraú
O Itapaje Lighthouse
Itarema
Almofala
Patos
Amontada
Aracatiará
Icaraí
CE-016
ATLANTIC OCEAN
N
Itapipoca
Mundaú
Umurim
Trairí
0   30 km
0   15 miles
Fleixeiras
Paraipaba
Lagoinha
Croatá
Paracuru
Key
Paved roads
Unpaved roads
BR-223
Pecém
São Gonçalo
do Amarante
Cumbucu
Icaraí
Caucaia
Iparana
FORTALEZA

North of
Fortaleza
Paracuru Area

north to Redonda. After that, it heads back to the Icapuí and the coastal highway. Not surprisingly, the schedule is highly variable.

Ask around and you'll find cheap, simple lodging in Redonda. We stayed at Fátima and Assis' place, hanging our hammocks in the back room over the snooker tables. The snooker room/dormitory doubles as a dance hall on Sunday afternoon, when couples shuffle around the cement floor to *forró* music. Redonda has no running water, but virtually every home has a well for bathing.

Redonda's *jangada* fleet numbers about eighty, plus a couple of motorboats. We arrived during lobster season, and Dona Fátima apologized profusely that she could serve us no fish; we had to settle for lobster or go hungry.

South from Redonda you'll pass the beaches of Picos and Barreiras. Our thirst got the better of us in Praia dos Picos, and we stopped at one of half a dozen huts for coconut water. The owner turned out to be a lobster fisherman, prematurely wrinkled from years of salt spray and sunshine. Two of his three children had blonde hair. He scurried inside to provide us with wooden benches and sent one of his sons shimmying up the nearest tree for coconuts. Rather than allow us to drink and eat directly from the husk, he insisted on bringing glasses and spoons for his distinguished guests. Such hospitality is typical not only of Ceará, but also of hinterlands throughout the northeast.

Continuing south, past Icapuí and Ibicuitaba (both served by a road, but some distance inland from the beach itself), the inshore bluffs and sandstone formations gradually disappear. The last settlement you'll find in Ceará is Tremembé, some 8 or 9km from Ibicuitaba and within sight of Tibau, Rio Grande do Norte. Tremembé has electricity and gets a few weekenders, but remains a fairly placid fishing town. Some of the lobster fishing here is done by divers. Using helmets and surface-supplied air, they'll spend four or five days at sea before returning with their catch. Freshwater fish abound in the nearby rivers but, as is typical in northeast beach towns, the residents absolutely refuse to eat them.

Just before reaching Tibau you'll have to cross a small river; there's a ferry of sorts operating during the day.

North of Fortaleza

The first decent beach starts 35km north of the city after about a one hour bus ride: Cumbuco. Not surprisingly, Cumbuco draws a lot of people on the weekends, but the beach is deserted beyond the point to the north for some 10km.

Paracuru lies 101km northwest of Fortaleza; eight direct buses run there daily (US$5, 2½ hours). This town of 30,000 boasts electricity, running water, several cheap hotels and rustic *barracas* on the beach. A real sleeper of a town when we first visited in 1984, Paracuru has since groomed itself as the Carnaval party headquarters of Ceará. Nevertheless, the beaches just east and northwest remain largely deserted most of the year. They are wide and open, flanked by low-lying dunes but without the characteristic sandstone bluffs commonly found south of Fortaleza. The wooden structures just offshore are *armadilhas*, crude but efficient fish traps tended daily by the locals. You can hike for hours east of town.

Northwest of Paracuru some 18km lies Lagoinha, a gorgeous beach town that has become extremely popular with weekenders and weekend daytrippers from Fortaleza. French pirates reportedly used the area as a hideout. There are several good pousadas, including Pousada do Milton right on the beach (US$30). Seu Milton is a longtime resident of the area, something of a local legend, and very friendly. Hiking is good in either direction from the busy town beach, with a beautiful dune directly to the east and Lagoa da Barra, a lake surrounded by towering sand-dunes, about 3km to the west. Go during the week to avoid crowds and *bugues* on the beach. There are three direct buses daily from the Fortaleza *rodoviária*, leaving at 07.30, 13.30, and 15.30 (US$5.50, three hours via Paraipaba).

From Lagoinha to Acaraú, a distance of some 115km, the coast is seldom visited, though accessible by bus from Fortaleza via the towns of Trairí, Icaraí, Acaraú and Itarema. The beach closest to Lagoinha is called Fleixeiras, followed 11km to the northwest by Mundaú. You can walk to Mundaú from Fleixeiras at low tide, or take the bus. Both Fleixeiras and Mundaú are accessed by two daily buses from Fortaleza via Trairí (US$6, four hours). In Fleixeiras, the most developed of the two, you'll find lodging at Pousada da Célia and O Coqueiro, both around US$15–$25, as well as the more upscale Hotel Solar das Fleixeiras. Next to the town church, you can visit the workshop where Chico Pires builds and repairs *jangadas*. In Mundaú, lodging can be found at Mundaú Dunas Hotel, Sombra dos Coqueiros, or Brisa do Mar, all around US$25. Another option in Mundaú is the Casa de Retiro Estrela do Mar, a Catholic religious retreat charging US$10 with a great view of the beach; you'll need to call ahead for reservations (tel: 085 351 1220). Roughly 6km east of Mundaú, and an easy day hike, is the fishing village and beautiful beach of Guajirú.

Continuing northwest along the coast, the primitive beaches of Baleia, Pracianos and Marinheiros are accessible via Itapipoca, reached by daily bus from Fortaleza. Further yet is Almofala, a fishing village at the very end of a dirt road 180km northwest of Fortaleza. The asphalt runs out at Itarema, 10km away and the last point on most maps of the area. A direct bus from Fortaleza goes once a day to Almofala via Acaraú (US$10). The village is partially ringed by sand-dunes, although they are somewhat less spectacular than those surrounding Jericoacoara or Canoa Quebrada. For fifty years, the town church, Nossa Senhora da Conceição, lay mostly buried by shifting sands until the winds – or Providence – uncovered it again in the 1940s. Coconut palms and mango trees ring the village; mangoes are so plentiful that the locals actually feed them to their pigs. Inland, much of the terrain has been planted with *carnaúba* palms, which produce the world's finest car polishing wax.

Almofala has no running water, no hotels, and no restaurants, but lodging

Above: *Fork lightning over Barcelos on the Rio Negro* (GR)

Below: *Sunset on the Rio Negro, north of Manaus* (GR)

LAZY DAYS ON THE RIVER
Above: *Water taxis, Manaus* (GR)
Below left: *Pushing the ferry off a sandbar in the Solimões River* (GR)
Below right: *Hammock accommodation on the* Dom Manoel, *which plies the Solimões
River from Manaus to Tabatinga* (GR)   Opposite: (GR)

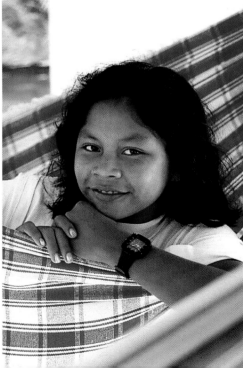

Above: *Teatro Amazonas (Opera House), Manaus* (GR)

Below: *Palacio de Justiça, Manaus* (GR)

in a local fisherman's home runs to about US$10 with two meals a day (provide your own hammock). Huts down by the beach can be rented long-term. We were the only outsiders in the village except for a fellow boarder, an itinerant projectionist who travelled the backlands showing 16mm films on whatever reasonably flat surface he could find. A whitewashed garden wall served as movie screen in this particular case. That night the whole town turned out for a Chinese martial-arts film, badly subtitled in Portuguese – the subtitles themselves were only partially visible. No one complained, however, and the projectionist had to explain what should have been obvious to us from the start: the villagers were, without exception, illiterate.

The beach south of Almofala remains absolutely deserted for 11km; there you'll find a freshwater lagoon surrounded by dunes and the tiny lobster-fishing community of Patos. The coast north of Almofala is even more remote, with the Itapajé lighthouse, at 17km, the only structure evident.

Beyond Almofala lies a string of deserted beaches like Barrinha and Praia Formosa, some semi-developed spots like Preá, and Ceará's most celebrated beach, Jericoacoara. Until a decade ago, Jericoacoara lay claim to being Ceará's – and perhaps Brazil's – most spectacularly secluded beach. Even in 1984, when we first visited, Jericoacoara had already acquired a certain mystique among off-the-beaten-track types. Jeri's saving grace was that it lay *so far* off the beaten track that very few people did anything but talk about it.

We landed there the first time via public bus from Fortaleza's main terminal, arriving at the town of Cruz eight hours later. After much lingering, we caught the twice-weekly *pau-de-arara* to Mangue Seco, a four-hour ride over dusty dirt roads. By then it was pitch black, so we hired two young boys to lead us down a forest path to the Atlantic. They pointed to a dim light in the eastern distance, the mast light of a lobster boat anchored off Jeri, and we were on our own. After an 11km beach hike, we tramped into town and rented a fisherman's hut. The next morning, we bathed at the town water-pump, surrounded by local children who followed us for most of the day.

Our second trip involved a six-hour bus ride from Fortaleza to Gijoca, some 10km southeast of Jeri. We spurned the offers of young villagers offering to guide visitors over the dunes, and instead headed north on our own. Rain had come to the northeast after a five-year drought, and between the dunes we sometimes found placid freshwater lagoons ringed by palm trees – the classic cinematic oasis.

Only twice did we meet people. It didn't take us long to realize that getting directions in the dune country of northwestern Ceará was an altogether different type of proposition than asking a Fortaleza banker the whereabouts of the city post office. For one thing, the locals here used *leguas* (leagues) rather than kilometres; they spoke with a pleasant but virtually undecipherable accent; they used a slight jerk of the head to indicate either that the village was just over the next dune, or that it was a day's journey; and finally, they knew Jericoacoara by a different name: *Serrote*.

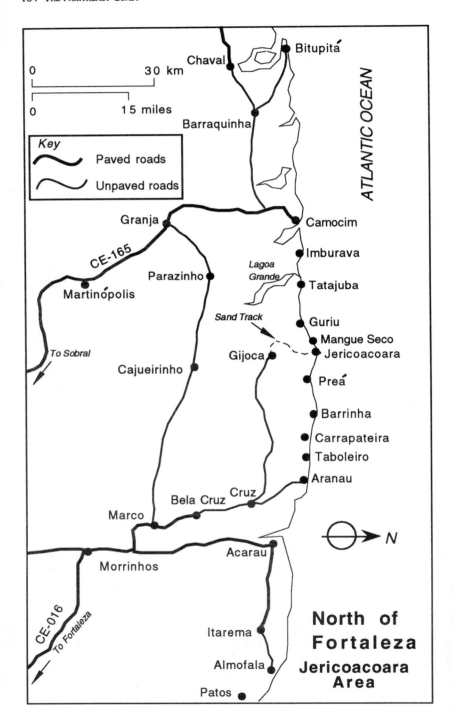

North of
Fortaleza

Jericoacoara
Area

But the setting sun proved a reliable compass and we trudged into Jeri just as the last light faded.

These days, getting to Jericoacoara is considerably easier. Indeed, a trip to Jericoacoara is as *de rigueur* in Ceará as riding the cable-car up Pão de Açucar is for tourists in Rio. I was frankly reluctant to return to Jeri when researching this edition, and there is no doubt that the once-bucolic fishing village has been forever changed by tourism. But while Jeri may no longer quite qualify as a hideaway, the landscape for many kilometres around the village remains idyllic and post-card gorgeous. As with so many other northeast beach towns, you can find solitude by simply slipping on your daypack and walking a bit. And, despite the hordes of travellers, long-time residents of the town remain affable, courteous and genuinely delighted when you take the time to chat.

To reach Jeri, take the Redenção buses which leave the Fortaleza bus terminal daily at 09.00 and 21.00 (US$15). The day bus will get you to Jeri in about 8½ hours, while the night bus makes fewer stops, arriving in about seven hours. The night bus is also cooler and less crowded. In either case, you'll have to disembark the bus in Gijoca (*aka* Jijoca) and transfer to a passenger truck (the *Jardineira*) for the 45-minute ride to Jeri; the price of the *Jardineira* is included in your fare from Fortaleza. The last half hour of the trip is over a soft sand track. The *Jardineira* leaves Jeri on the return trip daily at 06.00 and 22.00; buy tickets and catch the truck outside the Pousada Casa de Turismo, near the western edge of town at the base of the big sand dune. If you're coming by car, you'll only be able to drive as far as Gijoca. At that point, leave your car with one of the local pousada owners (about US$5) and either wait for the *Jardineira* or hire a truck or *bugue* to Jeri (roughly US$30 for up to six people).

Regardless of which bus you take, you'll be met by touts for the local pousadas, of which there are scores in the US$12–30 range. Jeri has only a few dirt streets, so you can easily canvass most places on foot. You can often bargain for better prices in the off-season. Most pousadas have electricity only until about 22.00. Good choices include the Isalana (on the main street), the Calanda, and the Pousada Casa de Turista. You can also rent houses fairly cheaply (ask around), or camp. Camping in the town itself is possible next to the Pousada do Véio and the Senzala Italian restaurant. There's a small phone office on the main street, and the Casa de Turista sells stamps, posts letters, and changes cash and travellers cheques. A small market on the main street sells bottled water and snacks. There are numerous small cafés, mostly specialising in fish dishes.

Jeri lies nestled at the base of massive white sand-dunes that roll inland as far as the eye can see. Palm trees flank the village, and there are places where the dunes have literally buried them up to their tops. You can still buy postcards showing a particular cluster of palms west of town that were evident during my first visit in 1984, but which have since been completely swallowed up by the shifting sands.

Just east of town, the women of Jeri still comb the rocks at low tide, collecting sea salt that has dried in tiny natural pockets. Village children pluck an occasional spiny lobster from out of the crevices at the water's edge. Here the dunes give way to sandstone cliffs reminiscent of Ceará's more southerly coast. Climbing to the top of this headland, as you must when the tide comes in, you pass gnarled clumps of cacti rooted in rust-coloured earth. Photos are obligatory at the Pedra Furada, a natural stone archway located on the beach just 2km east of Jeri, as are nightly walks up the principal dune just west of the village to watch the sunset. The dune-filled landscape surrounding Jeri was given protected status in 1984, and *bugues* are forbidden to use all but a few established tracks. About 23km further east is Preá, where you'll find simple lodging at the Pousada Azul do Mar (US$15) and several rustic restaurants and *barracas*. You can walk to Preá and nearby Lago Azul along the beach if the tide is low, or hire a *bugue* in Jeri (roughly US$10 pp).

West of town, the beach is broader and the headlands are replaced by low-lying dunes all the way to Mangue Seco, a small village near the beach about 2km from Jeri. The coast then remains deserted until Guriú, a picturesque fishing village wedged between the river and the beach. A raft stands by to pole hikers and buggies to the village across the mouth of the swift river. Roughly 10km beyond Guriú lies Nova Tatajuba, another coastal village ringed by gargantuan dunes. The village is usually referred to simply as Tatajuba, but the prefix is significant; the original town was engulfed many years ago by shifting sands. There are two simple pousadas here, the Verde Folha and the Pousada Tatajuba (US$12 and US$30, respectively). Just outside town is spectacular dune country, pockmarked with freshwater 'lakes' which form in the pockets during wet years. You can swim in one of the largest lakes near town, Lagoa da Tosta, and eat fried fish at the tiny *barraca* as waves literally lap at your feet. You can walk to Nova Tatajuba from Jeri, the hike taking about a day and requiring a single river crossing by raft at Guriú (US$3). Alternatively, you can hire a sailboat from Jeri to Nova Tatajuba. Contact Seu Manoel, who lives on Jeri's main street, two doors up from the Pousada Isalana. The trip takes about 1½ hours each way, depending on wind and tide, and will cost about US$100 for six people. The easiest way to reach Nova Tatajuba is to hire a *bugue* in Jeri (about US$20 pp, and you'll need at least three people). The ride takes about 1½ hours each way, with side trips up the highest dunes. Ask at your hotel, or inquire at the Jericoacoara Associação de Buggys (JAB), across from the Pousada Capitão Tomaz.

The beaches and villages west of Camocim, a port town and saltworks some 360km from Fortaleza, are still relatively unknown. Our guess is that they'll be the next beaches to be 'discovered' in Ceará. We've heard enticing rumours about Bitupitá, the final Cearense beach on the frontier with the state of Piauí. Camocim can be reached by daily bus from Fortaleza (US$16, 7½ hours).

NATAL

Like most capital cities in the northeast, Natal is likeable but not memorable.
A city of 600,000 people, it provides access to about 380km of coastline in
Rio Grande do Norte state. Natal doesn't currently attract the same crowds
of vacationing Brazilians that cities such as Fortaleza and Salvador do;
consequently, its dune-flanked beaches and fishing villages remain relatively
pristine. But that is changing rapidly as the state and capital city preen
themselves for tourism.

The locals are friendly even by northeastern standards, and some of the
older folk speak rudimentary English; the Americans established a large
airbase here during World War II from which to attack German strongholds
in Africa. Natal itself doesn't offer much to see and the city beaches are
rocky and dismal.

Getting there

Buses run daily to and from Fortaleza (US$20, nine hours), Salvador
(US$32, 20 hours), Recife (US$12, five hours), Rio de Janeiro (US$90, 44
hours), São Paulo, Belém, Aracaju, João Pessoa and hundreds of towns in
Rio Grande do Sul. The 'new' bus station – to distinguish it from the ancient
but centrally-located *rodoviária velha* – lies 7.5km from the centre, in the
Cidade da Esperança neighbourhood. Walk outside and catch the bus marked
'Via Tirol' to get downtown.

The airport, Internacional Augusto Severo, is located 15km from town
in the Eduardo Gomes district. Daily flights serve all the cities mentioned
above plus Belém. To reach the old bus station in the centre of town, catch
the bus marked Aeroporto outside the airport. Taxis to the centre will cost
about US$15.

Where to stay and eat

More and more hotels are popping up in Natal as it becomes more tourism-
oriented. You'll find most cheap lodging in the centre (known as the Cidade
Alta); from there, everything but the bus terminal is within walking distance.
There's a youth hostel, the Albergue da Juventude Ladeira do Sol, at Rua
Valentim de Almeida 10 on the Praia do Artistas, one of the town beaches
(US$10–15 pp), and two other hostels at Ponta Negra, a beach 14km south
of town. One of our favourite hotels in the centre is the Casa Grande at Rua
Princesa Isabel 529 (US$25–40). Another old favourite is the Hotel Bom
Jesus at Avenida Rio Branco 374.

Of the restaurants serving northeastern regional food, O Farol at Avenida
Governador Silvio Pedrosa 132 (Praia de Areia Preta) and Casa de Mãe at
Rua Pedro Afonso 230 (Praia do Meio) are among the best. The restaurant
in the Hotel Casa Grande also turns out tasty regional food.

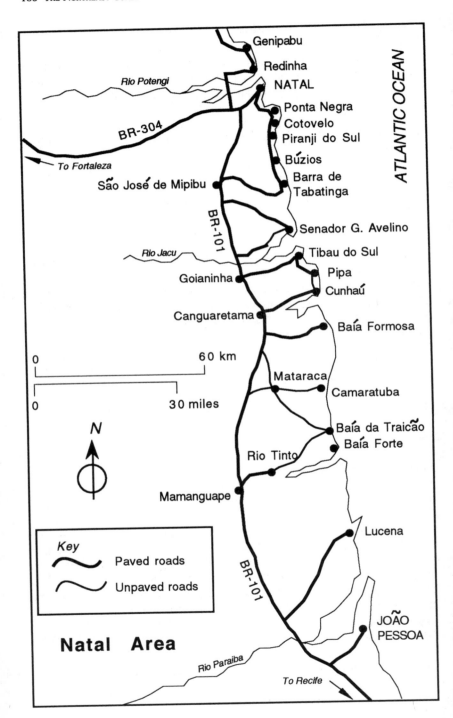

Natal Area

Information and useful addresses

Natal has never been an easy town for changing money, and you're pretty much relegated to the Banco do Brasil at Avenida Rio Branco 510 in the Cidade Alta. There's a câmbio changing cash and cheques, and you can also get cash advances on a VISA card. The Centro de Turismo is yet another converted prison, this one located on a hill overlooking the Praia do Meio, at the end of Rua Aderbal de Figueiredo. Here you'll get secondhand (though fairly reliable) tips on remote beaches in Rio Grande do Sul. There's also an information booth at the new bus station, and a quick-dial telephone number for information (Teleturismo), 1516.

Excursions

Everyone raves about Genipabu and its gigantic *duna*. Just 30km north of Natal, it's unquestionably pretty but hasn't qualified as a pristine, undeveloped beach for many years. Not surprisingly, the truly deserted coastline of Rio Grande do Norte lies much further afield from Natal.

Baía Formosa is a medium-sized fishing town providing access to some 20km of stunningly beautiful beach, extending all the way south to the border with Paraíba state. You can reach Baía Formosa on either of two direct daily buses (one at 11.30 and the other at 18.00) from Natal's new terminal (US$6, 2½ hours), and drops you off on the hill above the harbour. Return buses leave at 05.30 and 14.30 daily. If you're not planning to camp, your best bet is to bring a hammock and rent a local fisherman's cottage. Once the single *pensão* in town, the Miramar charges about US$10 pp for a dungeon of a room facing the sea. Overlooking the beach there's the Pousada dos Golfinhos at Rua Francisco Fernandes Freire 361 (US$25), and practically on the beach is the Pousada Sonho Meu at Rua Dr Manuel Francisco de Melo (US$25–40). Ask at the simple café across the street from the Miramar regarding house rental.Two restaurants in the main plaza (Praça da Conceição) serve good fish and northeastern regional dishes: O Pontinho da Vandete (view of the sea) and Restaurante Elila.

The bay itself blocks much hiking to the north, although a 4km walk will get you to the usually deserted beach of Barra do Cunhaú. You can hire *bugues* at the Pousada dos Golfinhos to take you as far north as Tibau do Sul (US$100 for four people, four hours), passing Praia da Pipa (see below). Walking south from Baía Formosa, you'll pass a few huts before landing on totally unspoiled beach which extends to Paraíba. Along the way you'll pass the beach and lighthouse of Bacopari (1km) and Praia do Sagi (3km). A hired *bugue* to Sagi from the Pousada dos Golfinhos will cost US$45 for four people, 2½ hours. The waves are just big enough to *pegar jacaré* (body surf), and the area is now attracting lots of Brazilian surfers during the summer. A rippling series of tall sand-dunes provides escape from the occasional wind. Bring plenty of fresh water – we never saw any, nor did we run into a single person on this shoreline. Despite the direct bus and its growing reputation as a surfing mecca, tourism is still fairly low-key at Baía Formosa.

To reach Pipa, probably the most scenic and famous of the villages north of Baía Formosa, you can either hire a *bugue* (see above), or you can take a direct bus leaving Natal's new bus terminal at 08.00 or 15.15 daily (US$4, two hours). Also, any bus travelling on BR-101 between Natal and João Pessoa or Recife can drop you off at Goianinha (tell the bus driver to stop) and you can take a daily bus from there to Pipa at 11.00. It's about a two-hour trip over a poor dirt roadway.

Pipa itself consists of about thirty simple houses, about ten pousadas, and a growing number of cafés and bars, all perched on a bluff overlooking the beach. Lodging options include the youth hostel, Albergue da Juventude Enseada dos Golfinhos, just north of town at Rua Projetada 19 (US$14 pp). In town on the main street you'll find the Pousada Troup Praiana, the Pousada Coco Brasil, and the Portal da Pipa, all around US$20–25. The Pousada da Pipa (owned by Chantal, a French woman), Praia do Amor, and Tropical all charge US$30, and the first two have beach views. You can also rent a fisherman's house and sling your hammock, or camp for US$3 pp next to the Espaço Verde restaurant. Other restaurants include the Colher de Pau and Casarão, both serving northeastern regional foods like *paçoca* and *carne-de-sol*. One fellow in town sells vegetables, and there are two tiny stores where you can buy other food items.

Pipa is a fishing village, but like Baía Formosa, its fishermen don't sail the jangadas typical of the northeast. The tides are spectacular here, exposing immense stretches of beach during the ebb, and virtually eliminating it during the flood. Instead of sand-dunes, you'll find impressive reddish-orange cliffs flanking the beach. Hiking is good in both directions, but carry lots of water; there are no settlements or springs nearby.

Many of the hotels and the youth hostel arrange boat or *bugue* trips north to Tibau do Sul, south to Cunhaú, all points in between, and south to Baía Formosa (about US$80 round-trip for four people). North of town is the Baía dos Golfinhos (Bay of the Dolphins), and a boat will take you there to see the namesake dolphins for about US$6 (one or two hours, arrange with the hostel). Buggy trips are offered as well. Also north of town and an easy kilometre walk is the Santuário Ecológico da Pipa, a small nature preserve featuring marked trails and great views of the ocean. You can hike the trails yourself or with a guide, and there's a snack bar and souvenir stand. South of town, a series of beaches (including the ominously-named Praia do Afogado, Drowned Man's Beach) stretches all the way to Barra de Cunhaú. You'll find simple pousadas at both Tibau do Sul and Barra de Cunhaú.

MACEIÓ

Maceió is a pleasant, not particularly interesting port city of 500,000. Vacationing Brazilians flock to the Praia da Pajuçara, a beach just 3km north of the centre that's famous as a *piscina natural*. Lined by a distant coral reef, Pajuçara turns into a vast, shallow pool at low tide, filled with scores of tourist-laden *jangadas*. A mere 45km to the north, however, independent travellers will begin to find the same 'natural swimming pools' in a far more tranquil setting. Visitors spend most of their city time near the beaches of Pajuçara, Ponta Verde, Sete Coqueiros and Jatiúca, all east of the city centre and all offering a variety of hotels, restaurants, and bars. Closer to the city centre are the beaches Praia da Avenida and Praia do Sobral, which are polluted but still have some budget hotels and beachfront restaurants nearby.

Getting there

Daily buses run to Maceió from Salvador (US$22, 10 hours), Recife (US$7, four hours), Aracaju (US$9, five hours), Rio de Janeiro (US$70, 36 hours), São Paulo, João Pessoa, Natal, Penedo and numerous other cities and towns. The bus station is located a good 4km from the city centre and hotels. Many local buses, including those marked 'Feitosa', make the slow trip to the city centre and Pajuçara beach area. Daily flights connect Maceió with Rio, São Paulo, and most other northeastern state capitals. The Campo dos Palmares airport lies 23km from the centre; catch the Rio do Largo bus, which runs downtown along Rua João Pessoa. Taxis to the centre and Pajuçara cost about US$20.

Where to stay and eat

Maceió's city centre has a couple of cheap hotels, but it doesn't make a lot of sense to stay here; downtown Maceió isn't very interesting, and the hotels near Pajuçara beach cost about the same or only a bit more. Good choices in Pajuçara include: Água Verde (Rua Commandante Almeida Guimarães 137), Hotel Glória (Rua Jangadeiros Alagoanos 1119), Hotel Miramar (Rua Conde de Irajá), Pousada Zeide (Rua Dr Antonio Pedro de Mendonça 315), and Pousada Saveiro (Rua Jangadeiros Alagoanos 805). All these pousadas cost about US$30–35. Also at Pajuçara is a youth hostel, the Albergue da Juventude Pajuçara at Rua Quintino Bocaiuva 63, which is close to the beach, organizes tours, and costs US$15 pp with breakfast. The next beach, Ponta Verde, has the youth hostel Albergue da Juventude Nossa Casa (Rua Prefeito Abdon Arroxelas 177, US$15 with breakfast), as well as a number of moderately-priced pousadas, including Mar e Sol (Avenida Robert Kennedy 1447) and the Bela Vista (Rua Mário Gusmão 1260), both around US$35.

Maceió is loaded with beachfront *barracas* serving seafood, and it's a good place to sample the tasty *agulhas fritas* (fried needlefish). Near the

JANGADAS

No other single image conjures up the northeast coast quite as evocatively as does the *jangada*. Jangadas are crude wooden fishing rafts rigged with a single cotton sail, and you cannot possibly wander this part of the coast without seeing scores of them.

Typically, the entire fleet of a small coastal hamlet will sail off in the morning, returning one by one in the afternoon with their catch. During these short trips, the fleet may split up, each raft fishing a separate area. Sometimes, however, depending on the season, the fleet will stay at sea for as many as five consecutive days. During these longer trips, the boats stay within sight of each other, returning to the village en masse.

Launching a jangada in heavy surf requires both strength and split-second timing; the raft is rolled out to the water on two logs, the crew boards, and then a shore crew waits for a light set of waves to begin the final push. We've seen jangadas pitch-pole back onto the beach more than once.

The typical crew of two to five *jangadeiros* per boat carry no compasses or sextants despite the fact that they sail well beyond sight of land even on the day trips. Instead, they rely on an intimate knowledge of winds and tides to bring them back to their own tiny speck of coastline. It's a feat that takes on heroic proportions once you've actually sailed on a jangada.

With about a half metre of freeboard, waves continually wash the deck in even the calmest of seas. There are no bunks; on the overnight trips, jangadeiros must curl up on a wooden deck never more than two metres wide. The only covered space is reserved for the catch and some meagre rations. At regular intervals, the *jangadeiro* must douse the cotton sail with buckets of water so that it holds the wind.

All of this is mere existence at sea – the business of fishing requires a whole separate set of skills. Depending on the season, *jangadeiros* may use either hook-and-line or nylon nets, and the catch is often a mixed bag of grouper, mackerel, skate, shark and eels. Once they're beyond sight of land, *jangadeiros* have only their depth-sounding leadlines and fisherman's sixth sense to locate the fishing grounds. I'm an ex-commercial fisherman myself, and I've asked *jangadeiros* to describe this process in detail. They can't possibly regard me as a competitor – I can't clear the breakwater without LORAN, radar and a full set of nautical charts; still, I get the kind of response you might expect from a chef asked to divulge his recipe for shrimp bisque.

The high point of the afternoon in most coastal hamlets is the return of the jangadas. Women, children and old men – in short, the only members of the village that aren't active *jangadeiros* – crowd around the boats as the catch is pitched ashore. If the fishing has been good, the surplus is up for grabs, and if you're bold you can join in the bargaining. I'd keep this to a minimum – never outbid the locals if they want the fish.

Similarly, I recommend against paying for unsolicited jangada rides in the truly remote coastal villages. By all means go for a jangada ride, but do so in Maceió or Recife or Canoa Quebrada; the experience will be the same, and you won't be undermining a fishing economy with tourist dollars, turning *jangadeiros* into sightseeing guides.

Jagandas

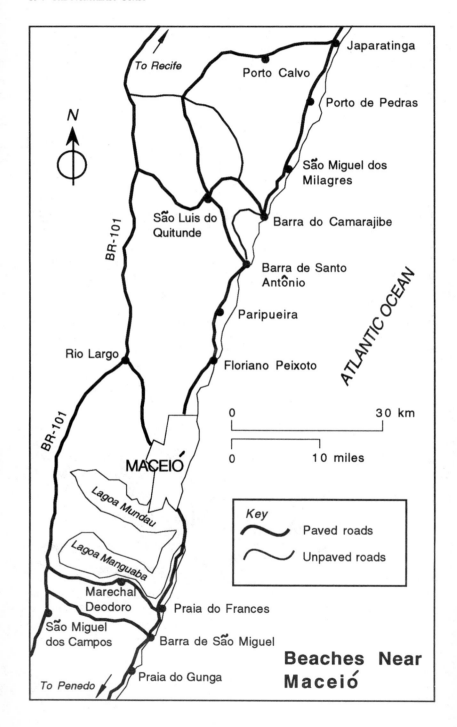

Beaches Near Maceió

city centre at Praia da Avenida, Lagostão at Avenida Duque de Caxias 1384 serves good seafood, including the namesake spiny lobster. Near the Pajuçara beach, O Komilão at Rua Domingos Lordsleen 848 and Clã Destinos at Rua Commandante Almeida Guimarães 482 both serve reasonably-priced local seafood dishes.

Information and useful addresses

Banco do Brasil at Rua do Livramento 120 changes cash and cheques, and advances cash on VISA cards. You can also try the local travel agencies; sometimes they're buying travellers cheques, sometimes not. The state tourism authority, Ematur, staffs an information booth at the airport, at Avenida Duque de Caxias 2014 near the beach downtown, and at Pajuçara beach. They are extremely helpful with current hotel listings (including prices). Local handicrafts, including hammocks, can be bought at the Mercado de Artesanato in the Parque Rio Branco, located downtown at Rua Melo de Morais 617. Artisans also set up stalls along the Avenida Dr Antonio Gouveia on Pajuçara beach.

Excursions

With so many beaches nearby, most vacationing Brazilians stay within 20km of town. Of the populated beaches, our favourite is Praia do Francês (with great bodysurfing) 22km south of the centre via *kombi* from Praia do Sobral, or via scheduled bus to Marechal Deodoro from the bus station. Garça Torta, 14km to the north, is especially fun on weekends; take the Fátima bus from downtown. At *barracas* at either beach, try the *agulhas fritas*, tiny fried fish with an elongated needle-like snout.

But for a truly idyllic stretch of deserted coastline, plan on hiking north from Barra de Santo Antônio, 45km north of Maceió. Buses run daily from the city terminal to Barra de Santo Antônio. Plenty of small boats are available here at the dock along the Avenida Pedro Cavalcanti, most of them taking visitors to nearby Ilha da Croa (US$8 pp). Hire one instead to take you across the Santo Antônio River; just on the other side you'll find a smaller village, fringed by coconut palms and the last outpost of civilization for the next two days of walking. Once on the beach, simply head north toward a second, much smaller fishing town, Barra do Camarajibe. Bring along plenty of fresh water; you'll find only one *fonte* (spring) after you leave Barra de Santo Antônio – and it's located just south of Barra do Camarajibe, where there's plenty of water anyway. Local maps put Antônio and Barra do Camarajibe 13km apart, but that's along the dirt road to Porto de Pedras; along the undulating coastline, it is considerably longer, demanding about two days of leisurely hiking.

The coast between Antônio and Barra do Camarajibe consists of a series of spectacular, crescent-shaped bays separated by headlands and bluffs to the east. Not a single human dwelling stands here, probably owing to the lack of fresh water. One of the beaches along this stretch is known locally as Carro Quebrado (Broken Car), presumably because of the rugged terrain.

Once in Barra do Camarajibe, where pousadas are now popping up, you'll have to find a boat to cross the river if you plan to continue along the coast. This stretch of beach, to São Miguel dos Milagres and thence to Porto de Pedras, is reportedly uncluttered and attractive. Buses run daily from Porto de Pedras back to Maceió.

SALVADOR

Until 1763, Salvador reigned as Brazil's capital city. Today it vies with São as the cultural capital of the country, and with Rio as the centre of tourism. Salvador boasts the best musicians (Caetano Veloso, Gilberto Gil, Gal Costa, Maria Bethânia and Moraes Moreira, among many others), the most churches (reputedly one for each day of the year), the most famous poets and authors (among them Jorge Amado), the richest and spiciest food, and the most vibrantly African influence of any Brazilian city. It also provides a home base from which to explore Bahia's 880km of palm-strewn shoreline.

Salvador lies at the entrance to the vast Baía de Todos os Santos, which lends the city its full name, Salvador da Bahia. Frequently referred to simply as *Bahia*, Salvador is a sprawling metropolis, but travellers find that most everything of interest lies close to the city centre. The centre is divided into two sections: the Cidade Baixa (lower city), where most businesses are located, and the Cidade Alta (upper city), the older part of town containing the major historical sites and cheap hotels. A century-old elevator joins the two cities. The heart of the upper city is the Pelourinho, the square where slaves were whipped in colonial times, now a picturesque maze of baroque architecture, cobbled streets, outdoor cafés, and vendors of all sorts. Everything in the upper city is within reasonable walking distance, but the bus system for all other parts of the city can be confusing. Ask at any of the Bahiatursa tourist information desks for help.

Getting there

Salvador can be reached on daily flights from all major Brazilian cities via the national airlines, including those offering air passes: Varig, Vasp, and Transbrasil. Daily flights also connect Salvador with Miami, Frankfurt, Lisbon, Madrid, Paris, and Asunción, Paraguay. Dois de Julho airport is 30km from the city centre, and taxis are expensive, roughly US$30 (buy tickets at the booth inside the airport). The air-conditioned *executivo* bus to the city centre, colloquially called the *frescão,* is much cheaper (US$2.50), but takes roughly 1½ hours to reach its final destination at the Praça da Sé, taking a coastal route past the beach and hotels in Barra. Catch the bus, marked 'Praça da Sé', on the sidewalk right outside the airport. There's a Bahiatursa tourist information booth located in the airport that can provide up-to-date information on transportation and lodging in Salvador; open daily from 08.30–22.00.

Salvador can be reached by daily bus from all the major Brazilian cities, including Rio (28 hours, US$50), São Paulo (30 hours, US$57), and Recife (13 hours, US$27). Salvador's bus station, located directly across the street from the city's huge Iguatemi shopping complex, is only 5km from the city centre, but you won't believe it if you take a bus there. The Rodoviária-Sé local bus takes at least 45 minutes of tortuous winding to negotiate this distance. Other buses, equally slow, run to Campo Grande, Terminal de Barroquinha, and Avenida da França. Except for the Sé bus, you'll still be let off some distance from the cheap hotel district in the upper city near the Pelourinho. Splurge and take a cab (about US$7) if you've got baggage; tickets for taxis are sold at a booth in the bus station. For the latest information on local transportation, check at the Bahiatursa tourist information booth inside the station, open daily 09.00–21.00.

Where to stay and eat

Except during Carnaval, when Salvador fills to overcapacity with revellers, you should have no problem finding reasonable lodging in the upper city, the throbbing centre of cultural life. Best deals are the youth hostels (*albergues da juventude*), four of which are located in the heart of the Pelourinho: Albergue do Passo, Albergue das Laranjeiras, Albergue Solar, and Albergue Pelô. These all run to about US$12–$15 pp, and are much nicer than many of the hotels in the area. Another good choice is the Hotel Pelourinho at Rua Alfredo de Brito 20, where a plaque in the lobby informs guests that Jorge Amado penned his novel *Suor* here as a student (perhaps not the best recommendation given the fact that *suor* means perspiration!). Other reasonably-priced hotels in the upper city include the Hotel Chile at Rua Chile 7, the Solara at Rua José Alencar 25, and the Themis in the Praça da Sé. Many other hotels are located near the beach in Barra district, a short bus ride from the centre.

Bahian cooking is a national treasure, and if you like spicy, African-inspired cuisine, you will eat better in Salvador than anywhere else in Brazil. See *Chapter Four* for a description of Bahian foods. Don't miss the quintessential Bahian finger-food, *acarajé*, a bean fritter fried in aromatic *dendê* palm oil then filled to order with a mixture of dried shrimp, peppers, ground cashews and spices. They're made and sold on streetcorners throughout the city by Bahian women (*baianas*) decked out in flowing white dresses and strings of beads. Line up behind the locals and when your turn comes let the *baiana* know how you want your *acarajé* (*com tudo* means 'with everything'), and how much pepper sauce you'd like her to smear on the fritter; you'll probably have an audience if you order yours *bem quente* (really spicy).

I could survive happily on *acarajé* alone, but travellers who want a bit more culinary latitude have literally hundeds of restaurants to choose from in Salvador. Places serving good Bahian cuisine in the upper city include Dona Chica Ka, Cantina da Lua, Novo Tempo, Bargaç and Temporo da

Dada (these are all splurges for budget travellers, but worth it). The Escola Senac cooking school at Largo do Pelourinho 13 offers a daily buffet of forty Bahian dishes for US$15. There is the usual assortment of *comida por kilo* places and other budget cafés throughout the city. One caveat: many travellers experience some intestinal discomfort with Bahian food. Dendê oil, which gives local dishes their heady aroma and bright orange colour, is practically indigestible, so go easy on your first day of sampling Bahia's exotic cuisine.

Information and useful addresses

Finding your way around Salvador can be challenging, at least in part because residents don't know or use street names on a regular basis. Many streets aren't signposted, and those that are frequently go by another name, as do many of the squares and plazas.

Bahiatursa, the state tourist agency, has a central office in the upper city just off Rua da Miseracórdia and not far from the Lacerda elevator; follow the signs from the street down a stairway to the agency's office overlooking the bay and lower city. They're open daily from 08.00–18.00, providing very helpful advice on city lodging (including private homes renting rooms), money changing, transportation, music, and cultural events such as music, *capoeira*, and *candomblé*. They offer free maps of the Pelourinho and upper city, and sell more detailed city maps. There's also a message board and a guide to weekly events. Bahiatursa also staffs information booths at the bus station, airport, and the Mercado Modelo in the lower city.

Banks are about the only option for changing cash and travellers cheques, but fortunately there are plenty of them with câmbios in all areas of the city frequented by travellers. Banco do Brasil changes money at the airport (open 08.30–21.00 Mon-Fri, 09.00–16.00 Sat, Sun, and holidays), as well as at branches in the Pelourinho, the lower city, the Iguatemi shopping complex (across from the bus station), and the Barra hotel district. Banco Econômico in the Pelourinho also changes cash and cheques. Ask at Bahiatursa for other money-changing options.

Excursions

Salvador's popularity with both Brazilian and European travellers means that remote coastline in the state of Bahia is getting tougher and tougher to find. Fortunately, if you avoid the holiday seasons and hike past the villages where visitors stay congregated, you'll still find plenty of the real Brazil.

North of Salvador

As you head north from Salvador towards the border with neighbouring Sergipe state, you'll discover a string of gorgeous beaches and fishing villages. These begin north of Imbassaí, and extend all the way to the border. The whole stretch of coastline was made more accessible in 1993 with the opening of the Linha Verde (Green Line) highway. Buses from Salvador cruise the Linha Verde's 142km on a daily basis, and you can't go wrong getting off virtually anywhere. You can also drive the Linha Verde in a rental car, but to reach some of the more remote beaches you'll have to leave your car in a village and proceed by *bugue*, bus or on foot.

Mangue Seco lies 223km north of Salvador, tucked amidst sand-dunes along the border with the state of Sergipe. Jorge Amado chose the pastoral setting for his novel *Tieta do Agreste* and several of his relatives still live in the village. Film crews invaded Mangue Seco in 1989 to make a television series based on the novel, and in 1995 returned to produce the movie version, starring Sônia Braga in the title role. Fame boosted tourism in Mangue Seco – so much so that the envious citizens of neighbouring Jandaíra voted to change their town's name to Santana do Agreste, Tieta's fictional village in the book and movie. Tourism, however, dropped off once the TV show and movie faded from public view, and Mangue Seco, though not exactly forgotten, remains bucolic.

Sand-dunes over 20 metres high dominate the landscape in Mangue Seco, and over the years their natural shifting has gradually buried palm trees, streets and even houses. You'll find six pousadas and four restaurants in this town of 300 people. The fanciest is the Hotel Village, with doubles costing US$40 and a swimming pool; the cheapest is the home of Doña Berenice, who calls her place Grão de Areia and rents rooms for US$20 for two people. In between are Telma's Pousada and the Hotel Mangue Seco, and two other pousadas in the town of Pontal across the river (Portal do Sol and Seu Fontes, costing US$10–25 for a double). The town's few pousadas fill up during Brazilian holidays. You can also camp anywhere along the beach, which lies about 1.5km from the village. If you don't feel like carrying your things, a tractor makes daily trips to and from the beach when the weather's good, charging US$1 pp.

Amado's novel described the difficult road conditions on the way to Mangue Seco, and things haven't changed a great deal since Tieta's time. The best access is via the town of Pontal in Sergipe, but even this road is a tortuous, bumpy track which demands four-wheel drive. You're far better off catching the bus for Pontal which leaves Estância daily at 16.00. The bus heads south to Indiaroba, then west for another 13km over a terrible dirt track straight out of Amado's novel. You can also catch the bus when it stops in Indiaroba. Once in Pontal, you still need to cross the Rio Real to Mangue Seco, a 10–20 minute boat ride costing US$1 pp. If you miss the last scheduled boat, you can either bargain for a ride (about US$15 per trip), or simply stay the night in Pontal and continue to Mangue Seco in the morning by road.

Mangue Seco – the town's official name is Santa Cruz da Bela Vista – is the most northerly village along the coast of Bahia. From Mangue Seco, you can hike the coast south past towering sand-dunes, or hire a *bugue* driver for the trip. Here begins a string of isolated beaches, accessed via the Linha Verde highway from the towns of (from north to south): Sítio do

Conde, Barra do Itariri, Baixio, Subaúma, Massarundupió, Porto Saúfpe, and Imbassaí. All of these towns lie between two and ten kilometres from the Linha Verde highway, and all are served either directly or indirectly by buses from Salvador. The towns themselves aren't great destinations, and some can get quite crowded on Brazilian holidays, but they serve as jumping-off points for many miles of deserted and semi-deserted beaches. Sítio is the most developed of these towns, and to the north (some 12km) lies the village of Siribinha, between the beach and the Rio Itapicuru. There's a pousada here, several tiny stores selling food and drink, and unlimited possibilities for camping. Green sea turtles lay eggs on the beach at Massarundupió, where an environmental group keeps tabs on them; there's a single pousada and camping is permitted.

South of Salvador
Morro de São Paulo, like Ceará's Jericoacoara, has finally been 'discovered'. Soon it may turn into another Canoa Quebrada, but its stunning beaches, clear water, and tranquil (as yet) fishing village still make Morro de São Paulo a deserving destination. It also has the distinction of an island setting, but it's one that you pay for dearly; virtually everything but fish must be shipped from the mainland so that food is extremely expensive. Stock up before leaving Salvador.

From Salvador, take one of the many daily buses to Valença. Because the buses drive all the way around the Baía de Todos os Santos, it's a 272km, five-hour journey. If you're successful in hitching a ride with a private motorist, you'll go via Itaparica Island, a much more direct route. Plan on spending the night in Valença if you get there much later than 17.00, when the last scheduled boat leaves.

Boats to Morro de São Paulo leave theValença dock seven times a day beginning at 07.30 and ending at 17.00; five return trips are made per day, from 06.00 to 17.00. The fare is US$2 and the trip takes about two hours. During the high season and on weekends, large boats leave directly from the Mercado Modelo in Salvador, reaching Morro de São Paulo in about four hours. From Valença, there are other, smaller craft bound for the island of Tinharé and Morro de São Paulo which follow no set schedule but will charge more. Check the ferry schedule with Bahiatursa in Salvador; additional boats run in the summer, but the island is besieged during that time with visitors.

Boats stop first at the village of Gamboa, surrounded by mangroves, picking up and discharging passengers, then continue on to Morro de São Paulo. The entrance is dominated by the huge stone portal of the fort and prison constructed here in 16.30. Continue up the steep hill to the village itself and a 19th century lighthouse.

The village consists of but a single street.You'll find lodging in a number of simple pensions or else rent a house from the locals. Beds are available here, so you won't need a hammock. Camping is possible along the beach on the eastern side of the island. Even with sea breezes, the place can be insufferably hot, but if you leave your shutters open be prepared for guests; huge swarms of bats fill the night skies around Morro de São Paulo. One of the draws here is the crystal-clear water, an anomaly along most of Brazil's coast. Virtually all of the eastern side of the island, extending 35km, contains white-sand beach. If Morro de São Paulo isn't laid-back enough for your tastes, continue to the neighbouring Ilha de Boipeba, a bucolic spot with about half a dozen pousadas. Boats to Boipeba leave Valença daily (four hours), as do boats from Morro de São Paulo (two hours).

Two final reminders: avoid Morro de São Paulo during Brazilian holidays, and bring as much of your own food as possible.

Continuing south along Bahia's coast, you'll reach Camamu, a pleasant town in its own right, and a good jumping-off spot for exploring the wild and idyllic Maraú peninsula. Buses run daily to Camamu from Salvador, via Valença. Camamu commands a gorgeous view of Brazil's deepest bay, a green maze of mangrove islands, and Maraú peninsula in the distance. The baroque church of Nossa Senhora da Assunção, built in 1631, oversees this vista, and the town's steep cobbled streets are full of colonial facades. With some thought to preservation, this unpretentious little town could become even prettier. There are two hotels, costing between US$20–50: the Green House (in the lower city by the docks); and the Rio Acaraí (a modern place with swimming pool and great views in the upper city; very reasonable in the off-season). The Green House serves cheap, hearty meals, including tasty fish *moquecas*. Women in festive white dresses sell Bahian bean fritters (*acarajé*) on the street corners, and there's a good, smelly fish market along the waterfront.

But people mostly come to Camamu to catch boats bound for Barra Grande, a small fishing and resort settlement at the northern tip of the Maraú peninsula. Although the peninsula is in theory accessible by road from Ubaitaba, the 80km of bumpy dirt road leading to Barra Grande is terrible, and getting worse yearly. Most rental cars won't make it, and even a good high-clearance car will take four hours to negotiate the distance. Even the bus no longer goes from Ubaitaba all the way to Barra Grande (although it will get you within about 12km). The easiest and most scenic way to visit Barra Grande is via boat from Camamu.

During the summer, the ferry *Sid Narref* makes two trips per day to Barra Grande, leaving the dock at Camamu at 09.15 and 18.15. Depending on tides, the trip takes about two hours and costs US$3 pp. The ferry returns to Camamu at 07.00 and 15.30. During the week, you could also try hitching a ride with the boat that ferries children back from school, the *Lágrima de Criança*. Boats also leave for Barra Grande from Igrapiúna, a town about 15km north of Camamu.

A number of smaller boats can also be hired for trips to Barra Grande.

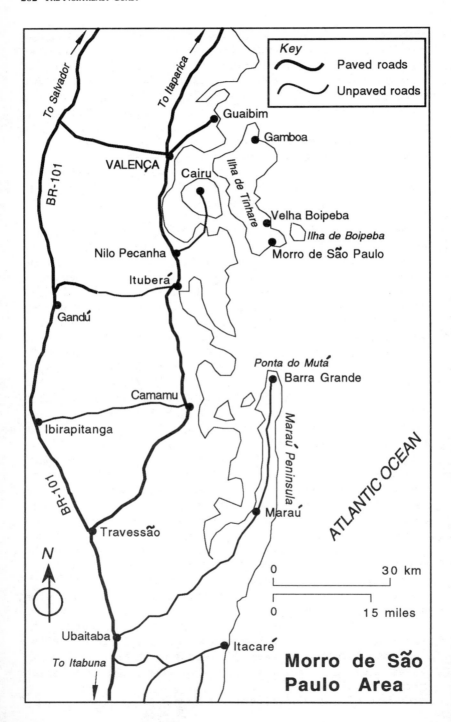

Key

Paved roads

Unpaved roads

To Salvador

To Itaparica

BR-101

Guaibim

Gamboa

VALENÇA

Cairu

Ilha de Tinharé

Velha Boipeba

Nilo Pecanha

Ilha de Boipeba

Iuberá

Morro de São Paulo

Gandú

Ponta do Mutá

Barra Grande

Camamu

Maraú Peninsula

Ibirapitanga

ATLANTIC OCEAN

BR-101

Maraú

Travessão

N

0 ⎯⎯⎯⎯⎯⎯ 30 km

0 ⎯⎯⎯⎯⎯⎯ 15 miles

Ubaitaba

Itacaré

To Itabuna

Morro de São Paulo Area

These will be your only option outside the busy summer months, but at least they provide a more personalised tour of the area. You'll often be approached by boat skippers with an offer during the off-season, but sometimes you'll need to comb the docks. One of the best skippers in town is Andre Barbosa, skipper of the *Feliz Natal* (Merry Christmas). He can be reached by calling his sister on 073 255 2200, or simply asking around on the docks. Andre will put together a day-long cruise for roughly US$18 pp, assuming three people.

The scenic two hour trip to Barra Grande passes first through the placid Baía de Camamu, a mangrove-lined waterway where fishermen tend their crab pots and silvery needlefish flit across the surface of the water like skipping stones. The closest beach is Ponta do Sono, followed by the tiny island called Pedra Furada, roughly an hour out of Camamu in the middle of the channel. Pedra Furada (Hole in the Rock) is a good place for a picnic, but so are many of the isolated islands and beaches nearby. These include Ilha de Campinho where, besides many kilometres of beach, there are three pousadas, a calm inlet, numerous summer homes and piers, and a rock quarry. On the other side of the bay is Ilha Grande and Praia de Goió, a gorgeous white-sand beach. Boat lovers will want to stop in the tiny mainland town of Cajaíba, where the men build massive wooden schooners which are famous throughout Brazil. The locals are justifiably proud of their boats, and you'll probably be invited to climb aboard a schooner under construction.

Barra Grande itself doesn't have much useable beach; it's crowded with elaborate fish traps made of sticks lashed together with reeds. But walk in either direction and you'll quickly find yourself on isolated beaches. Those on the bay side are predictably calm, while those on the ocean side are wilder and wave-battered. Much of the ocean side beachfront is also paved with solid, sharp rocks, but there are occasional sand-filled lagoons which are semi-sheltered and good for swimming. Rounding the peninsula's tip at Ponta do Mutá, the first you'll come to is the beach called Três Coqueiros, where there's a friendly pousada of the same name (tel: 073 255 2112). Owner Camilo Silva Reis rents out rooms with private bath for US$30, cabanas for US$15, and grassy campsites for US$5 pp. There's a restaurant and bar, and Seu Camilo can arrange for *bugue* rides anywhere on the Maraú peninsula. In the fishing village of Barra Grande itself, there are a handful of pousadas, including Tuburão, Meu Sossego, Maria de Firmino, and the Entrada do Sol. All of these cost about US$15–30, and most serve meals.

The entire Maraú peninsula is loaded with beaches, and those on the wave-swept ocean side are isolated even during the summer high months. There are pousadas for overnight stays at beaches like Cassange and Saquaíra, but camping is also possible. Other good, swimmable beaches on the peninsula include Bela, Taipus de Fora, Algodões and Arandi. All the way at the peninsula's southern end, near the picturesque town of Itacaré

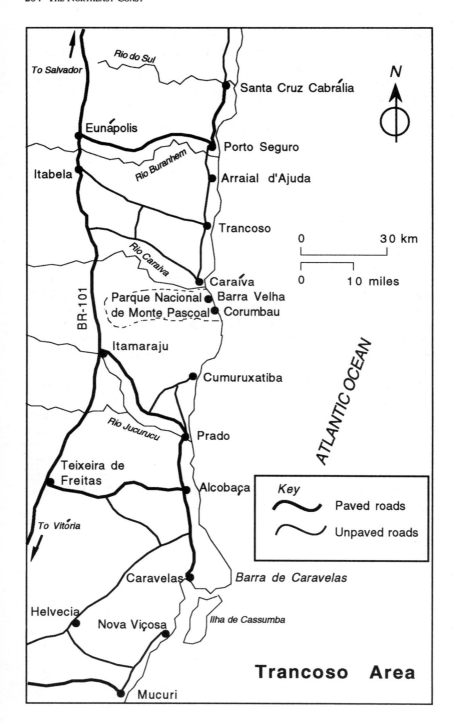

Trancoso Area

and the Rio Contas, is Praia de Piracanga, pounded by breakers.

To reach these areas, either hike or hire a *bugue* (try Seu Camilo at the Pousada Três Coqueiros, above).

Trancoso, some 743km south of Salvador, is Bahia's Canoa Quebrada, minus the huge sand-dunes. But as in Canoa, a short hike down the beach will soon put you far from the hip crowd and into some gorgeous scenery.

To reach Trancoso, catch a bus to the resort town of Porto Seguro (from Salvador US$30, 12 hours; from Rio US$35, 19 hours). If you miss a direct bus to Porto Seguro, almost any bus travelling between Rio and Salvador on BR-101 can drop you off in Eunápolis, from where you'll hop one of the frequent buses to Porto Seguro (US$3, 1½ hr). From the Porto Seguro bus station, local buses and taxis make the 2km run down the hill to town.

Porto Seguro is a bustling tourist mecca, with scores of hotels, pousadas, bars and dance clubs. Walk to the southern end of town and catch one of the tiny ferry-barges across the Buranhém River (US$0.75), from where buses make frequent runs to Trancoso (US$2), roughly 22km south on a dirt road. The road is narrow, deeply rutted, steep in spots, and impassable during heavy rains. When we first took the bus, a huge gash in the flooring afforded us an intimate view of both road conditions and the drive shaft. If you miss a bus, there are always *kombis* willing to take you there (a bus-load of 10 people runs to about US$50).

The bus first bounces its way into Arraial d'Ajuda (a terminally hip traveller's mecca shown on some maps as Nossa Senhora da Ajuda) before descending the final hill to Trancoso. The 22km trip takes about 1½ hours. Trancoso sits on a bluff above the beach, with an ever-burgeoning number of pousadas, bars, and organic-chic cafés. The palm-lined beaches just south of Trancoso, however, are nearly deserted and perfect for extended hiking. So are the beaches to the north, and you can hike along the shore all the way back to Arraial d'Ajuda, roughly 15km. If you walk the whole way, you'll have to cross two rivers, the Rio Taipe and Rio da Barra. You'll also pass two famous stretches of beach, Lagoa Azul and Pitinga, the latter a popular naturalists' beach. To the south, there are roughly 35km of isolated beaches (once you get a few kilometres past town) which can be explored on foot or by hired boat from Trancoso.

Trancoso itself grows every year, and Brazilian celebrities like singers Gal Costa and Elba Ramalho now own homes nearby. Still, it's a pleasant and lively place, particularly the shaded main square known as the Quadrado, which is closed to vehicular traffic. As with Morro de São Paulo, it's best to avoid the whole Porto Seguro-Trancoso area during Brazilian holiday season unless your goal is non-stop partying.

The fishing village of Caraíva, 42km south of Trancoso, has no electricity, no cars, no snack shacks along the beach, no post office, and but a single community telephone. A new road now connects the two towns, but it's a rough, poorly-maintained dirt track that becomes totally impassable after rains. Still, a bus valiantly attempts the trip twice a day, seven days a week, leaving Arraial d'Ajuda at 07.00 and 15.00; the bus stops in Trancoso to pick up passengers and then continues for another 2½ hrs to the banks of the Rio Caraíva, where passengers disembark. You'll then have to board one of the dugout canoes (US$0.75) which are poled across the river to Caraíva. No cars are allowed in the village. Buses return twice daily to Trancoso after dropping off passengers on the river bank. A second option – once the only way to reach Caraíva by road – is to catch the daily bus which leaves at 15.00 from Itabela, a town on BR-101 roughly 30km south of Eunápolis. The trip on dirt roads takes about four hours, dropping you off on the river bank. This bus immediately returns to Itabela, from where travellers can make bus connections anywhere on BR-101; there's also a daily bus leaving Caraíva at 06.00 for Itabela. If you're driving, you can use this route to reach Caraíva, turning off BR-101 onto the dirt road about 10km south of Itabela. Finally, boats are now making the trip to Caraíva from Trancoso and from Cumuruxatiba (see below).

There is a handful of pousadas in town, some with electrical generators: Pousada da Barra, Pousada da Praia, Recanto da Vera, O Caboclo, Casinhas da Bahia, Canto da Duca, Pousada da Lagoa, Luna and Pousada da Terra. Rooms at these pousadas range from US$10 to US$40, and if you're worried about space during Brazilian holidays you could call the community telephone at 073 868 1142. You can also pitch your tent at Carlito's simple campsite along the river (US$5), which provides a bathroom and water pump for showering. There are simple restaurants serving Bahian food, and the Canto da Duca offers vegetarian fare. Ouriços and the Pousada da Lagoa are more upscale, and offer a wide variety of dishes. Be sure to bring a torch (flashlight) for evening strolls in Caraíva.

The magnificent, isolated beaches south of Caraíva can be easily reached either hiking (south of the Rio Caraíva, there are no large rivers to be forded) or hiring a *barqueiro* to drop you off along the coast. Hiking the beaches south of Caraíva, you'll enter the Parque Nacional de Monte Pascoal, a 14,480-hectare park established in 1961 which encompasses a variety of habitats and is home to the Pataxó Indians. Barra Velha, about 6km south of Caraíva along the beach, is a small Pataxó tribal village among the palm trees which is accustomed to seeing hikers, and residents sell local handicrafts at reasonable prices. The hike to Barra Velha takes about four hours one-way. The interior of the park, which includes the point of land first sighted by Pedro Cabral upon his discovery of Brazil (540-metre Monte Pascoal), is difficult to reach from the coast and is best accessed via the western entrance along BR-101. Even so, there are as yet no established trails within the park. Continuing south another 6km along the beach from Barra Velha, hikers will arrive in Corumbau, another formerly remote village now being discovered by travellers. There are simple pousadas here, one luxury resort being developed, another Pataxó Indian village, and decent snorkelling along the reef, Recife do Pataxó. There's also a daily bus linking

Corumbau with Itamaraju on the BR-101 highway, and from there travellers can transfer to buses going north or south.

Further south, about two hours by boat from Corumbau, lies Cumuruxatiba, a popular resort town that has thus far avoided high rise hotels and maintains a degree of rustic charm. There are a couple of dirt roads through town, and during winter the place is practically deserted. Cumuruxatiba is reached by two buses daily from Itamaraju on the BR-101 highway; buses stop in Prado along the coast before heading north to Cumuruxatiba on a dirt road. If you're driving, there are two dirt roads leading to Cumuruxatiba; the best is a fairly level 32km road which cuts off from the road between Itamaraju and Prado. The other option is the direct road from Prado, about 30km, rough and very steep in some places which offers some beautiful glimpses of deserted coastline and great beaches, but is next to impassable after rains.

Cumuruxatiba (locals refer to their town as Cumurú) is loaded with pousadas in all price ranges, as well as simple restaurants serving good Bahian cuisine (try Restaurante da Isabel for delicious *moquecas* of fish or shrimp). You can camp at Aldeia da Lua next to the beach for US$7 pp, or the Corais campsite on Morro da Fumaça for US$4 per tent. The beaches near town aren't very good for swimming simply because they remain shallow all the way out to the offshore reef. Hike along the beach to the north, however, and you'll find some spectacular scenery, including Ponta do Moreira, a secluded palm-studded swimming spot at the base of a towering cliff (roughly an hour and a half from town). Contact Léo at Aquamar Turismo on the town beach about kayak and canoe rentals (US$4 per hr), horseback riding, and boat trips to Corumbau and Caraíva. Another outfit offering trips to Corumbau and Caraíva is R&S Turismo, tel: 073 873 1033.

Near the extreme southern tip of the state of Bahia, some 890km from Salvador, is Caravelas, a pleasant colonial port at the mangrove-lined mouth of the Rio do Meio. The town's narrow streets are quiet, and many of the houses and shopfronts still sport the beautiful Portuguese-style blue tile work, pastel colours, and carved wooden doors. There are excellent beaches north of town such as Barra de Caravelas (8km), Grauçá (9km), and Yemanjá. About 7km to the south is Ponta da Baleia, a deserted beach where whalers once butchered their catch; Abrolhos Turismo (see below) will take you there on horseback (US$10 pp).

Caravelas is most famous, however, as the jumping-off point for trips to the Parque Nacional Marinho dos Abrolhos, an officially protected archipelago some 80km offshore consisting of five islands, on only two of which may visitors set foot (Santa Bárbara and Siriba). Abrolhos is home to humpback whales, sea turtles, thousands of marine birds and numerous species of fish which inhabit the coral reefs surrounding the islands. Several tour operators in town offer boat trips to the islands, some of which include SCUBA diving. The islands were visited by Charles Darwin in the 1830s, and are today administered by IBAMA, which staffs an information office in the Praça Doutor Imbassay (tel: 073 297 1148). Practically next door in the same plaza is Abrolhos Turismo (tel: 073 297 1149), the biggest private tour operator offering trips to Abrolhos, and a good place for information on the marine park; staff will sit you down and show you videos of the park, both above and below the waterline, with a minimum of sales pitch. Other tour operators offering pretty much the same variety of trips to Abrolhos include Paradise Abrolhos (tel: 073 297 1150) and Abrolhos Embarcações (Avenida das Palmeiras 2, tel: 073 297 1172).

There is a dizzying variety of guided boat trips, both overnight and day, that you can make to Abrolhos, so it's best to check out the options once in Caravelas if you have the time. Abrolhos Turismo and Paradise Abrolhos both run day trips lasting from about 07.30 to 17.30 for US$95 pp, including park entrance fees, lunch (usually sandwiches) and soft drinks. They rent snorkelling equipment (mask, snorkel, and fins) for US$10. Overnight trips are available from all three of the tour operators listed above for about US$140 pp, including all meals. Humpback whales have a mating season from about July through to November, and it's at this time that the town and day trips fill up; you'll need to call ahead for reservations.

The SCUBA diving at Abrolhos is not world-class, but except for the island of Fernando de Noronha, it is one of the few decent dive sites in Brazil, and much cheaper than a trip to Noronha. The visibility is good, and the coral reefs, although suffering from the effects of sedimentation and over-fishing in the past, are worthwhile if you've got the time and a C-card. Divers will end up paying roughly US$45 pp for a two-tank dive in addition to the normal US$95 pp boat trip charge from most operators. Divers may want to check out the underwater video at the Abrolhos Turismo office before making a decision. Remember that in these clear waters you can see a lot simply snorkelling.

You can reach Caravelas easily via six daily buses from Teixeira de Freitas on BR-101, and also from Salvador. There are several reasonably-priced hotels in town, including the Hotel Navegantes and the Hotel Caravalense, both costing around US$30. The cheapest place in town is the Shangri-lá at Rua 7 de Setembro 219 (US$10 pp). Several hotels are located outside town at Praia de Grauçá, including Pousada do Juquita (US$12 pp). Another rustic cheapie well outside town on Yemanjá beach is the Pousada Yemanjá, with reed cabanas, no electricity at night, and mosquito nets (US$15 pp). There are a number of simple restaurants serving mostly fish dishes, including Encontro dos Amigos (Rua das Palmeiras 370, near the Hotel Navegantes) and Jubarte (Rua Marechal Deodoro 6). The most picturesque seafood joint, serving good *moquecas,* is the Museo da Baleia, on the beach at Praia de Grauçá; the name refers to the humpback whale bones, found along the beach, which festoon the place.

The Banco do Brasil in Caravelas does not change either cash or travellers cheques, but will give you a cash advance on a VISA card.

Deserted beach in Rio Grande del Norte

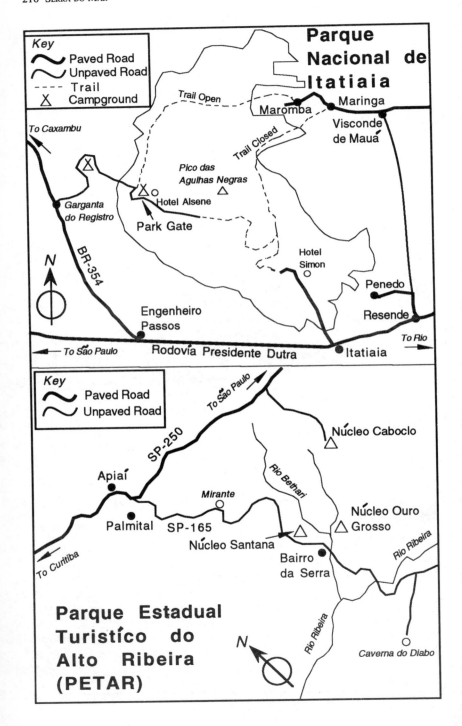

Key
~ Paved Road
~ Unpaved Road
- - - Trail
X Campground

Parque
Nacional de
Itatiaia

Trail Open

Maromba

Maringa

Trail Closed

Visconde
de Mauá

To Caxambu

Pico das
Agulhas Negras

Hotel Alsene

Garganta
do Registro

Park Gate

N

BR-354

Hotel
Simon

Penedo

Engenheiro
Passos

Resende

To São Paulo

Rodovia Presidente Dutra

Itatiaia

To Rio

Key
~ Paved Road
~ Unpaved Road

To São Paulo

SP-250

Núcleo Caboclo

Apiaí

Mirante

Rio Bethari

Palmital

SP-165

Núcleo Ouro
Grosso

Núcleo Santana

Rio Ribeira

To Curitiba

Bairro
da Serra

Rio Ribeira

Parque Estadual
Turistíco do
Alto Ribeira
(PETAR)

N

Rio Ribeira

Caverna do Diabo

Chapter Eight

Serra do Mar

Ric Goodman

The Serra do Mar is a 1,500km scarp running parallel to the Atlantic coast in southeast Brazil, separating the coastal strip, the *litoral*, from the *planalto* beyond, the traditional home of Brazil's coffee plantations. The mountains attain a height of 2,787m, in the case of Pico de Agulhas Negras, in Itatiaia National Park, one of Brazil's highest summits. The mountain system includes a number of ranges with individual names (such as Serra da Bocaina, Serra da Mantiqueira, Serra Negra, Serra Quilombo, Serra de Paranapiacaba) and is not confined to the mainland; the islands of the southeast coast, such as Ilha Bela and Ilha Grande, are part of the same range. The ecosystem supported throughout the region is known as *Mata Atlântica*, or Atlantic rainforest, which originally continued up the littoral as far as the state of Bahia. Vestiges of Atlantic rainforest exist even in isolated areas near Natal on the northeast coast.

The Serra is under immense pressure from the population centres of São Paulo, Rio de Janeiro, and Curitiba, as well as from mass tourism, farming, deforestation, poaching and *palmito* (palm heart) thieves. In response to this threat, the state agencies for environment in São Paulo and Rio have created a chain of state parks, ecological stations and biological reserves, forming a thread of protected areas along the length of the Serra do Mar. These areas are still subject to the ravages of developers, archaic land registration, and simple ignorance of the law, but the Serra nevertheless contains large tracts of virgin forest, often connected by trails used by the local population, varying in hiking time from a few hours to several days. One day it might be possible to walk the entire length of the Serra do Mar without having to ask permission of the land owners, but for now the trail system is far from complete.

This chapter concentrates on the best preserved nuclei of the Serra do Mar, considered the best parts of the Serra accessible to the determined traveller, the Parque Nacional da Serra da Bocaina, the Parque Nacional de Itatiaia, and the Parque Estadual Turístico do Alto Ribeira (PETAR).

Getting there

Gateway cities for Serra da Bocaina and Itatiaia parks are Rio de Janeiro and São Paulo. PETAR is easily accessible from both São Paulo and Curitiba. Daily buses from these metropolises will get you to smaller towns close to all three parks (eg: São José do Barreiro, Itatiaia, Apiaí and Iporanga). Detailed instructions for reaching the park entrances can be found in the sections on individual parks.

When to go

There is no prohibitive period in the Serra, but observe the following: if you are going to gain altitude, you will sooner or later walk into rain clouds. During the summer months the heat and humidity rush up the mountain wall and sometimes you're stuck with rain for days. It can rain in winter too, but it is generally a better season for travel. Be warned, at 2,000 to 3,000m things can be chilly, even though you're being roasted on the beach. You'll need a tent, sleeping bag, fleece and rainwear (as cheap and lightweight as possible). You'll also want a lightweight kerosene or all-fuel camping stove in preference to the damp wood.

One other word of warning: avoid Brazilian public holidays if you can while travelling in the Serra. New Year and Carnaval are times when the cities empty and the buses and pousadas fill up, loading all accessible space in the parks.

Information and useful addresses

There is no chance of changing money outside the gateway cities of Rio, São Paulo and Curitiba, so stock up before leaving for the parks. A good shop selling camping and other outdoor equipment in São Paulo is Half Dome, Rua Dr Vila Nova 321, Vila Buarque, São Paulo (tel: 011 255 4331).

For general information on the parks and biological reserves, contact: IBAMA (Instituto Brasileiro de Meio Ambiente dos Recursos Naturais Renováveis), Alameda Tietê 637, São Paulo (tel: 011 883 1300/011 852 8415); the Secretaria do Meio Ambiente do Estado de São Paulo, Rua Tapapuã 81, São Paulo (tel: 011 822 0766); or the Instituto Florestal, Rua do Horto 931, São Paulo (tel: 011 952 8555).

The only ready suppliers of detailed maps of the Serra do Mar (and Brazil in general) is IBGE (Brazilian Institute of Geography and Statistics) in São Paulo and Rio de Janeiro. The last updating of many 1:50,000 maps was during the 1970s. Take them with a pinch of salt; sometimes new paths will have appeared or been upgraded, a marked house has become a pile of foundation stones and so on. The topography, however, is generally reliable and these maps are often the best thing going. Maps cost US$8 a sheet. If they include any detail of military owned land they are restricted, and you'll need a copy of your passport or identity card to obtain them. If the map you need is out of stock, the staff is prepared to make a scale copy for the same price. IBGE's address is Rua Ubussui 93, São Paulo (tel: 011 822 2106) or Avenida Franklin Roosevelt 146, 20021-060 Caselo, Rio de Janeiro (tel: 021 210 1250; web site: http://www.ibge.gov.br and webmaster@cddi.ibge.gov.br).

The world-renowned serpent research station and museum of Butantã is located in São Paulo and it's a good place to bone up on your local snakes before heading out to the parks. The instute is located at Vital Brasil 1500, Butantã, São Paulo (tel: 011 814 3816/813 7222). Admission is US$1.20.

GEOGRAPHY

South America and Africa were one continent until they began to tear apart 200 million years ago. They finally separated only 40 million years ago, after the evolution of flowering plants, increased insect populations and the first appearance of mammals and marsupials. As they began to split, a granite ripple formed the Serra do Mar around 130 million years ago. The granite of the region is very old, formed more than a billion years ago. Compressions and elevations formed the great 800m high wall and the granites transformed into laminated gneiss. Enormous pieces of rock loosened and crashed into the sea and formed islands, such as Ilha do Cardoso. On the lee side, the slopes are much kinder, and the planalto, or high plain, continues inland, its moderate temperatures ideal for the coffee plantations and cattle rearing of the interior.

The flat strip between the Serra and the sea consists of deposits of sediment washed down from the hills and up from the sea. These banks continue to grow out into the sea, forming estuaries and bay mouths. Stabilised by vegetation, tongues of sediment eventually separate the sea from lakes or brackish mangrove lagoons, where the fresh water of the river is topped up from the sea at high tide. You can find examples of these *restingas* all along the Serra coast, for example Marambaia and Jacarepaguá in Rio de Janeiro. Ilha Comprida near Iguape in the south of São Paulo is a *restinga* in the making.

THE PEOPLE

The original inhabitants of the area are called the Sambaqui people, after the name for large piles of broken sea shells on the coast found to contain human skeletal remains and communal garbage. The Portuguese colonisers found therein a prime source of lime and raided the mounds for whitewash production, destroying many. There are finds from one of these mounds in the Museu do Sambaqui, in Joinville (state of Santa Catarina), which has been dated to 2980–40BC.

These early inhabitants were supplanted by Guarani Indian culture, speaking dialects of the Tupi-Guarani family. Many of the place, plant and animal names in Brazil are from this linguistic base. The Guarani forged the first links between the planalto and the littoral, through pathways that were used to visit related groups with whom they traded and married. Upon the arrival of the Portuguese, these Indians were the first to be contacted and persuaded to help the colonisers build their empire. Once the tribes started to desist, they were enslaved, trapped between the cruelty of the *bandeirantes* and missionary policy, whose soul-saving activities ignored the cost in human lives.

The Serra do Mar was the first obstacle that the bandeirantes had to surmount to reach the interior and their initial quarries: gold, gem stones, labour, and the subsequent products of coffee and sugarcane. When the indigenous population ceased to be sufficient, African slaves were imported. Slaves were used to improve the structure of trails through the forest with stone, and to carry gold from the interior to the coast, where it was loaded onto boats and sent to Portugal. Escaped and freed slaves formed settlements known as *quilombos*, hiding from the colonisers, and becoming strongholds and symbols of resistance. The mixture of Indian, African and European blood produced a distinct culture of countryside settlers, the *caboclo*. Sometimes these people, living near to the coast or rivers are known as Caíçaras. Living from the forest, the Caíçaras retain many traits of their Indian ancestry, for example using dugout canoes, fish traps and plant poisons to kill fish. The estuarine life is dominated by the phases of the moon, as the low tides are the only times their traps can be accessed. They thus have a reputation for being lazy and sleeping all day, while in fact they are active during the night. Their main sources of food are hunting, foraging, collection from the forest and slash-and-burn agriculture.

There are many people living all along the Serra today whose right to be there is in legal dispute. Land rights and agrarian reform are two of the big themes of present-day Brazil. Occupied land is considered owned, which encourages its possession, until the title is disputed by someone richer, more powerful, or possibly more violent, than the current possessor. Often two equally legal but conflicting claims show on the registry. With the opening up of the coastal roads and the continual increase in population and demand for leisure space, local people are often moved off their homesteads, giving way to big hotels and condominiums. Allocating land to park status prohibits hunting and extractive use of the forest in order to preserve threatened species. The indigenous peoples are starting to come up with replacement ideas, such as the Reserva do Rio Silveiras near Bertioga, where for ten dollars a native guide will walk you round the forest for an hour and demonstrate some of his or her knowledge. This sort of small scale sustainable industry is set to grow in the near future.

Inside park boundaries, the legal presence of squatters is disputed. Those there before the park limits were drawn often have the right to stay. Indeed, it has been recognised that not only do subsistence farmers do little damage to an ecosystem, they can also play a useful role in guarding the forest. The problems can and do come when outside demand for poached animals, skins, wood, and minerals encourage deforestation.

NATURAL HISTORY OF THE MATA ATLÂNTICA
Flora
In some isolated areas of the Serra do Mar, there are patches of *pinheiros do Paraná*, the most exotic and majestic of all the pines (*Araucaria augustifolia*). Related to the monkey-puzzle, this tree is well known as the source of pine-nuts (*pinhões*), roasted and consumed during the festival of Junina. These opportunistic trees take hold on open grass-land and are the primitive first stage of development of Atlantic rainforest. Letting little light pass through to the forest floor, the trees make sure that not many other plants stand a chance of taking hold beneath. It is said that at one time one could ride a horse at night through these pine forests. There are two other pines in Brazil (yellow-woods, genus *Podocarpus*) but in these forests *Araucaria* can account for 95% of the vegetation.

Eventually, of course, shrubs and small trees do take hold, and as the lower community becomes denser the pines no longer find conditions favourable for reproduction. The understorey becomes dominated with *imbauba*, *cedro* and *maté*, and the forest canopy becomes continuous. These conditions give right of passage to umbrophilic species, such as palmito and tree ferns, hallmarks of true Atlantic forest, while the occasional 300 year old pine protrudes through the roof, keeping sentinel until it dies. You will see patches of these trees in various places, especially above 1,600m; but if you're intent on seeing an entire forest, then the canyons of the Aparados da Serra in the state of Rio Grande do Sul is where you should head.

There are various differences between Amazon and Atlantic forest. The former occurs mainly on the plain while Mata Atlântica is found at higher altitudes. In the Amazon forest, average temperatures are high all year round, 26°C, with a maximum of 39 and a minimum of 22 degrees. In the Atlantic forest, the average is 14–21°C, depending on latitude and altitude. Temperatures rarely drop below freezing, although it sometimes manages to snow in the south, the event normally producing front page news. The soils differ also, with intrinsically fertile tertiary sediments coming from the Andes to fill the Amazon basin (although much of this fertility is rapidly leached off by heavy rainfall) while in the Serra do Mar, eroded crystalline rock such as granite and gneiss give a thin covering on often steep slopes. Precipitation is fairly similar, varying in both areas between 2,000 and 3,000mm annually, the mountain aspect forcing out the water from the moist sea air. Crossing as it does five states from south to north, the Mata

Atlântica has a variation of climate from one end to the other, and so the character of the forest changes along the length.

Go to any *churrascaria* barbecue in Brazil, and *palmitos* (palm hearts) will probably be on the menu. This species of palm (*Euterpe edulis*), is native to the Mata Atlântica and is significant as a case study for ecologists, conservationists and observers of Third World economies. Palmito palms live at up to 800m in altitude, grow up to 20m high and live up to 100 years. They mature and start to reproduce when they are around ten years old, but many of them do not reach that stage – boy, are they good to eat! The shoots between the trunk and the fresh leaves are taken, dehusked and cut into bite-sized pieces. To access the top of a thin 15m high tree it is necessary to cut down the whole thing. It is illegal to cut palmitos without an IBAMA licence, but this restriction has meant a growing black market in the trade, with armed gangs of palmito poachers roaming the forest, hacking down the young trees and selling them to the licensed manufacturers. Shady businesses don't bother heating the hearts for the required 45 minutes to eliminate botulism, and it is common to find invented IBAMA registration numbers or source addresses on the supermarket jars. A dismal estimate of only 10% of palmitos sold in São Paulo having a legal source was cited in one newspaper. Attempts are being made to hybridise palmito palms with another related species native to the north of Brazil, which would regenerate quickly and take the heat off the forest, but for the time being, the lesson is: don't touch the ones less than 2.5cm in diameter, or better, not at all. *Bom apetite*!

The common name of *xaxim* is given to the tree fern *Dicksonensis*, endemic to the Atlantic forest. A similar situation to the palmito exists with these trees; they are poached, often with the co-operation of the landowners, for their fibrous trunks, which are used as domestic plant holders and sold in markets and nurseries. Of course, the scale of the business is an order of magnitude smaller, but the threat both to the species itself and to ecologically related species is real enough. By the way, a fern in Portuguese is a *samambaia*, a tree fern is a *samambiacus*. Learn something every day.

The *imbauba* (*Cecropia*) is a characteristic Mata Atlântica tree. I've heard it described in English as a pumpwood or trumpet tree, but I'm not sure of this terminology. Its huge, hand-shaped leaves are silver on their undersides, and the banana bunch-shaped red fruits serve as food for tree sloths. They also shelter other symbiotic residents – ants that live in their hollow trunks and protect the tree. They're native from Central America to southern Brazil and are a true 'pioneer' tree, able to grow only where there is sunlight, such as where the forest has been cleared. Two or three hundred years ago the tree was rare in the region, but now it's characteristic. It is said that an infusion of imbauba leaves is good for heart and blood problems, and you can find it in the herb shops of São Paulo. (Maybe this is why the speedy sloths love it?) The germinated fruit is edible, 'but not agreeable'.

In much of the Mata Atlântica, and abundant in the Serra do Mar, are purple flowered trees, the *quaresmeira* (*Tibuchina granulosa*), so named for the time of flowering, Lent (although they also flower in July). The Quaresmeira is also commonly seen in cities, planted for its flowers.

Inside the forest you will be surrounded by epiphytes of all descriptions. The most easily recognised are the bromeliads, cupped onto the side of trees and rocks, being filled with water and all the forest debris in the air. The characteristic bromeliad is the ruby-flowered *Vriesea spectrum*, which when in flower produces a red shoot around 50cm long with its flowers.

Birds

Three eagles seen in the Serra do Mar are the *gavião de penacho* (*Spizaetus tyrannus*), the monkey-eating hawk *gavião pega macaco* (*S. ornatus*), and the formidable *gavião real* (*Harpia harpyia*), or harpy eagle. Only existing in primary forest, where they are threatened by hunting and deforestation, harpy eagles survive on a diet of sloths, monkeys, young deer and parrots, and are capable of carrying them all to the treetops. Attentive and persistent observers can occasionally see one flying over the forest. All three eagles are important in maintaining natural animal populations, especially of simians.

Somewhat at the other end of the grace and looks scale, but rather more common than eagles, are the guans or *jacus*, represented by the *jacupemba* (*Penelope superciliaris*). Known in English as the rusty-margined guan, the jacupemba is a brown, turkey-like bird with a white stripe above its eye (which gives it its name –*supercilio* means eyebrow in Portuguese) and a red throat. An alarmed guan is possibly the noisiest bird in the forest, screeching at full volume before blasting out of the canopy. Its rarer cousin, the black-fronted piping guan or *jacucaca* (*Pipile jacutinga*), sports a blue beak, a red wattle on the throat and white feathers on the back of its head. Both are hunted for their meat, by both men and panthers. Men imitating the guan's calls can attract unsuspecting panthers; I'm not sure which is more surprised when they meet.

The acauã (*Herpetotheres cachinnans*), or laughing falcon, is another noisy bird, and easy to recognise by its black zorro mask, its cream coloured body and black wings. Many legends describe the various calls of the acauã, one popular tale saying that the male sings 'quero casar', the female replying 'quero gritar'. (*No comment.*)

More noises emit from the *araponga* (*Procnias nudicollis*), commonly known as the *ferreiro,* the blacksmith. Its ring, sounding like the blow on an anvil, is written something like 'heins' (applications to update the next edition welcome). White and similar to a pigeon, it is one of the common birds of the forest.

Amongst the commonly seen colourful birds is the seven-coloured tanager (*Tanagara fastuosa*), and its close relative the *pintor verdadeiro*, in magnificent blues, yellows and orange. Hummingbirds are never too far away, the *beija-flor preto e branco* or black jacobim (*Melanotrochilus fuscus*) being the most common. This species feeds on nectar, insects, spiders and flies, robbing spider's webs for the protein they contain. Its body is mostly black, with white from under the wings to the tail. Parakeets with blue wings screech away in groups, giving your presence away instantly. The threatened red-breasted parrot (*Amazonia brasiliensis*) is also present, and is the basis for Disney's amiable freeloader Zé Carioca.

Mammals

There are many primates living in the Serra do Mar, but all are quite difficult to see without patience and luck. Brown howler monkeys, *monos barbados*, (*Alouta fusca*), which have a reddish brown coat, survive only in the densest forest, their growls providing a terrifying backdrop to the atmosphere of the forest.

The *mono carvoeria* (*Brachyteles arachnoides*), the largest of the New World primates, can weigh up to 13 kilogrammes. They have black hairless faces, and are very curious about people. I have passed them on branches less than three metres away in Bocaina Park. Like most of the wildlife in the forest, they are most active at dawn, so you'll have to get out of bed to stand a chance. And there's the *macaco prego* (*Cebus apella xanthosthernus*), so called because its penis is the shape of a nail, or so they say.

The tiny golden lion tamarin, or golden capuchin monkey, *mico-leão vermelho* (*Leontopithecus rosalia*), endemic to Rio de Janeiro state, is one of a number of threatened tamarins, and one of the symbols of threatened Mata Atlântica habitat. There are considered to be around only 150 golden lion tamarins left in the wild. They prey on small invertebrates as well as wild fruits, and their young have the incredible facility to become independent of their mother within five days. Other closely-related tiny primates exist: *micos* and *saguis* (*Callithrix* sp.) can be encountered occasionally, and if you have no luck in the wild you could do worse than to visit the Botanical Gardens in Rio.

Small, delicate deer, the *veado catingueiro* (*Mazama gouazoubra*), are found in all forested areas of Brazil. Their small horns are not shed, and can continue to grow for many years. They survive to about 15, living a mostly solitary life.

The three-toed sloth, *bicho perguiça*, (*Bradypus tridactylus*) is to be found primarily in imbauba trees. It has two layers of fur, one short and one long, the latter growing algae and harbouring a variety of insects.

Various wild cats inhabit the Serra. Most are near extinction and are rarely seen. *Jaguatirica* (*Felis pardalis*) has the same wide distribution, colour patterns and behaviour as three other species – the small forest cat (*Felis tigrina*), the large forest cat (*Felis geoffroyi*), and the *gato maracajá* (*Felis wiedii*) – and so are extremely difficult to distinguish. Bigger than all of these is the cougar or puma, *suçuarana* (*Felis concolor*), growing up to 105kg. Capping them all is the *onça pintada* (*Panthera onça*), which eats deer and rabbit. Residents I've talked to have seen these panthers, but they're extremely rare. There are occasional conflicts, with the onças taking cattle belonging to the farmers, as commonly happens when big game territory is threatened.

Snakes

Yes, there are snakes in the Atlantic forest, although I've come across them rarely, and then they've mostly been slipping away from me.

The *jararaca* is responsible for 88% of fatal snake bites recorded in Brazil. The latin generic name *Bothrops* means 'pit', referring to the cavities located between the eyes and nose which look like an extra pair of nostrils. Thus the name 'pit viper'. Snakes of this genus are nocturnal, seeking out their hot-blooded prey by sight, 'smelling' through their tongues, and sensing heat through their pits. All 30 species are venomous. Most are black with white patches, and grow to a maximum of two metres.

The rattlesnake is responsible for almost 9% of the snake bites in Brazil. Known here as *cascavel* (*Crotalus durrisus*), rattlers are also around two metres when fully grown and have a white diamond pattern on their backs.

The infamous bushmaster, or *sururucu* (*Lachesis muta*), lives largely in the Amazon but a subspecies also exists in the Mata Atlântica. It is the largest of the American poisonous snakes and grows up to 4.5m. An object one third of the snake's mass can pass through its digestive system. It has alternating dark brown and light brown triangles running down its back.

The mystery man in the snake world is the coral snake (*Micrurus frontalis*). With more than 30 subspecies, this venomous snake lives all over Brazil in places frequented by man. Miraculously, corals only account for half a percent of accidents, as they are only dangerous if molested. The vast majority have black, red and white stripes hooped all the way down their bodies, in different orders, but this is not the only colour scheme. The non-venomous false coral, which does a famous job of imitating its poisonous cousin, is from another genus, but it is difficult to tell them apart. The *only* way to be sure is through their dentition; real corals have their fangs at the front of the mouth, false have them at the back, in a position unable to inject venom. But don't hang around for a closer look!

No visit to São Paulo would be complete without a tour of the Snake Farm at Butantã, near the Cidade Universitária. The only research station of its kind in Latin America, the facilities include three outdoor snake pits (most lively on a sunny day), hospital, helipad, library and store room full of thousands of pickled reptiles. The museum is full of live specimens and skeletons, including a 5.1m anaconda with 482 ribs; the largest example ever found anywhere was 11.68m in length (disbelieve all others). The exhibition will teach you everything you never knew and is highly recommended. Take a Butantã USP bus from Clínicas, and ask the *cobrador* to let you down before you get into the university campus. The Instituto Butantã is on Vital Brasil, walk up through the forest. Museum entrance US$1.20.(tel: 011 814 3816 or 813 7222).

PARQUE NACIONAL DA SERRA DA BOCAINA

Inland from Parati, Angra dos Reis and Mambucaba on the coast, the Parque Nacional da Serra da Bocaina offers the best opportunity of getting to know the landscape of the Serra do Mar on foot. Created in 1961, the national park covers 100,000 hectares, the majority in Rio do Janeiro state, and a small portion in São Paulo state. The highest point of the park is the Pico Tira Chapeu at 2,132m. The northern limits of Bocaina are Cunha, São José do Barreiro and Bananal. Further north of these you are in the Paraíba Valley; the word Bocaina means literally the space between two mountains.

The principal path through the park is known as the Trilha do Ouro, the Gold Trail. The trail was originally built by slaves in the early 18th century to bring gold down to the coast, from where it was loaded into Lisbon-bound boats. Parati at that time was more important than Rio, and thousands of slave hours went into creating this major link to the interior. The trail can be traced through Minas Gerais state, the last marked 30km stretch linking Ouro Branco and Ouro Preto, 500km to the north. Today the Minas landscape has been decimated by mining and deforestation for smelting, but the 100km stretch over the Serra do Mar to the coast at Mambucaba is still intact, and offers a very attractive walk, passing stretches of virgin forest, at least three powerful waterfalls more than 50m high, and a number of farms inhabited long before the national park boundaries were drawn. The superb views give out over pristine Serra do Mar beauty – an unbroken canopy dotted with purple *quaresmeira* flowers, falcons and eagles soaring overhead. On clear days one can see right down to the base of the hills and out over Parati and the Atlantic, where the stone path meets the *planicie*, the alluvial plain before the sea, and where the river Mambucaba ceases its dramatic final gush down the mountain shelf.

To visit the park, permission must be obtained from the park administration in São José do Barreiro, either in writing or in person, at least ten days in advance of any entrance to the park. The permit must be presented at the park gate, 26km up road from São José do Barreiro before entering. Depending on just how much advance notice you give, the permit is either kept in the head office or sent up the road to the park gate for collection. In practice, you could try to persuade the staff to write this document on the same day you enter, as long as it's within their working hours. For written permission, write to: Administração do Parque do Serra do Bocaina, São José do Barreiro - SP, CEP 12830-000. The telephone number is 0125 77 1225.

Getting there

The gateway to the park is the town of São José do Barreiro ('Saint Joe the Muddy'). To reach São José, you have a number of options on public buses. From São Paulo, the Passaro Marrom bus leaves Tietê rodoviária at 07.00

and 16.00 daily, arriving at 11.30 and 20.30 respectively (US$12). The alternative is to take the same bus company's 08.30 service to Cruzeiro, changing there to get the daily 11.30 bus to Areias, proceeding to São José. Paid in three separate instalments, the whole lot should add up to around US$14.50, and gets you in at 13.00.

If coming from Rio, or any other direction, then get to Resende, where you can take the Tupi bus at 06.00 or 16.00, arriving in São José an hour later (US$4). This bus returns to Resende an hour after its arrival in town. Various other schemes can no doubt be thought of, for example coming by way of Barra Mansa and Bananal. All these routes are good for car access; however if you are doing a one way trip across the mountains you have the obvious problem of returning the circuitous 250km to pick up your car.

Once standing on the main Rio-Santos road next to the beach, you have the choice of going to Parati or Angra dos Reis to connect to your onward destination. Local buses are frequent enough not to need a timetable here. From Parati to São Paulo, Reunídas buses go at 11.00 and 23.30, frequently full at weekends, but you can catch services to the main São Paulo-Rio highway, the Dutra, and connect from there. From Angra to São Paulo there is only one bus at 22.00, a ride from hell to be avoided if at all possible. I once suggested to the driver that it was dangerous to drive so fast: 'Sim, senhor, isn't this road terrible?' was his affable reply. Eval buses from Angra to Rio run hourly and take three hours (US$9). Of course, getting straight out of Parati or Angra might not be what you want to do; both have numerous options for sightseeing: hotels, food, islands and beaches.

A 26km unlevelled dirt road runs from São José's town centre to the entrance of the park proper. Without your own transport, you could hire a taxi if it's dry (talk to Zé Milton at the only tour agency in town, see below) or walk – it is not unpleasant, but there's little water and few sites suitable for a tent on the way, other than by the road side. If you drive, you are ill advised to attempt it without 4WD except in perfectly dry conditions. The road is terrible after a night of rain, and the park receives 14 nights of rain a month, with an annual average of four metres. Take your brolly. An alternative is to hold out for a lift from one of the locals living near or in the park; there are a number with trashed pick-ups that come into town for supplies, normally having to be repaired every kilometre of the way. Sometimes the IBAMA jeep is going and they're happy to take you along if there's space. You might have to wait around for a day to get a ride. Horses could also be negotiated; they are expensive, however, and you'd have to pay for their handler as well, plus their return time if you're going one way. Bicycles would do well as far as the final descent to the coast, where the path is too degraded to think about biking it. (This will probably stand as an invitation for someone to try; don't invite me.)

Where to stay and eat

There's a choice of places to sleep; the Pousada Régis by the bus station is reasonable at US$20 a night, and in the corner of the square is the Hotel Morrison, run by a fan of the late Doors singer. Both campsites are some distance from town, three and nine kilometres, so camping doesn't present itself as a reasonable option, unless you have your own transport.

Information and useful addresses

São José do Barreiro is a charming little town, and not a bad place to get stuck in. Stretching at least four blocks in each direction from the main square, you can spend time visiting the church, the two bars, the two general stores and the bakery, catching up on the local gossip while you're about it. The Park Administration is also in town, just start up the track to the park, and it's on the right. Not only are you obliged to pay a visit for permit reasons, but they can also offer you a basic sketch map of the Trilha do Ouro hiking trail, anonymously drawn and donated, which proves very useful. Some of it is inaccurate and out of date, but not as out of date as the 1:50,000 scale map which covers Bocaina (Rio Mambucaba), obtainable from the IBGE. The latter doesn't show the entire trail, but it could be copied from IBAMA's wall before you set off. The sketch is adequate if you're not intent on going off-piste, in which case nothing short of a satellite navigation system is going to be much good.

MW Trekking (Praça Col Cunha Lara, s/n, São José do Barreiro,12830-000 SP, tel: 012 577 1178), a travel agency on the main square, offers guided tours into the park. Owner Zé Milton speaks good English, and has a number of set itineraries on fixed dates to visit the park, lasting two or three days, but can do tailor-made excursions if you wish. Obviously it is cheaper to go as part of a group – if it is possible to contact others before arriving. Try calling a few weeks in advance to let him know; there might be other people interested in going around the same time. It's worth dropping in whatever the case, he's more than happy to chat and give advice, and his walls are covered with some great photos he's taken in Bocaina.

Excursions

The most beautiful and challenging trail in the park is the Trilha do Ouro. The following description of the Trilha do Ouro gives approximate distances in kilometres. Total walking time is given in hours from the park gate, excluding rest time.

Having got yourself to the park gate, the 4WD road continues another 25km into the park, to Fazenda Barreirinha, but to ride this section would be to miss one the best preserved sections of forest along the trail and two of the principal waterfalls, Cachoeira do São Isidro (3km, 1 hr), and Cachoeira das Posses (8km, 2 hrs). Both waterfalls require that you walk away from the track, and down to the river. You pass above the Valley Bonito and start up a hill that takes you past a turn for the Fazenda do

Veado (10km, 2½hrs). Keep to the main track and you'll eventually emerge out on a ridge of bracken. There is a small makeshift chapel further along this part with *macumba* images in it (21km, 4½hrs). Do not disturb these images. The practice of *macumba* is very widespread through the backcountry here, brought here by the black slaves and never effectively flushed out by Catholicism. I have listened on more than one occasion to priests steering their congregations away from their alternative saints.

Soon the track veers to the right and starts to descend through a saddle. Come off the motor road and take the short cut small trail heading down to the farm house visible in the lap of the valley 300m away; if you miss it, the road eventually arrives at the same destination.

This is Fazenda Barreirinha, (25km, 5 hrs) marked as Fazenda do Sertão on the IBGE map. Tião and Wander and their seven children offer food, lodging, showers and camping space. The house contains no less than 15 beds within its wooden walls, but it is rarely full (except, perhaps, when Carnaval might bring a group here from the city). The facilities are priced separately, full board at US$30, camping at US$1. The choice is yours. A good excursion from here is the 40 minute tramp straight up the hill to catch the view looking down into the bay of Ilha Grande and Parati.

Continuing past the small locked church, you start to walk on the original stones of the Trilha de Ouro. Along the way you pass a very small patch of forest with a trickling stream exiting as a waterfall and crossing the path (30km, 6 hrs). Just here is another suggested camp. Much of the land around here is farmed, a few cattle and some maize being the norm, although some fruit is harvested as well, such as the oranges and *goiabas* of the Fazenda Central (35km, 7¼hrs), which comes after a 2km stretch of cooling forest, worth spending some rest time in; another great camp, you can also spend time absorbing some of the huge copious wild strawberries that are abundant here.

Crossing a stream and following the muddy descent, the path arrives at an open pasture by the bank of the Mambucaba river, which at this point is a good 30m wide. This fazenda (37km, 8 hrs), which also forms part of Fazenda Central, is run by Sr Zé Candido, who offers basic food and beds with mattresses and blankets.

Don't cross the river here, but walk behind the farm and again find the trail which proceeds parallel to it. Shortly you'll hear through the trees the sound of the largest of the park's waterfalls, the Cachoeira do Veado (41km, 9 hrs). If there were a symbol for the park, this would be it. Crashing over 60m into the Mambucaba River, the Deer Falls are a wonderful place to camp, stay, bathe, fish and recount campfire tales. The best site is on the flat ground just across the log bridge, with the top of the falls visible over the trees. A trail leads up for a much closer look, and it is possible to swim in the pool beneath the falls.

The trail crosses the river just beyond the camp gound, on a long, bouncy log bridge, and follows to the left through some maize fields to ascend to the path that must be taken up into the forest again. A last view is possible back at Veado across the valley, before disappearing into the forest for a few hours. The path here is original stone work, which unfortunately hasn't been repaired for a good while; with constant use by horses and heavy rain, the clay on which the stones are laid is waterlogged in places and rather treacherous. You're advised to pick up a stout stick to help you down the 9km (4 hrs) between Veado and the suspension bridge on the plain below (50km,13 hrs). On the way are two rivers that must be forded, and while you're at it you can swim in them. They also provide an opportunity to put on repellent against the blood-sucking *borachudos*, pium flies that are much more tenacious than any mosquito, and which start to become more prevalent as you approach the coast. A plateau is reached before you exit the forest where there are banana clearings. The common non-indigenous herbaceous plant growing all along the side of the path is butterfly ginger (genus *Alpinia*), named for its flamboyant white flowers which appears in the summer months and fill this stretch with perfume. The root is comparable to cooking ginger. The mud here is unavoidable, and it is sometimes better to rid yourself of your boots and go barefoot.

The suspension bridge marks the boundary to the national park, as it lies on the 100m contour. Nothing can now be built legally above this line anywhere in Brazil. There is a while to go yet before reaching the beach. The jeep track slowly widens and the occasional car is seen serving the various farms; it might be possible to catch a lift (to the town of Pereque, an uninspiring concrete dump) that lets you down before reaching the main road. Mambucaba (65km, 16 hrs) itself is on the other side, with a small beach and a pretty colonial church.

PARQUE NACIONAL DE ITATIAIA

Itatiaia was the first national park created in Brazil, in 1937. Its summit stands 2,787m above sea-level, and it is one of the few places in Brazil where you find yourself above the tree line, with an outside chance in winter of a thin covering of snow. There are two parts to the 30,000-hectare park, each quite different. The lower portion of the park is easily accessible, contains numerous pousadas and hotels, and boasts a number of short trails leading to waterfalls. The upper portion is more difficult to reach, less frequently visited, and contains the most challenging trails, many leading to spectacular views of the Paraíba Valley.

Getting there
The lower and by far the more accessible area starts just behind the town of Itatiaia which itself lies on the main Presidente Dutra highway, 174km from Rio and 257km from São Paulo. Take a bus from either city to Itatiaia and follow the directions given below under *Excursions*.

The elevated part of the park is tougher to reach, and takes some initiative to get to without a car. First, you must catch a bus from Rio or São Paulo towards either of two cities in the state of Minas Gerais, Caxambu or São Lourenço, via Engenheiro Passos, jumping off at the spot known as Garganto do Registro. This is the high mountain saddle between the states of São Paulo and Minas Gerais, and from here begins a very unpaved road ascending the final 17km to the park entrance, which you'll have to walk or hitch. Many trucks stop at the Garganta do Registro, but it is illegal to take passengers, and private car drivers are scared of picking up hitchers, unless they're locals who understand that a gringo with an enormous backpack is probably harmless.

Returning from the upper portion of the park, you can simply double back to the Garganta do Registro, or else take an old farm track which eventually descends the mountains to the town of Maromba; this route is explained below in *Excursions*. A bus passes Maromba and the neighbouring town of Visconde de Mauá at 08.30 daily to descend to Resende, on the Dutra highway, from where frequent buses go to Rio and São Paulo. The ascending Tupi bus brings residents back home from Resende at 16.30.

Where to stay and eat

There are a number of pousadas and hotels within the lower portion of the park, with standards up to the five-star Hotel Simon, owned by the state tourist agency, Embratur.

Excursions

To visit the lower portion of the park, a well-maintained, paved road begins behind the town of Itatiaia, accessed by bus from Rio or São Paulo. This road is similar to that which goes around Tijuca park in the city of Rio, and takes you up through Mata Atlântica to a number of short trails to see various waterfalls: Véu da Noiva, Maromba, Poranga, and Itaporoni. Without your own transport, jump off the bus from either Rio or São Paulo as close as you can to the footbridge that crosses the main road, and wait for the midday public bus that goes all the way up to the museum (which is being rebuilt at the time this was written). The bus gets up far enough into the park to enable you to walk the rest. A 12km trail starts from the road and trudges up to a viewing platform, the Mirante, and comes out at the five-star Hotel Simon.

To explore the upper portion of the park, begin at the summit jumping off point, the Garganta do Registro (see *Getting there* above for details). Stop here for traditional *mineiro* sweets and a fresh water spring before hiking (or hitching) the 17km to the park entrance. Feeling dizzy due to the rapid rise from the beach, you cross the 2,000m contour, the trees shrinking and eventually disappearing altogether. A wonderful camping area is found on the right – open, clean and free. There is also the Hotel Alsene, a climbers' lodge with basic dormitories, food and showers. It is also a good place to find a guide for the park if you wish.

One kilometre further up the road is the park entrance gate. The park admits guests starting at 08.30. A nominal fee, currently US$1.25, is charged upon entrance. The rule is that you must repass the gate before 16.30; that is, no camping in the park. IBAMA closed the park to overnighters for a number of reasons: lack of funding prevents effective policing against forest fires, the vandalising of two out of the three shelters available in the park, and maintenance of the eroded footpaths that traverse the park to Visconde de Mauá and Itatiaia. An underpaid staff of 24 is now down to eight, so it doesn't look like the situation will be reversed soon.

That having been said, the trails open to the public present considerable challenges to the day visitor. The big attraction is the peak of Agulhas Negras. Two kilometres past the park gate, the Abrigo das Rebouças, an out-of-use climbers' hut, marks the start of the trail. Turning left off the jeep track, you must first cross the small dam over the Rio Campo Belo, before finding the obvious path. After 30 minutes, you arrive at the only bifurcation on the trail. Keep right and continue another 15 minutes until the rock wall presents itself. There is a rope hanging down to help you up to the first shelf, thereafter the next two hours must be taken with care and balance. As in any mountain environment, make sure you have with you spare food, map, compass, torch, whistle and first-aid. On a clear day the top gives views over the Paraiba Valley towards the Serra do Mar and Bocaina.

There are two other points worthwhile visiting if the weather is too rotten to ascend Agulhas Negras: Pedra do Altar and Asa do Hermes, which are certainly less frightening. Back at the turn, take the left branch and the trail descends to lovely views of the Aiuruoca valley, on the north of the park.

On the other side of the valley, to the west, are the Prateleiras (The Shelves) attaining 2,600m. The trail begins where the jeep path finishes, and veers to the right, from where you can see the peak after 20 minutes. It is a climbing haunt popular for its huge steps accessible on this side.

With park traverses closed, there is another way of getting out of the park without doubling back down to the entrance. From near the Hotel Alsene, an old farm track begins to descend the rear slopes of the park towards Fazenda da Cabeceira do Aiuruoca, re-entering the forest for a time. You must head for the peak 2195, and skirt around the north side of it. From there it is a steady descent along a 7km ridge until reaching the town of Maromba, which offers lodging and food. Maringá and Visconde de Mauá, lined up on the same road, also offer pousadas and good things to eat. Visconde de Mauá is a developed 'ecotourism' point, and a variety of trails head out of town to the abundant waterfalls. There are a few campsites around here, probably the most pleasant being the pined Santa Clara, 2km from Maromba, for which you must cross the footbridge over the river of the same name. From these towns, daily buses will return you to the Dutra highway, from where you can return to Rio or São Paulo.

PARQUE ESTADUAL TURÍSTICO DO ALTO RIBEIRA (PETAR)

At the far end of São Paulo state, west of the city, lies an unbroken stretch of preserved forested mountains, geologically still the Serra do Mar, but with the local name of Serra de Paranapiacaba. Their forests are preserved in sections with different access points: Fazenda Intervales, Carlos Bothelo and Jacupiranga. All but the first exclude casual visitors; there is little or no infrastructure, no finance nor will to develop the area and admit *ecotourismo* to the forest proper.

The one exception to this is the Upper Ribeira valley, home to Brazil's highest concentration of limestone caves, formed by the seabed that was pushed up by the mountains and the continual downpour it receives. PETAR also contains numerous rivers and waterfalls, and offers some of the best close-up looks at Mata Atlântica-type forest, with various short marked and unmarked day trails through the forest to points of interest, varying in length from five minutes to six hours.

Frequently referred to as the poorest part of the state, with minimum industry, agriculture and infrastructure, the park was created as the result of a battle between the fast growing environmental lobby and supporters of a proposed hydro-electric dam on the Ribeira River. For now, the area remains protected from further development, but the unemployed of the area haven't lain down yet. While 90% of its area is still involved in land conflict of some kind, the unemployed local populace is banned from the extractive industries that the forest potentially offers. Tourism offers one possible solution if kept at an appropriate level. Similar to coral reefs, caves have a fragility that is easily disturbed by enthusiasm and ignorance. Many of the caves are restricted to registered speleologists (for reasons of safety), but enough remain accessible to guided or unaccompanied travellers to make visiting a great experience. Travelling through the valley is a treat too; the fast and richly forested mountain streams crash into the powerful Rio Ribeira, flanked by banana plantations and punctuated with dugout canoes, plus the odd small colonial church.

The central focus to PETAR is the Núcleo Santana, 25km east of the town of Apiaí, 316km southwest of São Paulo. The big attraction here is the Caverna de Santana. The second 'nucleus' of PETAR is Ouro Grosso with its namesake cave, while a third 'nucleus' lies north of the range (Núcleo Caboclo), featuring numerous caves, some of them open to non-speleologists.

Getting there

Ideally you should have your own transport – a bicycle would work well – but you can reach PETAR by public transport if you don't mind waiting for the local buses. In any case, you must get to either Apiaí or Iporanga by bus from São Paulo or Curitiba, and throw yourself at the mercy of the local bus service that runs the 40km between the two, jumping off either at Bairro da Serra or Santana, clearly marked along the unpaved roadside. The 'schedule', as best as I can discern, is as follows: on Tuesdays, Thursdays and Saturdays the bus leaves Apiaí at 16.00, arrives in Iporanga and departs again at 18.00 for the return trip. On Mondays, Wednesdays and Fridays, however, the service starts in the town of Registro, and only does the one way trip from Iporanga to Apiaí. Don't count on this.

Where to stay and eat

Camping is easy in Núcleo Santana (see *Excursions* below for details), but there are a number of options if you're not up to camping. Bairro da Serra has the luxurious Pousada das Cavernas (tel: 011 822 0398/822 6329) or the simpler Pousada Rancho da Serra with dormitory rooms and shared bathrooms; they also rent out inner-tubes for river running. Call in advance on the neighbourhood telephone (055 561 188) to reserve rooms. Larger dormitories can be found at Alojamento do Vandir, popular with school groups but quiet during the week (ring the same number for reservations). In Apiaí and Iporanga your choice is limited, but beds are available.

SOS MATA ATLÂNTICA

The rainforest of the Atlantic coast is the second most threatened in the world (after that in Madagascar). What remains today is less than 9% of its original area. In the five years between 1985 and 1990, half a million hectares of primary forest were destroyed, which in proportion to its area is three times faster than the rate of destruction in the Amazon, according to IBAMA. At this rate, it will be completely destroyed in 50 years. Of 10,000 known plant species found in the forest, 50% are endemic, and of its 130 mammal species, 51 are not found elsewhere. Of 202 threatened species in Brazil, 171 inhabit the Mata Atlântica. In addition, 70% of Brazil's human population live in its domain.

The threats to the Mata Atlântica come from various directions: illegal farming and deforestation, ineffective land legislation, palmito thieves, tourism developments for wealthy *paulistanos*. Other significant threats in the wings are the Petrobras oil refinery 25km east of Angra dos Reis, and the two nuclear reactors 40km west of Angra, built on a known fault line. Nevertheless, the refineries have the capacity to supply 20% of Brazil's electricity, and thus are next to impossible to shut down unless the political will arises.

Facing these top line statistics is SOS Mata Atlântica, a non-governmental organisation created in 1986 to defend the remaining forest, including its cultural and historical landscape. Supported by donations from a membership of around 30,000, corporate sponsorship and international support from organisations such as the WWF, SOS supports numerous projects, including the first satellite mapping of the area, education schemes and legal aid for land disputes. They also publish a bimonthly newspaper, free of charge from their headquarters.

Write to SOS Mata Atlântica, rua Manoel da Nobrega 456, São Paulo (tel: 011 887 1195). Drop into their shop and buy the T-shirt. There is also a library open to the public if you wish to know more about the forest.

Information and useful addresses

If stuck in Iporanga, near the church to the right of the town hall is a museum owned and lived in by Clayton Lino, an authority on the area and its caves. In Bairro da Serra across from Alojamento do Vandir, the Brazilian Speleological Society (SBE) operates a small store selling spelunking equipment, including lanterns and batteries. The store is open only on weekends and holidays.

Excursions

The Núcleo Santana lies 25km east of Apiaí and four kilometres before Bairro da Serra. The campground beside the Bethari River can hold up to 160 people in total, two areas, so if you are arriving on an important holiday it's best to call in advance either the gatehouse (tel: 015 552 1875) or headquarters in Apiaí (tel: 015 552 1528). The overnight cost is US$4, with showers, toilets, and manual clothes-washing facilities. Day entrance costs US$2, with use of the barbecue sites, thatched shelters and tables.

Visits to the principal cave of Santana must be conducted by park guides, and their fee is included in the entrance ticket. Guides supply lanterns. The cave's estimated 15km is only open up to 800m of its length, but it is still considered to be one of the region's best assets. Another trail leading out from the campground is the Trilha do Bethari, and 3.6km up the steep hillside along this trail you pass two waterfalls, Cachoeira das Andorinhas, and Cachoeira do Betarzinho. The trail crosses the river five times on the way, and for this reason the waterfalls are not accessible after heavy rain when the river is in spate. Also accessible from this trail are the caves of Morro Preto and Agua Suja where visits are unrestricted. Across the footbridge from the camp, up an easy 380m path, is the entrance to the Cachoeira and the Caverna do Couto, 200m deep and with free access. Remains of a previous civilisation have been discovered in this cave, but I am unclear if the notice outside the cave means that it was actually inhabited; other cultures generally used caves for ritual purposes, preferring not to inhabit their damp atmospheres.

The next Nucleus is Ouro Grosso, on the opposite side of the river from Bairro da Serra. The entrance is unmarked; find JJ's Bar and follow the track almost opposite. Only 4WD vehicles can cross the river. The tree trunk footbridge certainly looks a safer bet. The track continues for a kilometre to the visitor centre. Restricted visits to the Caverna Ouro Grosso require an official guide and technical equipment. Inside are waterfalls and swimming pools. Outside, a two-kilometre trail leads down to some ancient fig trees in the forest. There is no camping here; you are best off staying in the Núcleo Santana campsite or sleeping in Bairro da Serra.

The third nucleus (Núcleo Caboclo) is to the north of the range, off the SP-250 highway. Turn off at the sign to Espirito Santo, about 30km to the north of Apiaí, and the dirt road continues another 18km to the campsite. Holding around 60 campers, the site has toilets and showers but not the luxury of electricity. Camping is currently free. The unrestricted cave is Gruta do Chapéu, and the four requiring guides are Chapéu Mirim 1 and 2, Gruta das Aranhas and Gruta da Água Sumida. Other caverns in this region are restricted to official parties.

One other cave of note in the region is the Caverna do Diabo, 5km off the Iporanga-Eldorado highway. A concrete, railed walkway leads 300m into the illuminated grotto. There is a US$2.50 entrance fee. There are cabins that sleep up to ten people (US$80), but no restaurant while it's under reformation. A luncheonette at the junction is the nearest source of nourishment.

PARQUE NACIONAL
DA SERRA DA BOCAINA

HvW97

Appendix One
BRAZILIAN PORTUGUESE
Sally Crook and Ric Goodman

Brazilians speak Portuguese in a more lilting way than the Portuguese themselves, and their speech is thus often easier to understand than the guttural string of consonants Europeans use.

As in Spanish, there are two renderings of the verb "to be". *Ser* (*sou, é, somos, são*) is more or less for characteristics or permanent states, and *estar* (*estou, está, estamos, estão*) for temporary states. Many written words can be guessed from English or Spanish and some Spanish speakers may be lucky enough to get along quite well with a mixture of *português* and *espanhol*, popularly known as *portanhol*. Examples include many words ending with -ion in English and -on in Spanish which are similar in Portuguese but end in -ão (plural usually -ões) – *televisão*, *razão* (reason), *verão* (summer). As in many other latin languages, "o" and "a" denote the masculine/feminine adjective.

Widely used in Brazil are the diminutive endings -inho and -zinho, to express either size (*casinha*, a little house), affection (*filhinha*, a little daughter), emphasis (*pertinho*, very near), scorn (*que filminho monotono*), or for no apparent reason. Likewise the suffix -ão increases size, eg *fogo* (fire), *fogão* (oven), or emphasis – *abraço* (a hug) goes to *abração* (a big hug).

Take care, though, for some similar Spanish and Portuguese words have completely different meanings: *Niño* (Spanish = child) versus *ninho* (Portuguese = nest); *pretender* means "intend" rather than "pretend" (*fingir*) and it is best not to describe an ordinary man as *ordinário* as this implies he is common or vulgar.

The letters "k", "w" and "y" are not found in Portuguese words. With a couple of exceptions, the only consonants which can be doubled up are "c" (the first pronounced hard and the second soft), "r" and "s".

PRONUNCIATION

ã + a vowel followed by m = nasal (similar to a vowel in English followed by "ng").

c = ss before i or e; k elsewhere

ç = ss

cc = ks

ch = sh

g = soft j before i or e; hard g elsewhere

j = soft j (as in French)

lh = ly (as in Spanish ll)

nh = ny (as Spanish ñ)

o or ô = oo when unstressed

o or ó = o when stressed (as in hot)

ou = o sound (as in both or window)

õ + a vowel followed by m = nasal (similar to a vowel in English followed by "ng").

qu = k before i or e; kw elsewhere

s = z or sh (at end of syllable)

x = sh or s

z = soft j

double vowels are pronounced separately:

compreendo = compree-endo

cooperação = coo-operassaoo

WORDS AND PHRASES

please	*por favor*
thank you	*obrigado/a* (I'm obliged)
you're welcome	*de nada* (ie. "it's nothing" – reply to thank you)
yes	*sim*
no	*não*
perhaps	*talvez*
excuse me	*desculpe* (or *da licença*)
good	*bom / boa* (m/f)
better	*melhor*
bad	*mau/má*
worse	*pior*
yesterday	*ontem*
today	*hoje*
tomorrow	*amanhã*
day	*dia*
night	*noite*
morning	*manhã*
good morning	*bom dia*
good afternoon	*boa tarde*
good evening/night	*boa noite* (meeting as well taking leave)
hello	*olá, oi*
goodbye	*até logo* (until soon), *até mais* (until more)
pleased to meet you	*prazer* (pleasure)
how	*como*
how much	*quanto*
how much (cost)/is this	*quanto custa / e isso*
what	*(o) que*
what's this called	*como se chama isso*
what's this	*(o) que e isso*
who	*quem*
when	*quando*
where	*onde*
where is	*onde fica / onde está*
do you know	*você sabe*
I don't know	*não sei*
I don't understand	*não entendo*
never	*nunca*
now	*agora*
before	*antes* (*de*)
after	*depois* (*de*)
large	*grande*

small	*pequeno/a*
larger	*maior*
smaller	*menor*
high	*alto/a*
low	*baixo/a*
a lot (very, much)	*muito/a*
a little (not much)	*pouco/a*
nothing	*nada*
there is/is there	*tem*
there is no	*não tem*
too much	*demais/muito/a*
enough	*bastante/suficiente*
that's enough!/stop	*pare!*
more or less	*mais ou menos*
I	*eu*
you	*você* (*tu* only used in southern Brazil)
what is your name	*como se chama*
my name is	*eu me chamo/nome*
how are you	*como está, como você 'ta, como vai*
everything OK?	*Tudo bem?* (The commonest exchange heard
everything good	*Tudo bom* in Brazil upon greeting, formal
	or informal)
I am well	*estou bem* [shtow be(ng)] (or a reply to *como está* might
	be *bom obrigado/a* = well, thank you)
I would like (to)	*gostaria de*
give me	*dá me*
sea	*mar*
to swim	*nadar*
on the beach	*na praia*
swamp, marsh	*pântano*
lake	*lago*
river	*rio*
valley	*vale*
hill	*morro*
mountain	*montanha*
forest	*mata*
scrub/bush	*mato*
city, town	*cidade*
small town	*vila*
village	*aldeia*
house	*casa*
shop	*loja*
supermarket	*supermercado*
market	*mercado*
hotel	*hotel*
boarding house	*pousada*
church	*igreja*

school	*escola*
square	*praça*
hospital	*hospital*
first aid	*primeiro socorros*
doctor	*médico*
ill	*doente*
it hurts/aches	*dói*
malaria	*malária*
headache	*dor de cabeça*
stomach ache	*dor de estômago*
diarrhoea	*diarréia*
fever	*febre*
bank	*banco*
money	*dinheiro (money)*
change	*câmbio*
small change	*troco*
(hard) currency	*divisas*
travellers cheques	*cheques de viagem/travel*
street, road	*rua*
road	*estrada*
railway	*estrada de ferro*
aeroplane	*avião*
bus	*ônibus*
car	*carro*
lorry, truck	*caminhão*
train	*trem*
lift/ride	*carona*
book	*livro*
newspaper	*jornal*
magazine	*revista*
film (roll of)	*filme*
(dry) battery	*pilha*
map (topographical)	*mapa*
city map	*plano*
(bed)room	*quarto*
bed	*cama*
mosquito net	*mosquiteiro*
bathroom, toilet	*banheiro*
toilet paper	*papel higiênico*
shower	*chuveiro*
cold/hot water	*água fria/quente*
light	*luz*
candle	*vela*
sheet	*lençol*
blanket	*cobertor*
towel	*toalha*

matches	*fósforos*
breakfast	*café da manha*
lunch	*almoço*
dinner	*jantar*
restaurant	*restaurante*
to eat	*comer*
eggs	*ovos*
meat	*carne*
pork	*carne de porco*
beef	*carne de vaca/bife*
chicken	*frango* (as food)
fish	*peixe* or *pescada* (as food)
beans	*feijão*
bean stew	*feijoada*
vegetables	*verduras*
rice	*arroz*
fruit	*fruta*
manioc	*mandioca*
roasted manioc flour	*farofa*
juice	*suco*
bread	*pão*
coffee	*café*
tea	*chá*
milk	*leite*
water	*água*
drink (verb)	*beber*
drink (noun)	*uma bebida*
drunk	*bebido/a*
beer	*cerveja*
sugar spirit/hooch	*cachaça/pinga*
sun	*sol*
rain	*chuva*
rain shower	*pancada*
wind	*vento*
dry season	*estação seca, inverno*
rainy season	*estação das chuvas, verão*
man	*homem*
woman	*mulher* (also = wife)
child	*criança*
mother	*mãe* (*mamãe* = mummy)
father	*pai* (*papai* = daddy)
sister	*irmã*
brother	*irmão* (pl. = *irmãos*)
Sunday	*domingo*
Monday	*segunda (-feira)* (2nd fair)
Tuesday	*terça (-feira)* (3rd fair)
Wednesday	*quarta (-feira)* (4th fair)

Thursday	*quinta (-feira)* (5th fair)
Friday	*sexta (-feira)* (6th fair) [seshta fayra]
Saturday	*sábado* (Sabbath or 7th day)

January	*janeiro*
February	*fevereiro*
March	*março*
April	*abril*
May	*maio*
June	*junho*
July	*julho*
August	*agosto*
September	*setembro*
October	*outubro*
November	*novembro*
December	*dezembro*

Numbers

Each part of a cardinal number is changed to ordinal when referring to a place in a sequence (eg: 2112th = two thousandth hundredth tenth second), so it is simpler to call the 11th floor of a building *andar numero onze* than *o decimo primeiro andar,* for instance. For days of the month only the first is an ordinal number (first of May, but two of May etc). Therefore, one can get by with only the cardinal numbers and *primeiro/a* (= first) and the ordinals for the days of the week.

1	*um/uma*	30	*trinta*
2	*dois/duas*	40	*quarenta*
3	*três = tres*	50	*cinquenta*
4	*quatro*	60	*sessenta*
5	*cinco*	70	*setenta*
6	*seis* (or *meia* [= half])	80	*oitenta*
7	*sete*	90	*noventa*
8	*oito*	100	*cem*
9	*nove*	101	*cento e um/uma*
10	*dez*	200	*duzentos/as*
11	*onze*	300	*trezentos/as*
12	*doze*	400	*quatrocentos/as*
13	*treze*	500	*quinhentos/as*
14	*quatorze*	600	*seiscentos/as*
15	*quinze*	700	*setecentos/as*
16	*dezesseis*	800	*oitocentos/as*
17	*dezessete*	900	*novecentos/as*
18	*dezoito*	1000	*mil*
19	*dezenove*	1001	*mil e um/uma*
20	*vinte*	2000	*dois mil*
21	*vinte e um/uma*	3000	*tres mil* .... etc
22	*vinte e dois/duas*	1,000,000	*milhão*

Appendix Two
FURTHER READING

History, the country, the people
Bastide, Roger (1978). *The African Religions of Brazil*. Johns Hopkins. Rich in detail, this is still the definitive work on the subject. Recommended reading for anyone visiting the northeast, where Afro-Brazilian religions flourish.

Bramley, Serge. *Macumba*. City Lights Books, San Francisco. Best paperback read of the spirits and practice of this thriving Afro-Brazilian religion.

Freyre, Gilberto (1964). Translated by Samuel Putnam. *The Masters and the Slaves*. Alfred A Knopf, New York. Freyre remains Brazil's best-known sociologist/historian. This is his classic tome interpreting the development of Brazilian society. Fascinating and well-documented, it's nevertheless skewed by Freyre's conservative sympathies. He is an unrepentant supporter of military rule, for instance, and also tends to look the other way when it comes to Brazilian racial discrimination.

Wagley, Charles (1971). *An Introduction to Brazil*. Columbia University Press, New York. Somewhat dated, this is still a fine description of social classes, the community, family and education, religion and state.

Natural history
Amazon Wildlife (1992). APA Insight. Well written and well illustrated guide to all things natural concerned with the Amazon Basin.

Cousteau, Jacques-Yves and Mose Richards (1984). *Jacques Cousteau's Amazon Journey*. HN Abrams, New York. Beautiful photographs.

Dunning, J S and R S Ridgely (1982). *South American Land Birds: A Photographic Aid to Identification*. Harrowood, London. With 1,112 colour photographs, range maps, and identifications of over 2500 species, this is *the* birder's field guide for not only Brazil but the entire continent.

Forsyth, Adrian and Ken Miyata (1984). *Tropical Nature*. Charles Scribner's Sons, New York. A highly readable book for the lay reader on rainforest ecology in Central and South America.

Perry, Donald (1986). *Life Above the Jungle Floor*. Simon and Schuster, New York. Biologist Perry lived for weeks in a platform high in the jungle treetops, where hundreds of fascinating plants and animals have gone unappreciated or even unnoticed by traditional biologists.

The Amazon, its people and problems
Denslow, Julie Sloan and Christine Padoch, editors (1988). *People of the Tropical Rainforest*. University of California Press, Berkeley. A host of experts discuss not only jungle people but also agriculture, rainforest ecology and the politics of exploitation. Much of the book deals with Amazônia. Superb colour photographs.

Hecht, Susanna & Cockburn, Alexander (1990). *The Fate of the Forest, Developers, Destroyers and Defenders of the Amazon*. The definitive analysis of the current dynamic of the forest, sorting much of the fact from the myth. A must.

Hemming, John (1978). *Red Gold: The Conquest of the Brazilian Indians.* Harvard University Press, Cambridge, Mass. A disturbing historical treatise on Portugal's exploitation and slaughter of Amazonian Indians.

Hemming, John (1987). *Amazon Frontier: the Defeat of the Brazilian Indians.* Harvard University Press, Cambridge, Mass. More on the decimation of Amazon tribes, picking up where *Red Gold* left off (1755) and continuing through 1910.

Kandell, Jonathan (1984). *Passage through El Dorado.* William Morrow and Company, New York. An insightful and thoroughly researched look at the development of the Amazon basin, mingled with travelogue.

Kelly, Brian and London, Mark (1983). *Amazon.* Harcourt Brace Jovanovich, New York. A compelling account of rainforest politics and destruction.

Shoumatoff, Alex (1978). *The Rivers Amazon.* Sierra Club Books, San Francisco. Shoumatoff is extremely well versed in Amazonian flora and fauna, backcountry travel, Brazilian politics and Amerindian affairs. He's also a superb travel writer who spends lots of time in remote corners of Brazil. This remains one of the best books on the Amazon.

Stone, Roger D (1985). *Dreams of Amazonia.* Viking/Penguin, New York. Stone is a member of the World Wildlife Fund with over 20 years experience in Brazilian Amazônia. A well-researched look at exploitation and development within the Amazon basin, from the early Spanish explorers to Henry Ford and Daniel Ludwig.

Wagley, Charles (1976). *Amazon Town: A Study of Man in the Tropics.* Oxford University Press. Originally published in 1953, this is a classic study of the *caboclo* way of life in Itá, Amazonas. Fascinating accounts of local customs, religions, myths, and survival along the great river. This edition has an update on the town.

Travel literature

A great many 'adventure travel' books centred on the Amazon owe more to the imagination than to reality. These are notable exceptions.

Fleming, Peter (1934). *Brazilian Adventure.* Reprinted by JP Tarcher/Houghton Mifflin. A travel classic which follows the English journalist on his search for jungle explorer Colonel Fawcett in the Mato Grosso. Fleming's observations are often dead-pan funny and any traveller in the Pantanal will be surprised at just how little things have changed over the past 60 years. Very British public school humour.

Harrison, John (1986). *Up the Creek.* Bradt Publications. A hilarious and harrowing account of a two-man journey up the Jari River by canoe. A good deal of practical advice on jungle camping, canoeing, hunting and fishing. Required reading for anyone considering such a trip; for those of us with more sense, Harrison's vigorous writing makes it fine armchair adventure.

Holman, Alan (1985). *White River, Brown Water: A Record-Making Kayak Journey Down the Amazon.* The Mountaineers, Seattle. A journal-type account of the longest continuous solo descent of the Amazon. The writing is unremarkable, but there's plenty of practical information for kayak and canoe enthusiasts on what to bring and how to pack.

Kane, Joe. *Running the Amazon*. A good account of the first kayak descent of the Amazon from source to mouth.

Matthiessen, Peter (1961). *The Cloud Forest: A Chronicle of the South American Wilderness*. Penguin Travel Library, New York. Matthiessen's itinerary took him to the Andes and Tierra del Fuego as well as Brazil, but he spent a lot of time in the Brazilian Amazon and the Pantanal, and there are fine descriptions of the flora, fauna and Indians of the area, all conveyed in Matthiessen's characteristically clean, unpretentious prose.

O'Hanlon, Redmond (1989). *In Trouble Again: A Journey Between the Orinoco and the Amazon*. Atlantic Monthly Press, New York. O'Hanlon is a connoisseur of the bizarre, and Amazônia has inspired him to new heights of wit and derring-do.

Popescu, Petru (1991). *Amazon Beaming*. Abacus. A stimulating account of Loren McIntyre's kidnapping and time spent with the Amerindians. The beaming of the title is the village chief speaking to McIntyre by telepathy. Riveting.

Shoumatoff, Alex (1986). *In Southern Light: Trekking through Zaire and the Amazon*. Simon and Schuster, New York. No one currently writing can match Shoumatoff when it comes to Amazonian travelogues. The first half of this book recounts his search for the source of the Amazon warrior legend on the Nhamundá River.

Portuguese instruction

British texts tend to stress European Portuguese; try to get one of the American books, which are invariably slanted towards Brazilian usage.

Dennis, Ronald D (1979). *2200 Brazilian Idioms*. Brigham Young University. Brazilians pepper their speech with slang and idiomatic expressions, and this book is lots of fun for those who already know the basics of the language.

Fernández, Oscar (1965). *Living Language Conversational Portuguese*. Crown Publishers, New York. A 2-cassette (or 4-LP) language course that comes with a conversation manual and a dictionary. Uses a phrasebook approach, so it should be supplemented by a grammar text. Several native speakers are used so that you can appreciate regional differences in pronunciation. Retails for about US$15. Make sure you buy the 'South American' version rather than the 'Continental'.

Foreign Service Institute (FSI). *Portuguese Programmatic Course – Brazilian*. Two volumes. US Department of State. The most comprehensive cassette course, with 45 cassettes and 1,400 pages of text. Recommended only for those who really want to immerse themselves in Portuguese. Volume I costs US$130, Volume II sells for US$115. Order from the National AudioVisual Center, Information Services PF, 8700 Edgeworth Drive, Capitol Heights, MD 20743-3701. (Barron's *Mastering Portuguese* course is a slightly modified version of FSI's Volume I. It's a 12-cassette programme with a 620-page text, selling for US$75).

King, Larry D and Margarita Suñer (1981). *Para a Frente!* An Intermediate Course in Portuguese. Cabrilho Press, Los Angeles. Intended for those with some basic knowledge of Portuguese who want more. Lots of slang, idioms, and current Brazilian readings.

Leroy, Claude E (1964). *Português Para Principiantes*. Two volumes. University of Wisconsin-Extension, Madison. A good text with emphasis on dialogue, grammar, and stories.

Lima, Emma Eberlein and Lunes, Samira. *Português, um curso para Estrangeiros*. EPU, São Paulo 1981. Why be taught the lingo by the gringos? Totally in Brazilian, from the grammar basics with lots of very Brazilian humour. Emphasis on communicating from page one. Recommended.

Nitti, John J (1974). *201 Portuguese Verbs*. Barron's Educational Series, Woodbury, New York. Every conjugation for every verb you're likely to need.

Thomas, Earl W (1974) *A Grammar of Spoken Brazilian Portuguese*. Vanderbilt University Press, Nashville. The best textbook on the subject we've yet seen.

Guidebooks

Box, Ben, editor (published annually). *South American Handbook*. Footprint Handbooks, Bath. What can you say about 'The Bible'? Easily the most comprehensive guide to Latin America and perhaps the best guidebook ever published anywhere. Regional and town maps, hotel and restaurant listings, travel, health, and background information. The Brazil chapter runs to 272 pages.

Jordan, Tanis and Martin Jordan (1982). *South American River Trips, Volume II*. Bradt Publications. Required reading for anyone planning a river trip on their own. The Jordans do their travelling via inflatables, but kayakers, canoeists and just plain jungle campers will benefit as well from the couple's practical advice on everything from staying dry in camp to shooting rapids. Spiced with anecdotes from the authors' river trips in Peru, Suriname, and Venezuela. The Brazilian section is by John Harrison, with advice on the Guaporé and Teles Pires rivers. Worth trying to get hold of.

Quatro Rodas (published annually) *Guia Brasil*. Editora Abril, São Paulo. Over 700 cities and towns, listed alphabetically, with 70 detailed maps. Information includes hotels, restaurants, bus stations, airports, banks, currency exchange houses, tourist bureaux, sights etc. An invaluable reference, but keep in mind that only the ritzier hotels tend to be listed for the larger cities. You can buy this guide at virtually all news-stands, bookstores, bus stations, and airports in Brazil.

Quatro Rodas (published annually) *Viajar Bem e Barato*. Editora Abril, São Paulo. A somewhat smaller version of the *Guia Brasil*, written with budget travellers in mind. Not quite as much detail as in the bigger edition, but perhaps better overall in describing the areas of most interest to backcountry travellers, and you won't have to wade through all the five-star hotel listings.

Health and safety

Dawood, Richard (1989). *Travellers' Health*. OUP, Oxford. Helpful, concise, and up to date information on all aspects of staying healthy abroad.

Dessery, Brad, and Marc Robin (1992). *The Medical Guide for Third World Travelers*. KWP Publications, San Diego. A detailed field reference actually written by medical professionals who've spent years tramping through Latin America.

Hatt, John (1993). *The Tropical Traveller*. Delightfully idiosyncratic but thoroughly useful advice for anyone travelling in the Third World. Full of anecdotes, often hilariously funny, it's worth reading for pleasure as well as the carefully researched information on every relevant subject.

Howarth, Jane Wilson (1995). *Healthy Travel: Bugs, Bites and Bowels*. Cadogan.

Seah, Stanley S K, M D (1983). *Don't Drink the Water: The Complete Traveler's Guide to Staying Healthy in Warm Climates*. Canadian Public Health Association.

Fiction

Amado, Jorge (1962). Translated by William L Grossman and James L Taylor. *Gabriela, Clove and Cinnamon*. Bard/Avon, New York. Amado has long been Brazil's best-loved novelist. Many of his books deal with city life in Salvador (*Dona Flor and Her Two Husbands*, for example). Yet he can also evoke, better than any sociologist, the flavour and pace of life in small-town Brazil. *Gabriela* takes place in Ilhéus, Bahia, along the northeast coast, and it's one of the world's great love stories.

Amado, Jorge (1979). Translated by Barbara Shelby Merello. *Tieta*. Bard/Avon, New York. This time Amado's bawdy heroine does battle with land developers bent on destroying a sleepy fishing village on the northeast coast. The novel's locale, near the Bahia/Sergipe border, remains unspoiled, and backcountry travellers may want to visit Mangue Seco, Tieta's favourite wind-swept beach (see *Chapter Seven* for details).

Souza, Márcio (1980). Translated by Thomas Colchie. *The Emperor of the Amazon*. Bard/Avon, New York. A wildly picaresque satire set in the rubber-boom era. Souza is a resident of Manaus and one of Brazil's most controversial new authors.

Vierci, Pablo (1987). Translated by Sarah Nelson. *The Impostors*. Bard/Avon, New York. An hilarious novel of river travel, greed, lust, and corruption along the Amazonian backwaters.

THE GLOBETROTTERS CLUB

An international club which aims to share information on adventurous budget travel through monthly meetings and *Globe* magazine. Published every two months, *Globe* offers a wealth of information from reports of members' latest adventures to travel bargains and tips, plus the invaluable 'Mutual Aid' column where members can swap a house, sell a camper, find a travel companion or offer information on unusual places or hospitality to visiting members. London meetings are held monthly (Saturdays) and focus on a particular country or continent with illustrated talks.

Enquiries to: Globetrotters Club, BCM/Roving, London WC1N 3XX.

242

INDEX